The First Book of

Word for Windows™ 6

The First Book of
Word for Windows™ 6

Sandra E. Eddy

John E. Schnyder

alpha
books

A Division of Prentice Hall Computer Publishing
201 W. 103rd Street, Indianapolis, Indiana 46290 USA

For Elizabeth Eddy.

International Standard Book Number: 1-56761-352-7
Library of Congress Catalog Card Number: 93-72391

95 94 93   8 7 6 5 4 3 2 1

Interpretation of the printing code: the rightmost number of the first series of numbers is the year of the book's printing; the rightmost number of the second series of numbers is the number of the book's printing. For example, a printing code of 93-1 shows that the first printing of the book occurred in 1993.

Screen reproductions in this book were created by means of the program Collage Plus from Inner Media, Inc., Hollis, NH.

Printed in the United States of America

Publisher
Marie Butler-Knight

Associate Publisher
Lisa Bucki

Managing Editor
Elizabeth Keaffaber

Development Editor
Mary Cole Rack

Manuscript Editors
Editorial Plus
Barry Childs-Helton

Cover Designer
Susan Kniola

Interior Designer
Roger Morgan

Indexer
C. Alan Small

Production Team
Gary Adair, Diana Bighan,
Brad Chinn, Tim Cox, Meshell
Dinn, Mark Enochs, Howard
Jones, Beth Rago, Carrie Roth,
Marc Shecter, Greg Simsic

*Special thanks to C. Herbert Feltner for ensuring the technical
accuracy of this book.*

Contents

3 Manipulating Text   83

4 Proofing Your Document   109

Introduction

Who This Book Is For

This book is for anyone who wants to start working with Microsoft Word for Windows 6.0 with a minimum of effort. It is designed to cover all basic and most intermediate functions of Word for Windows. Every chapter in the book provides you with basic concepts, step-by-step procedures, tips, and shortcuts.

What Is Word for Windows?

Word for Windows is a sophisticated and extensive but easy-to-use word processor based on the Windows graphical user interface, a display format that allows you to select commands, functions, and even other applications by pointing to parts of the screen with the mouse. However, if you do not have a mouse, you can still access every Windows command and feature by using your keyboard.

It is easy to select commands in Word for Windows. All the commands that you will use are organized under menus—just select the menu and Word displays the commands for that menu. If there is a shortcut key combination for the command, it is displayed next to the command.

After you have used Word for Windows commands to create and edit a document, you can use the built-in spell checker, grammar checker, and thesaurus to proof and refine your document.

Although Word for Windows is extremely complex, it is easy to use. If you hit any roadblocks, you can use its extensive and context-sensitive help facility. *Context-sensitive* means that when you ask for help, Word for Windows displays a help screen related to the command or feature you are trying to use. The help facility also includes an index of topics and a search facility.

Selecting Menus and Commands

Word for Windows allows you to select a command from a menu in one of two ways: by pointing and clicking with the mouse or by typing a key combination from the keyboard. In either case, before you select a command, you must first select a menu.

To select a menu and command with the mouse, simply point to the menu name and click on it with the left mouse button. When you see the list of commands available for that menu, point and click on the command name you want.

To select a menu and command with the keyboard, first press the Alt key to activate the menu bar and then type the underlined letter in the menu name—called a *selection letter*. When you see the list of commands, type the underlined letter for the command you want. (You do not have to press Alt again.) For example, to select the File menu and the Print command, press Alt to activate the menu bar and press F to select the **F**ile menu. Then press P to select the **P**rint command. (Note that in this book the underlined letter is boldfaced and the underline is omitted.) We remind you what the key sequence is by showing it in parentheses, for example, "Select the File menu and the Print command (Alt, F, P)."

As a shortcut, we often omit the word menu when a menu is immediately followed by a command. For example, "Select the File Print command" means to select the File menu and then select the Print command.

Conventions Used in This Book

The First Book of Word for Windows 6 uses some special conventions and features that make it easier for you to learn Word for Windows. The following sections describe each special convention and feature.

Terminology

Throughout this book, the term *Word* is interchangeable with *Word for Windows*. When we refer to Word, we mean Microsoft Word for Windows, version 6.0.

If you are told to select or choose a command, you can use either the mouse or the keyboard to do so.

Key Commands

Throughout this book, you'll see sets of keystrokes that are entered either in succession or simultaneously, shown in a font that resembles the keys of your computer. Keystrokes that you enter in succession are separated by commas. The comma means that you press the key and release it before pressing the next key in the command. You do not press the comma. For example, when you see the [Alt], [F], [P] command succession, press and release the [Alt] key, press and release [F], and then press and release [P]. Keystrokes that you enter simultaneously are separated by plus signs (+) just as you will find in Word menus. This means that you hold down the first key while you are pressing the second one. For example, when you see the Ctrl + P key combination, hold down the Ctrl key and press the P key while continuing to hold down Ctrl. (Incidentally, both of the preceding commands enable you to print a document.)

Typographic Conventions

To make your learning easier, we have incorporated certain typographic conventions. Keys that we want you to press or options we want you to select are shown in color—for example, "Press ↵Enter or select OK."

Text that we want you to type appears in color, boldfaced. For example, "To start Word for Windows from the DOS prompt, type winword." You type w i n w o r d and press ↵Enter.

When a term is presented to you for the first time, it is displayed in italics.

In Word for Windows, you'll see underlined letters in menus, commands, and dialog boxes. The underlined letter is the selection letter—the keyboard key that you press to activate a menu or command. In this book, the letter appears boldfaced rather than underscored. Note that to activate a menu, you must press Alt and the keyboard letter.

Special Features of This Book

To help you learn about Word for Windows and to emphasize important points, this book incorporates special features. Each feature has its own distinctive icon to help you identify it.

QUICK STEPS

Quick Steps are step-by-step instructions summarizing the sequence of tasks needed to perform a common Word for Windows procedure. The left column explains the actions that you perform. The right column explains Word for Windows' response.

TIP: *Tips* provide helpful ideas and advice or give a shortcut for a Word for Windows command. Notes provide additional information that is useful to know.

FYIdeas give practical, creative ways to use Word for Windows to solve a business problem or perform a task.

Cautions alert you to pitfalls and potential problems.

Toolbar Buttons

Word for Windows' *toolbars* are especially easy to use. Located above the Ruler, the Standard toolbar consists of 22 *buttons* representing the most frequently used tasks in Word for Windows. To use a toolbar button, just move the mouse pointer to the appropriate button and press the left mouse button. Word either performs an action or displays a dialog box into which you can enter information needed to perform an action. Including the Standard toolbar and the Formatting toolbar, which is right below it, Word also provides six other toolbars that you can display on the screen if you wish. Added to that are other toolbars that appear on the screen when you use particular Word features.

In this book, whenever you learn about an action that is represented by a default button on a toolbar, you'll see the toolbar button and a short explanation. You will also find explanations of specific toolbars throughout this book.

Acknowledgments

We had a great deal of help and support from the beginning through the end of this project. We acknowledge the special efforts of Mary Rack, Elizabeth Keaffaber, and Barry Childs-Helton. Special thanks go to Marie Butler-Knight and Lisa Bucki.

Thanks to family and friends who provided unending support every step of the way.

A very special thank-you to Indy, Toni, and Bart. They were always there to cheer us up.

Trademarks

All terms mentioned in this book that are known to be trademarks or service marks are listed below. In addition, terms suspected of being trademarks or service marks have been appropriately capitalized. Alpha Books cannot attest to the accuracy of this information. Use of a term in this book should not be regarded as affecting the validity of any trademark or service mark.

Avery is a registered trademark of Avery International Corporation.

CompuServe is a registered trademark of CompuServe, Inc.

Courier is a registered trademark of Smith-Corona Corporation.

Epson is a registered trademark of Epson America, Inc.

Helvetica and Times Roman are registered trademarks of Linotype AG and/or its subsidiaries.

Hewlett-Packard, HP, and LaserJet are registered trademarks of Hewlett-Packard Company.

Microsoft is a registered trademark and Windows and Toolbar are trademarks of Microsoft Corporation.

WordPerfect is a registered trademark of WordPerfect Corporation.

Ways to Start Word for Windows

- In Windows, double-click on the Word for Windows icon.
- From DOS, type `cd\winword` and press ↵Enter. Type `win winword` and press ↵Enter.

Mouse Actions

- Point—Move the mouse so that the mouse pointer is located where you want it on the screen.
- Click—Quickly press and release the mouse button once.
- Double-click—Quickly press and release the mouse button twice.
- Drag—Press and hold the mouse button down while moving the mouse.

Opening a Menu

Using the mouse, click on the name of the menu that you want to use; using the keyboard, press Alt and the underlined letter of the menu name.

Word's Buttons

- OK—Closes a dialog box after completing a command.
- Cancel—Closes a dialog box before completing the command. All settings return to their prior state.
- Close—Closes a dialog box before completing the command. All settings that you have changed remain changed.
- Help—Get help about the functions or actions related to this dialog box.

1

The Word for Windows Environment

Starting Word for Windows

Before you start Word for Windows, you'll have to start your computer and make sure that your surge protector and your peripherals, such as your printer, are also switched on.

NOTE: Before you can use Word for Windows, your computer must have Microsoft Windows and Word for Windows installed. Unless both of these programs are installed on your computer, Word will not work. For Word for Windows installation instructions, see Appendix A.

There are several ways to start Word for Windows. You can start the program from within Windows or from DOS, and you can use the mouse or the keyboard. The following Quick Steps provide three methods of starting Word for Windows.

Using the Keyboard to Start Word from Within Windows

1. If you have not started Windows at the DOS prompt, type win and press ⏎Enter.

   Windows displays a series of screens.

2. Press Alt.

   Word places a highlight on the second line of the window.

3. Press F, the underlined letter in the **F**ile command.

   Windows highlights the word **F**ile and opens the **F**ile menu (see Figure 1.1).

4. Press R, the underlined letter in the **R**un command.

   Windows opens the Run dialog box, shown in Figure 1.2). A dialog box is a small box into which you enter or add information in order to complete an action.

5. On the Command Line in the dialog box, type **c:\Winword\winword.** Press ⏎Enter.

   Word starts and displays its opening screen (see Figure 1.3).

Selection letters Each menu name contains an underlined letter, as do most commands and box labels. Often it's the first letter, but because many words start with the same letter (like **F**ile and F**o**rmat), sometimes a letter within the word is underlined instead. These are called *selection letters*, and they are referred to by that name throughout this book.

Windows File menu

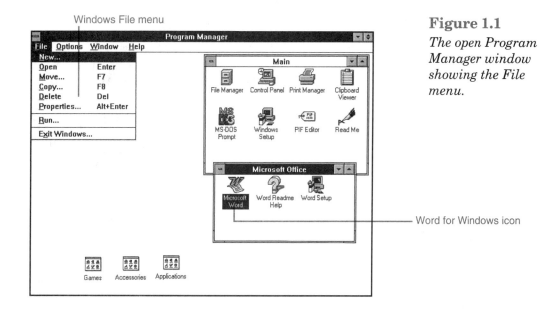

Figure 1.1
The open Program Manager window showing the File menu.

Word for Windows icon

Select OK or press Enter to complete the action.
The heavy border indicates that this is the default.

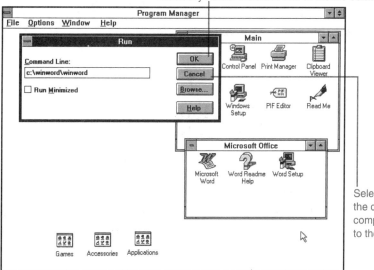

Figure 1.2
The Run dialog box showing the command line. Type c:\winword\winword in the Command Line box to start Word for Windows.

Select Cancel to escape from the dialog box. The action is not completed and you return to the previous window.

Figure 1.3

*The opening
screen of Word
for Windows.*

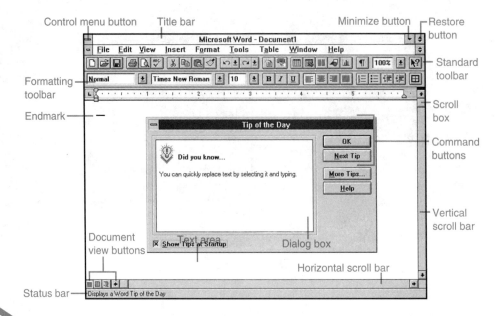

Control menu button   Title bar   Minimize button   Restore button

Standard toolbar

Formatting toolbar

Endmark

Scroll box

Command buttons

Vertical scroll bar

Document view buttons

Dialog box

Horizontal scroll bar

Status bar

TIP: Whenever you see a button (like OK) surrounded by
a heavy black border, this is the default choice. To accept
the default choice, press ↵Enter.

Using the Mouse to Start Word from Within Windows

QUICK STEPS

1. Double-click on Microsoft
   Office group icon.

2. With Windows already
   started, find the Microsoft
   Word icon on the Windows
   screen, move the mouse
   pointer to it, and then
   double-click by pressing

   The mouse pointer temporarily turns into an hourglass, indicating that the
   computer is processing and
   you must wait. Then Word
   starts and displays its

the left mouse button twice in succession. (The secret to double-clicking is to click twice rhythmically, rather than too rapidly.) opening screen, shown in Figure 1.3.

TIP: If you have trouble double-clicking, move the mouse pointer to the Microsoft Word icon and click (press and release the mouse button once). Then you can either press ⏎Enter or point to the File command and click; then point to the Open command and click. Note that you can change mouse clicking speed in the Windows Control Panel.

If you plan to use Word almost every time you use Windows, you can start Word automatically. Just copy its icon into the Startup window, which contains icons for all the applications that you wish to make active when Windows starts. Then just move your mouse pointer to the Word for Windows icon, press and hold down the Ctrl key, and drag the icon into the Startup window.

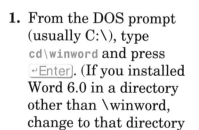

Starting Word from the DOS Prompt

1. From the DOS prompt (usually C:\), type `cd\winword` and press ⏎Enter. (If you installed Word 6.0 in a directory other than \winword, change to that directory instead.) DOS changes to the directory \winword. (You'll see C:\WINWORD.)

continues

> *continued*
>
> **2.** Type win winword and press ⏎Enter. | Windows opens; then Word starts automatically, first displaying its introductory screen and then its opening screen (see Figure 1.3).

TIP: You can also start Word from within Windows by pressing the arrow keys until you highlight the Microsoft Word icon in the active window. Then press ⏎Enter.

The Word Program Window

When Word for Windows starts, its display covers the entire computer screen. Any window this large is called a full screen or a maximized window. Figure 1.3 shows a maximized window and all its components. Before you create your first document, it is important to learn about the parts of the Word screen, what each component does and how it works. These components are shown in Figures 1.4 through 1.9.

Title bar—This horizontal rectangle at the very top of the screen displays the program name followed by the name, if any has been defined, of the current document. If the document is unnamed, Word names it DOCUMENTn, where n indicates a number that increases by 1 with each new unnamed document. (See Figure 1.4.) The Title bar includes these components:

Application Control menu—Click on this button to open a menu listing commands that manipulate the current program.

Minimize button—Click on this small button to reduce the program to an icon, often used to run another program while Word is active without taking up screen space.

Maximize/Restore button(Word)—Click on this button to switch between a Word window that encompasses the entire screen (i.e., it is maximized—the maximum size) and a smaller window. When this button is an upward-pointing arrow, the window is restored; click on the button to maximize the window. When this button is an arrow that points up and down, the window is maximized; click on the button to restore the window.

Control menu button   Program name   Document name   Minimize button

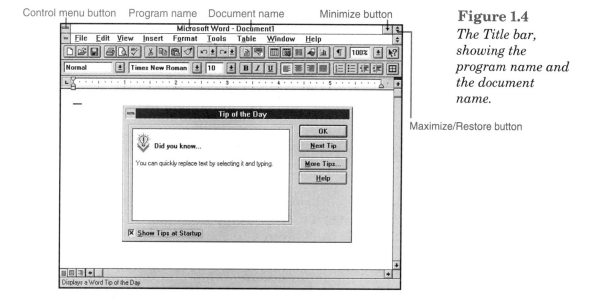

Figure 1.4
The Title bar, showing the program name and the document name.

Maximize/Restore button

Menu bar—This horizontal rectangle beneath the Title bar displays the main Word commands. Point to a word on the Menu bar and click, and a menu of commands is displayed, as shown in Figure 1.5. The Menu bar includes the following:

Document Control menu—Click on this button to open a menu that contains commands that manipulate the current document.

Maximize/Restore button (document)—Click on this button to open a document window within the Word window. To restore the Word document window to its previous full size, click on the Maximize/Restore button.

Figure 1.5

The Menu bar, which displays Word's main commands, also includes the Document Control menu button and another Maximize/ Restore button.

Document Control menu button   Restore Button

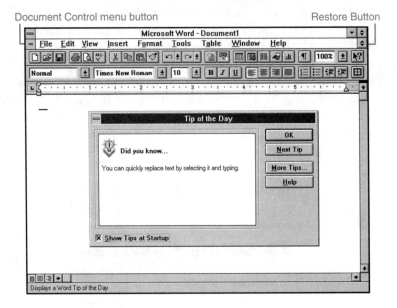

Standard Toolbar—This series of buttons, shown in Figure 1.6, provides the Word commands that you use most often. The inside back cover of this book shows an exploded view of all 22 of the Toolbar's default buttons, and Chapter 12 explains how you can customize the Toolbar.

Formatting Toolbar—This series of buttons and drop-down text/list box combinations are used to control the appearance and size of text, as well as character and paragraph formatting. Figure 1.7 shows you its features.

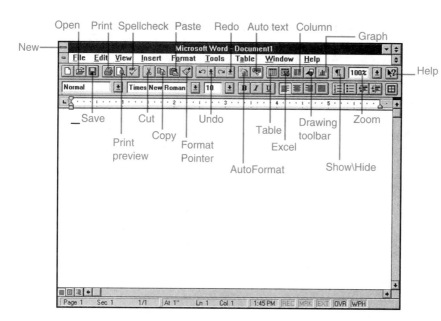

Figure 1.6
The Standard Toolbar shows the default buttons with which Word starts. You can customize the buttons on the Toolbar.

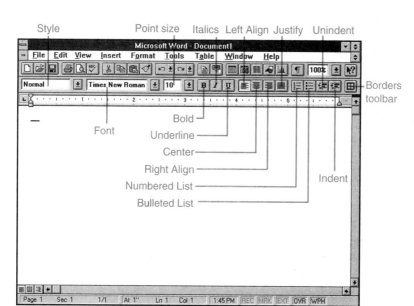

Figure 1.7
The Formatting Toolbar displays the current appearance of the paragraph and the current type and size of the text.

Ruler—This rectangle (shown in Figure 1.8) displays the current margin and tab settings. Use the Ruler to change these settings, to determine paragraph indentation (if any), and to widen or narrow columns of text.

NOTE: In Chapter 2, you'll find out about Word's vertical ruler for Page Layout mode, one way of viewing Word documents.

Figure 1.8

The Ruler displays and defines margins and tab positions.

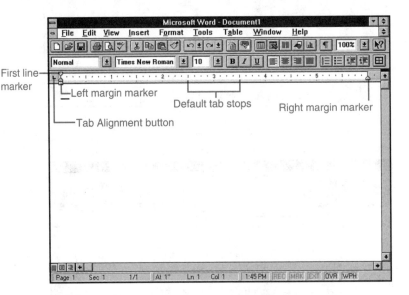

Text area—This area, shown in Figure 1.3, displays your document as you work. The vertical blinking line is the insertion point, which shows the location of the next character that you type. If you have not typed anything in the text area, the endmark, the horizontal line that marks the end of the document, is located below and to the right of the insertion point. The selection bar, from which you can select a line of text in the current document, is an invisible vertical area near the left margin.

When you first start Word, you'll see a Tip of the Day, which is a small tutorial. You'll learn more about the Tip of the Day in the "Getting Help" section of this chapter.

Scroll bar—There are two types of scroll bars, the vertical bar at the far right of the text area and the horizontal bar at the bottom of the text area (see Figure 1.3). The arrows at the ends of the scroll bar and the scroll box (the little box within the scroll bar) allow you to move around the document in the text area. The scroll box, which is sometimes called the scroll box, also indicates your current location in a document. You'll learn about moving around a document in Chapter 2.

Status bar—This area, shown in Figure 1.9, actually contains three types of information. The left section shows the page location: current page number, section number (explained in Chapter 5), and current page number versus the total number of pages in the document. The middle section is the location of the insertion point. The first number is the distance from the top edge of the page to the insertion point in inches. The second number is the number of the line on which the insertion point is located. The third number is the column, or characters counted from the left margin, in which the insertion point is located. The right section shows your current computer system time. (Use the Windows Control Panel to change the system time.) This section also displays indicators of certain Word features or modes. If the indicators look dim, they are not available; if they look black, the features or modes are available for use. For example, if you press the Ins key, the word OVR appears darker than the other indicators. (OVR represents overwrite mode, which is described in Chapter 2.)

Figure 1.9

The Status bar contains information related to the current document and also displays messages.

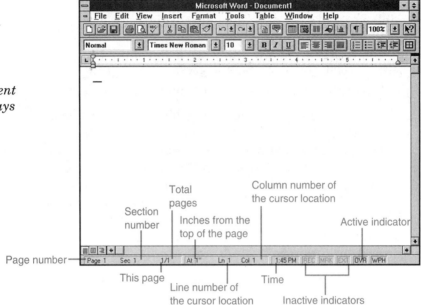

Sometimes the Status bar also displays messages. For example, if you open a command menu, the Status bar changes in order to show a description of each of the commands.

Understanding Word Menus

All Word menus are found in the Menu bar, which is divided into menus containing related commands and submenus. Word's menus are known as pull-down menus, which means that after you select a command from the Menu bar, a menu opens or "pulls down" from the Menu bar. (Figure 1.10 shows an example of a pull-down menu.) Once Word opens a pull-down menu, you can select a command by clicking on it, or you can close the menu by clicking anywhere outside the menu. To select a command using the keyboard, press the letter that is underlined. To close a pull-down menu using the keyboard, press the Esc key.

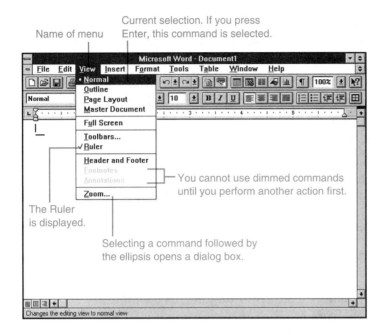

Figure 1.10
*The View Menu,
an example of a
pull-down menu.*

The menus are:

File—These commands manage documents. Use this menu to save, create, retrieve, and print documents, and to define page layout.

Edit—These commands manipulate text. You can copy, cut, and paste text; or you can search for and/or replace text. Use the Undo command to erase the last editing change and use Go To to move to a specific place in the document.

View—These commands control how your document appears on-screen. You can show your document in Normal, Outline, or Page Layout mode and in various sizes. You also can customize Word toolbars, display or hide the Ruler on-screen, and/or work on a document on the full screen (i.e., without the menu bar, toolbar, rulers, or status bar displayed). You also can use this menu to add footnotes (additional information that enhances, but is not part of, your document) and/or annotations (reviewers' comments).

Insert—These commands allow you to insert other documents, files, special symbols, graphics, and more into your document. You can also use this menu to create a table of contents, figures, and/or authorities or an index.

Format—These commands control the appearance of characters and paragraphs in your document. Use this menu to set tabs, apply styles, and change the number of columns.

Tools—These commands provide miscellaneous features. You can check spelling and grammar, find synonyms, hyphenate words in your document, work with macros, create envelopes, and so on.

Table—These commands create and control tables and their rows and columns in your document.

Window—These commands let you choose a document to view from a list of open documents. In addition, you can use this menu to open and arrange multiple windows.

Help—These commands offer you immediate help with the program.

Here are some additional facts about the commands in menus:

- Related items on a menu are grouped together and separated from other groups of items with a horizontal line.

- If a command looks dimmed or grayed, you cannot use it at this time. You may have to use another command first before you can use this command. For example, to use the **C**opy command in the **E**dit menu, you must first select text to copy.

- If a command is preceded by a check mark, the command can be turned on or off. For example, in the **V**iew menu, the **R**uler command is turned on (will be displayed on-screen) when a check mark is next to it and turned off (will not display on-screen) when there is no check mark next to it.

- If a command is preceded by a dot, the command function is the current selection. For example, in the **V**iew menu, only **N**ormal, **O**utline, **P**age Layout, or **M**aster Document can be the current setting.

- If a command is followed by an ellipsis (three consecutive periods), you will have to enter or select some choices in a dialog box after choosing the command. Figure 1.11 shows a typical dialog box and its different parts.

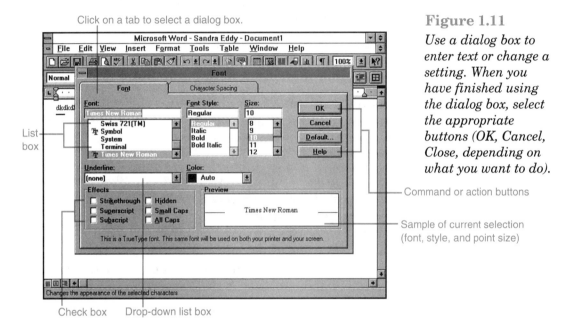

Figure 1.11

Use a dialog box to enter text or change a setting. When you have finished using the dialog box, select the appropriate buttons (OK, Cancel, Close, depending on what you want to do).

The Parts of a Dialog Box

Often, selecting a command causes Word to display a dialog box. The dialog box often contains other types of boxes and buttons, as shown in Figure 1.11 and described in Table 1.1. The following list explains the use of each element of a dialog box:

Text boxes—Boxes in which you enter text, such as a file name. Type and edit your text just as you would in a document window.

Drop-down list boxes—Boxes from which you select an item. To use a drop-down list box, select the list arrow (the underlined down arrow) at the right side of the box to reveal a list from which you can choose. To close a drop-down list box without selecting it, select the list arrow again.

List boxes—Boxes from which you select an item. To use a list box, which has a vertical scroll bar on its right side, select the desired item. If the item that you wish to select is not visible, scroll up or down the list.

Text/list boxes—Boxes that are combinations of text boxes and list boxes. You can either type a value in the text box or select a value from the open list.

Option boxes—Boxes into which you can either type a value or use the up or down arrow at the right of the box to increase or decrease, respectively, the value shown in the box.

Radio buttons—Small buttons that look like circles. When a group of options is preceded by radio buttons, you can select only one button, or option, from the group. Radio buttons work like buttons in a car radio: you can push only one at a time to select only one station at a time. When you select a radio button a large black dot will appear in its center, indicating that the option is selected.

Check boxes—Small square boxes that display an X when a feature is turned on, and are blank to show the feature is turned off. When a group of options is preceded by check boxes, you can select several options from the group.

Command buttons—Rectangular-shaped buttons that can be selected only separately. There are four command buttons that you will see most often: OK, Cancel, Close, and Help. Table 1.1 describes the purpose of each button. Some dialog boxes contain other command buttons, which will be described as they occur.

Button	Purpose
OK	Close a dialog box after completing the command.
Cancel	Close a dialog box before completing the command. All settings return to their prior state.
Close	Close a dialog box before completing the command. All settings that you have changed remain changed.
Help	Get help about the functions or actions related to this dialog box.

Table 1.1
Some Word Dialog Box Buttons

You can give commands and move around in Word for Windows using either the mouse or the keyboard. The mouse is easier to use because you can issue commands just by moving the mouse pointer to a certain area of the screen and clicking one of the mouse buttons. If you are a beginner, the best way to build your knowledge of Word is by using the mouse. After you have used Word for a while, you will learn keyboard shortcuts and will probably issue commands with a combination of the mouse and the keyboard.

TIP: If you need to see the contents of the window underneath a dialog box, move the mouse pointer to the dialog box title bar and drag the dialog box to another part of the window.

NOTE: Throughout this book, instructions for selecting a command from a menu are given as follows:
Select Menu name Command (**F**ile **N**ew, for example) where Menu name represents the name of a pull-down menu on the Menu bar (**File**) and Command is the name of a command on the pull-down menu (**New**). The selection letter which is underlined on your screen is shown in bold type in this book.

Working in Word with a Mouse

A mouse is an input device that you use by sliding it around on a desktop or other flat surface. As you move the mouse, a mouse pointer moves around on-screen.

The mouse pointer assumes different shapes, depending on where it is on the Word screen. Some of the most common shapes follow:

- When the pointer is located in the text area, it looks like an I-beam.

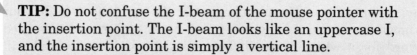

TIP: Do not confuse the I-beam of the mouse pointer with the insertion point. The I-beam looks like an uppercase I, and the insertion point is simply a vertical line.

- On a window border, the pointer is a two-headed arrow. You can use this type of pointer to change the size of the window—horizontally, vertically, or both (when you move the pointer to a corner of the window).

- Outside the text area, the pointer is an arrow that points diagonally to the left (see Figure 1.12). Use this arrow to point to parts of the window and click or double-click the mouse button to cause an action. You can point to:

  Buttons, which are small boxes usually containing pictures that remind you of the action to be taken or the format to be changed.

  Icons, which are small illustrations of the applications or components to be run or activated.

  Or you can point to menus from which you can choose commands.

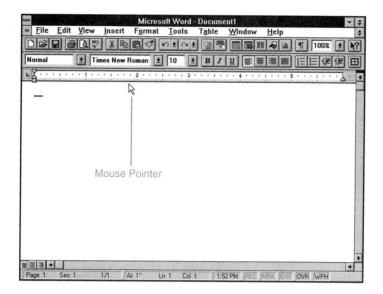

Figure 1.12

This mouse pointer selects buttons, icons, and menus to cause an action.

- When the pointer (pointing diagonally to the right) is in the selection bar in the left margin, you can highlight an entire line of text at once. See Figure 1.13.

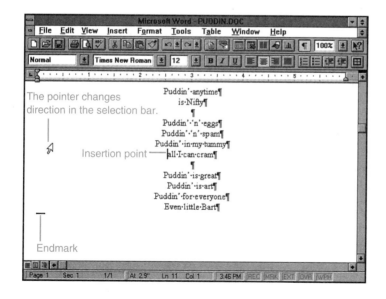

Figure 1.13

From the selection bar, you can highlight a line of text.

• When Word is executing a command, the mouse pointer looks like an hourglass. This signals that you have to wait to enter the next command or take the next action.

Throughout this book, you will learn about specific actions you take by moving the mouse and then pressing a mouse button. Unless otherwise mentioned, use the left mouse button. These mouse actions are described in Table 1.2.

Table 1.2
Mouse Actions

Action	Description
Point	Move the mouse so that the mouse pointer is located where you want it on the screen.
Click	Quickly press and release the mouse button once.
Double-click	Quickly press and release the mouse button twice.
Drag	Press and hold the mouse button down while moving the mouse.

The following Quick Steps show you how to use a mouse to access Word menus.

Selecting Menus and Commands with the Mouse

1. On the Menu bar, click on the name of the menu that you want to use.

   Word opens the menu and displays all the available choices.

2. Click on the name of the desired command.

   Word either performs an action or gives you more choices.

3. Click on the OK button to perform the action, or click on the Cancel button to take

no action. If the Cancel button has changed to a Close button, some changes have already occurred.	Word returns you to the place in your document from which you started the command.

TIP: You can access many Word commands even more quickly by clicking on the appropriate Standard Toolbar button. See the inside back cover of this book for a description of all the Standard Toolbar buttons.

Using the Mouse with Dialog Boxes

Often, selecting a command causes Word to display a dialog box as discussed earlier and illustrated in Figure 1.11. The mouse provides the easiest way to use a dialog box and its associated boxes (discussed earlier) and buttons, some of which are described in Table 1.1. The following Table explains how to use the mouse with each special element within a dialog box:

Dialog box element	Mouse action
Text boxes	Place the mouse pointer in the text box and click the left mouse button to move the insertion point to the text box. Type and edit your text just as you would in a document window.
Drop-down list boxes	Click on the list arrow (the underlined down arrow) at the right side of the box to reveal a list from which you can choose. To close the box without selecting it, click on the arrow again.

Table 1.3
Using the Mouse with the Elements of a Dialog Box

continues

Table 1.3
Continued

Dialog box element	Mouse action
List boxes	Click on the desired item. If the item that you wish to select is not visible, scroll up or down the list using the vertical scroll bar on its right side.
Text/list boxes	Place the mouse pointer in the text box and click the left mouse button to begin typing text, or click on a value from the open list.
Option boxes	Either place the mouse pointer in the text box and click the left mouse button to begin typing a value, or click on either the up or down arrow in the box at the right to increase or decrease, respectively, the value shown in the box.
Radio buttons	To select a radio button, move the mouse pointer to the radio button and click with the left mouse button. A large black dot appears in the button, indicating that the option is selected.
Check boxes	To select an option, move the mouse pointer to its check box and click with the left mouse button. To cancel the selection, click on the check box again to remove the check.
Command buttons	OK, Cancel, Close, and Help, the buttons you see most often, are described in Table 1.1. Some dialog boxes contain other command buttons, which will be described as they occur. Move the mouse pointer to the command button and click with the left mouse button.

Working in Word with the Keyboard

If you don't have a mouse or are not comfortable using it, you can execute commands in Word by using just the keyboard. However, if you have a mouse, you'll probably find that you use a combination of the mouse and the keyboard.

Word has many commands; you activate them by pressing single keys, key combinations (pressing two or three keys simultaneously), and key successions (pressing two or three keys one after another). In this book, key combinations are shown as two or three keys, each separated by a plus sign (+); and key successions are shown as two or three keys, each separated by a comma (,). For example, the key combination used to save a file is ⇧Shift + F12, and the key succession used to open the **F**ile menu is Alt + F.

If you plan to use the keyboard to access menus, look at the Menu bar for a moment. Notice again that each menu name contains an underlined letter as explained earlier. These are called *selection letters* because the keyboard user presses their equivalents on the keyboard to select the menus.

NOTE: Word accepts either uppercase or lowercase letters in key combinations or key successions.

The following Quick Steps show how to select menus and commands with the keyboard.

Selecting Menus and Commands with the Keyboard

1. To select a menu, press and release the Alt key (because this is a key succession, you don't have to hold down the Alt key). Then press the selection letter for the menu you want. For example, to select the File menu, press F.

   Word opens the menu and displays more choices with more underlined selection letters.

continues

continued

2. To select a command from the menu, press the selection letter in the command you want to use.

   Word opens the menu and displays more choices with more underlined selection letters.

3. When you have finished using the command and associated dialog boxes, press ⏎Enter to complete the command or press Esc to cancel the command or close the menu.

   Word returns you to the place in your document from which you started the command.

When you open a menu, some commands have key combinations or successions displayed to the right. For example, if you use the **Print** command, you'll see: **Ctrl+P.**

In this case, this combination is just another method of exiting Word (and almost any other Windows application). Press the Alt key and the F4 key simultaneously to exit. As you view other menus, you'll notice that some (but not all) commands have key combinations or successions.

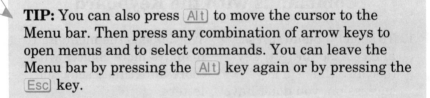

TIP: You can also press Alt to move the cursor to the Menu bar. Then press any combination of arrow keys to open menus and to select commands. You can leave the Menu bar by pressing the Alt key again or by pressing the Esc key.

Using the Keyboard with Dialog Boxes

Although the mouse is usually the easiest way to move around in a dialog box, you can use the keyboard, too. Table 1.5 describes the keys commonly used with dialog boxes. In general, to use the keyboard with a dialog box, press Tab to move from upper left to lower right through the options or press ⇧Shift + Tab to move in the opposite direction. To close a list and move to the next entry, press Tab or ⇧Shift + Tab. To clear an entry, press the ←Backspace key.

A dialog box can itself contain other types of boxes or it can contain buttons, as shown earlier in Figure 1.11 and Table 1.1. The following section explains how to use the keyboard with those boxes and buttons.

> **TIP:** To quickly select one check box from a list of check boxes, press Alt and the selection letter for that box.

Box	Keyboard Action
Text boxes	Press ⇧Shift (or ⇧Shift + Tab) to move to the text box. Then type and edit your text just as you would in a document window. To exit a text box and move to the next text box, press Tab or press Alt + the selection letter of the box to which you wish to move.
Drop-down list boxes	Select the list arrow (the underlined down arrow located at the right side of the box) by pressing any combination of arrow keys, Alt + ↓ or Alt + ↑. When a list of choices is revealed and your choice is highlighted, either move to the next option in the dialog box or press ↵Enter. To close the list, press Esc.
List boxes	Select the desired item by pressing any combination of arrow keys, Alt + ↓ or Alt + ↑, to scroll through the list.
Text/list boxes	You can either type a value in the box's text box or select a value from the open list by pressing any combination of arrow keys, Alt + ↓ or Alt + ↑.

Table 1.4
The Use of Typical Dialog Boxes

Table 1.4
Continued

Box	Keyboard Action
Option boxes	Either type a value or press any combination of arrow keys to cycle through the valid values for this option. When your choice is highlighted, either move to the next option in the dialog box or press ⏎Enter.
Radio buttons	To select a radio button, press any combination of arrow keys. When your choice is highlighted, either move to the next option in the dialog box or press ⏎Enter.
Check boxes	For each option that you wish to select, press the selection letter. Press the same letter to clear the box. When you have made your choice, either move to the next option in the dialog box or press ⏎Enter.
Command buttons	To select the default command button (usually OK), press ⏎Enter. To select another button, if a letter is underlined on the button, type that letter. Otherwise, press Tab⇥ or ⇧Shift+Tab⇥ until the button is selected; then press ⏎Enter.

Table 1.5
Commonly Used Keys, Key Combinations, and Key Successions

Key	Description
⏎Enter	Indicates that a command is complete. Pressing ⏎Enter is equivalent to clicking on OK.
Tab⇥	Moves to the next field, box, button, or option.
⇧Shift+Tab⇥	Moves to the previous field, box, button, or option.
↑	Moves one item up a list or up one line of text. Increases the value of a measurement.
↓	Moves one item down a list or down one line of text. Decreases the value of a measurement.
Alt+↓ or Alt+↑	Opens a selected drop-down list box. If or an option on a list is highlighted, selects it. If an option on a list is not highlighted, cancels the display of the list.

The Toolbars and Rulers

The Toolbars and Rulers provide shortcuts for using Word quickly and efficiently. You can use the default settings or create your own.

Word provides several toolbars, which you can display or hide on your screen:

Standard Toolbar—The Standard Toolbar (shown in Figure 1.6) is an easy way to use Word's most common commands. Just click on the appropriate button, and Word takes it from there. Throughout this book, as you find out about the commands represented by buttons on the Standard Toolbar, you'll get a look at the button. The inside back cover of this book shows an exploded view of all 22 Standard Toolbar buttons. You can customize the Standard Toolbar so that you can easily access the commands you use most often.

Formatting Toolbar—The Formatting Toolbar has commands that affect the way text appears in your document. Using this Toolbar, you can change the appearance and size of text, and you can format and enhance text characters. You'll learn more about text formatting in Chapters 6, 7, and 8.

Borders Toolbar—The Borders Toolbar has buttons that allow you to define borders, line styles, and shadings for parts of a document. You'll find out about borders in Chapters 6 and 10.

Database Toolbar—The Database Toolbar has buttons that allow you to work with Windows database applications, especially for mail merge. You'll find out about mail merge in Chapter 14.

Drawing Toolbar—The Drawing Toolbar provides many drawing tools and commands from which to choose. For information about graphics in Word, refer to Chapter 11.

Forms Toolbar—The Forms Toolbar enables you to add various forms to a document. You can create a table by using the Forms Toolbar, but most of the other buttons on this Toolbar are beyond the scope of this book. You'll learn about building and editing tables in Chapter 10.

Microsoft Toolbar—The Microsoft Toolbar provides buttons with which you can access eight other Microsoft applications.

Word for Windows 2.0 Toolbar—The Word for Windows 2.0 Toolbar displays an updated version of the Word for Windows 2.0 Toolbar, which preceded the Word 6.0 Standard Toolbar.

For information on customizing most of the Word Toolbars, see Chapter 12.

The Ruler controls the overall appearance of the document. You can set the alignment of paragraphs, adjust line spacing, and change tab positions and alignment.

Getting Help

Word has a very complete on-line help facility, which you can access in the following ways:

- Press F1 from any screen to display the main menu of the help facility. Then either click on a button or press the selection letter for each of the following:

  Contents—Select this option to view a synopsis of help topics.

  Search—Select this option to view information about a topic that you select from a list. You can either type the first few letters of a topic or select it from a list.

  Back—Select this option to return to the previous topic. When you first start help, this button is dimmed. (It is not currently available because you have no previous topic in this help session to which to return.

History—Select this topic to see a list of topics that you have "visited" in this help session. When you exit help, Word erases all the history entries.

Index—Select this option to view the index of help information for Word.

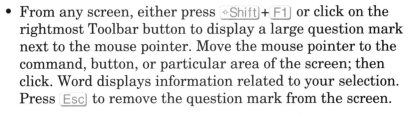

TIP: Quick Access with Jump Terms   From within Help use either the mouse or the keyboard to select a jump term, green, underlined text that reveals specific information about a help topic. To use the mouse, point to the jump term and either click on it or hold down the mouse button. To use the keyboard, press the Tab⇕ key to highlight the term or press ⇧Shift+Tab⇕ to move back to the prior term. Press ↵Enter and Windows displays the available information.

- From any screen, either press ⇧Shift+F1 or click on the rightmost Toolbar button to display a large question mark next to the mouse pointer. Move the mouse pointer to the command, button, or particular area of the screen; then click. Word displays information related to your selection. Press Esc to remove the question mark from the screen.

- Click on Help or press Alt, H to open the Help menu. Then you can select from the Contents, Search for Help on, Index, Quick Preview, Examples and Demos, Tip of the Day, WordPerfect Help, Technical Support, or About Microsoft Word categories. The Word Help window operates in about the same way as the main Word screen. For example, there is a scroll bar on the right side of the window and if the window does not encompass the entire desktop, you can move it by moving the mouse pointer to the title bar and dragging it.

To leave the help facility, back up screen by screen (either click on Back or press B)) until Back is dimmed. Then select File Exit. You can also use File Exit to exit quickly from any help screen.

Learning Word with Quick Previews

If you select **Q**uick Preview from the **H**elp menu, Word displays the titles of three on-line demonstrations. To choose a demonstration, either click on its button or press ⟨Alt⟩ plus the underlined letter in its title.

Seeing Examples and Demos

Examples and Demos provides lessons ranging from Getting Started to Automating Your Work. To travel through the lessons, follow the prompts. Either click on a button, press ⟨Alt⟩ and the underlined letter, or tab to a lesson. You can display the Examples and Demos menu by pressing ⟨Alt⟩, ⟨C⟩; then select an option to go to another area of the tutorial or press ⟨Alt⟩ + ⟨E⟩ to exit.

Viewing the Tip of the Day

When you started Word for the first time, a Tip of the Day dialog box popped up on your screen (see Figure 1.3). There are several ways of working with The Tip of the Day, which shows you a Word shortcut. You can keep viewing tips every time you start Word, or you can turn this automatic feature off by checking or unchecking the Show Tips at Startup check box. When the dialog box is open, you can click on the Next Tip button to keep viewing tips, or you can click on More Tips to open a dialog box from which you can select tip categories. If you have turned off this display, and want to start reviewing tips again, select Tip of the Day from the Help menu. In the Tip of the Day dialog box, check Show Tips at Startup.

Getting WordPerfect Help

If you are a WordPerfect user, Word for Windows provides a list of WordPerfect commands and three ways to get help. You can open the help facility to get help about a particular command, you can see a demonstration of how to use the command, and you can set WordPerfect help preferences (e.g., from setting the speed of the demo to simulating the movement of the mouse). When the WordPerfect dialog box appears, just click on a command in the Command Keys list box and then click on a button at the bottom of the dialog box.

Answering Your Technical Support Questions

To find out how to reach Microsoft Technical Support team and what to do when you reach them, click on Technical Support.

Getting Information About Microsoft Word

When you click on About Microsoft Word, you get information about the application, information about your computer system, and a list of those who contributed to this version of Word. Especially important is System Info, which allows you to view a list of system components and to check your current memory usage.

Quitting Word

There are several ways to quit Word. You can

- Choose the File menu and select the Exit command (Alt), F, X).

- Double-click on either the Application or Document Control menu buttons (the two buttons at the top left part of the screen).

- Press Alt+F4.

  If you change your mind, click on Cancel or press the Esc key.

NOTE: When you issue a command to exit word, if you have made any changes to a document, Word displays a dialog box. To save the changes, either press Y, click on the Yes button, or press Enter. For detailed information on saving a file, see the next chapter.

Setting Word Preferences

From the **T**ools menu, select **O**ptions (Alt, T, O). Click on any of the tabs: View, General, Edit, Print, Save, Revisions, User Info, Compatibility, File Locations, Spelling, Grammar, or AutoFormat.

Status Bar Indicators

Black indicators are on; dimmed indicators are off.

- REC—The Word macro recorder is turned on or off.
- MRK—Mark Revisions is on or off.
- EXT—The Extend Selection key (F8) is on or off.
- OVR—Overtype mode is on (black); insert mode is on (dimmed).
- WPH—WordPerfect help is on.

Displaying Formatting Symbols

- Click on the Paragraph button on the Standard toolbar.
- From the **T**ools menu, select Options (Alt, T, O); click on the View tab; and select All under Nonprinting Characters.

Saving a Document

From the **F**ile menu, select Save or Save As; or from the Standard toolbar, click on the Save button (third from left). If prompted, type the file name and press ↵Enter.

Retrieving a Document

From the **F**ile menu, select **O**pen; or from the Standard toolbar, click on the Open button (second from left). Then type the file name and press ↵Enter.

Creating Your First Document

In Chapter 1, you were introduced to the Word Program window and its components, and you learned how to use the mouse and the keyboard to get around Word for Windows. Next you'll learn how to put some of these components to work in creating your first document, from typing the first words to printing the final copy.

The Document Window

When Word starts, the text area (also called the *document window*; see Figure 2.1), is empty, except for the insertion point, the endmark, and the I-beam mouse pointer. The document window is the area in which you'll create and edit all your documents. If you have more than one document open, the window in which you are currently working is known as the active window.

Notice that the Title bar reads Microsoft Word—Document1. Because you are just starting your first document and haven't named it yet, Word automatically gives the document the default, or starting, name, which is Document1. At any time, you can give the document a name of your choice by saving it. (You'll learn about saving documents later in this chapter.) If you haven't named your document by the time you try to exit the program, Word asks if you want to save changes to Document1, even if it contains only one character. If you select Yes, Word displays a dialog box into which you can type a file name for the document. If you select No, Word exits without saving Document1.

Figure 2.1

A new document window in Word for Windows.

Insertion point

I-beam mouse pointer

Endmark

Text area

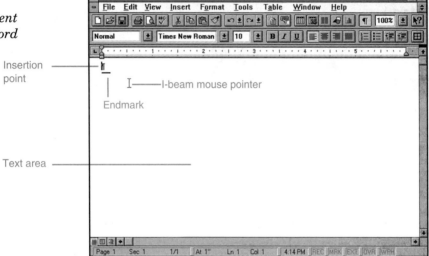

In Chapter 1, you learned that the Toolbars and the Ruler provide shortcuts to using Word efficiently. As a beginner, you'll find the Toolbars and the Ruler useful so make sure that all of them are displayed on-screen before you start typing text. Later, as you get more comfortable with Word, you can decide whether to keep the Toolbars and the Ruler open or use Word's commands instead. Chances are you will keep them even if you use commands almost exclusively.

To turn on and off the Ruler and the Toolbars, use Word's **V**iew menu (see Figure 2.2). From the **V**iew menu, you can also choose **N**ormal, **O**utline, **P**age Layout, and **M**aster Document views (which you'll learn about shortly); create headers and/or footers (see Chapter 5); and add footnotes and/or annotations to your document. You can also use the **Z**oom command as a form of page preview, with one difference, you can edit your document while it is zoomed. See Chapter 9 for a description of the Zoom command.

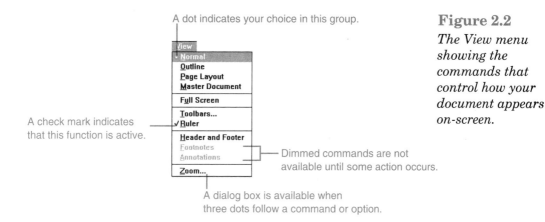

A dot indicates your choice in this group.

A check mark indicates that this function is active.

Dimmed commands are not available until some action occurs.

A dialog box is available when three dots follow a command or option.

Figure 2.2
The View menu showing the commands that control how your document appears on-screen.

The following Quick Steps show you how to turn the Ruler on and off.

Turning the Ruler On and Off

1. Select View from the Menu bar or press Alt, V.

   Word opens the View menu. A check mark or bullet preceding any command or function on a list indicates that this command or function is either turned on or is on display.

2. To switch between displaying and hiding the Ruler, move the mouse pointer to the **R**uler command and click, or press R.

   Word either places a check mark next to the selected option or removes the check mark.

TIP: Another way to open a new document window is to click on the New button on the Standard Toolbar.

The following Quick Steps show you how to turn a Toolbar on and off.

QUICK STEPS — Turning Toolbars On and Off

1. Select View from the Menu bar or press (Alt), (V).

   Word opens the **View** menu.

2. Select the Toolbars command.

   Word displays the Toolbars dialog box, as shown in Figure 2.3.

3. Check or uncheck check boxes in the Toolbars group.

   Corresponding Toolbars are displayed or hidden.

Figure 2.3

The Toolbars dialog box in which you can select Toolbars for display and set customized Toolbars.

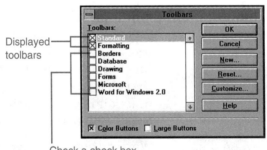

Displayed toolbars

Check a check box to display a toolbar.

NOTE: Word's starting Toolbars are Standard and Formatting. All other Toolbars are hidden except when you display them.

An Overview of Setting Preferences in Word

Word provides a mind-boggling array of settings that affect almost every aspect of using Word: the screen display, the document's appearance on-screen, the printing of a document, the use of Word's commands, and more. When you first start Word, the default settings are activated. However, you can change these settings, including the look of the new document window, to suit your particular needs.

Word provides a straightforward method for displaying and/or changing the default settings. Using the **O**ptions command in the **T**ools menu, you select one of 12 categories (indicated by tabs). After you select a category, Word displays the settings pertaining to that category. You then select the settings you wish. Because you will be selecting some of these categories in this chapter, an overview of the 12 categories is presented here.

From the **T**ools menu, select the **O**ptions command (Alt, T, O). In the Options dialog box (see Figure 2.4), you will see a list of categories from which you can select. Click on the ↓ to scroll through the list. Each of the categories is explained in the following list:

- The View dialog box controls how your document looks on-screen. For example, you can turn on and off the vertical and horizontal scroll bars and the Status Bar. See Chapter 1 and this chapter for more information about the parts of the Word screen affected by the View category.

Figure 2.4

The Options dialog box in which you can select and change your preferences.

Dialog box for the General category.   Click on a tab to open the appropriate dialog box.

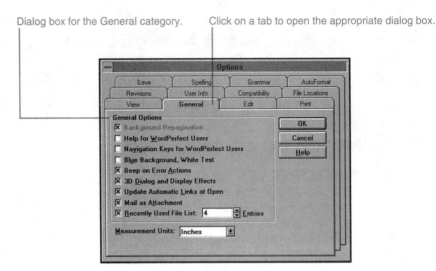

- The General dialog box enables you to display or change some general settings, such as defining the measurement unit with which you want to format or choosing the number of prior files on the File menu. If you are familiar with WordPerfect, use the General dialog box to select whether WordPerfect help is enabled.

- The Edit dialog box controls some of your editing options. For example, you can decide whether you use drag-and-drop text editing or allow typing as little as one character to replace a highlighted block of text.

- The Print dialog box allows you to adjust print settings, such as whether hidden text, footnotes, and annotations are included in your printed output. You can also control how paragraphs are split between pages. Chapter 9 is devoted to printing Word documents, and Chapter 7 includes a section on hidden text.

- The Save dialog box provides a way to review or change save options. For example, at predetermined intervals, you can have Word automatically save the document on which you are working; you can save a backup copy whenever you save a document; or you can decide whether to provide Summary Info for a document. You'll learn about saving documents later in this chapter.

- The Revisions dialog box allows you to determine how Word handles revisions. This is particularly useful if a group of people is working on a single document; it allows each member of the group to identify his or her new text and deleted text.

- The User Info dialog box shows you personal information, such as your name, initials, and mailing address, and allows you to change it.

- The Compatibility dialog box enables you to select certain options for the current document. For example, you can substitute an available font for one that is not available. You an also select file formats and decide whether to use some "foreign" format features for your Word documents.

- The File Locations dialog box allows you to view or modify the directories in which files are located.

- The Spelling dialog box, which enables you to define custom dictionaries for a specific document, is described in Chapter 4.

- The Grammar dialog box allows you to determine how strictly your grammar will be reviewed. Chapter 4 contains information about Word's grammar checker.

- The AutoFormat dialog box enables you to set a variety of automatic formats for the current document.

Entering and Viewing Text

Once the document window appears on-screen, you can start entering text. As you type, text appears to the left of the insertion point (the vertical blinking line). You don't have to press the Enter key when the text reaches the right margin because Word automatically controls the amount of text that appears on a line. If you are near the right margin and the word you are typing won't fit on the line, Word moves the word to the beginning of the next line. This is known as *word wrap*.

TIP: If you press ⏎Enter, Word starts a new paragraph. To undo this, all you have to do is press the ⬅Backspace key once. To start a new line without starting a new paragraph, press ⇧Shift+⏎Enter.

By default, Word aligns text with the left margin of the page and keeps the text at the right side of the page ragged (not aligned with the right margin). This is *left alignment* or *left justification*. Word also provides *right alignment* (the text is aligned with the right margin and ragged on the left), *centered alignment* (the text is balanced on either side of a center point), and *full justification* (the text is aligned with both left and right margins). Chapter 6 contains detailed information about alignment.

Paragraphs and New Lines

Whenever you want to signify the end of one paragraph and start a new paragraph, press the ⏎Enter key. Word places a paragraph mark (¶), a special nonprinting symbol, at the end of the first paragraph. You can turn on and off the display of paragraph marks and other nonprinting symbols, as you will learn shortly.

Some documents require that you override the word-wrap feature and define your own lines. For example, if you are writing a poem, you might want to specify the number of lines in each paragraph. To create new lines within a paragraph, press ⇧Shift+⏎Enter. Word places a newline mark (↵) at the end of the line.

To display the paragraph and newline marks as well as other nonprinting symbols, click on the Show/Reveal button, the large paragraph symbol on the Standard Toolbar. You can also control the display of nonprinting symbols from the Options dialog box for the View category. You'll learn how to use this dialog box and find an overview of its features later in this chapter.

Insert Versus Overtype

When you enter text in Word, you have a choice of two typing modes, Insert or Overtype. In Insert mode, every time you type a character, everything to the right of the insertion point is pushed ahead. No text is deleted as you type. Insert mode is the default typing mode.

In Overtype mode, text to the right of the insertion point is erased as you type new text. To get to Overtype mode from Insert mode, press the [Num Lock] key. To switch back to Insert mode, press [Num Lock] again. Word's Status bar indicates whether you are in Insert or Overtype mode. When the Status bar displays a black OVR, you are in Overtype mode. If OVR looks dim, you are in Insert mode. Table 2.1 lists all the Status bar indicators and gives a description of each.

NOTE: When you press the same key to switch between two modes or settings, it is called a *toggle key*. You will find several toggle keys used by Word.

Indicator	Condition Indicated
REC	The Word macro recorder is turned on.
MRK	Mark Revisions is on.
EXT	The Extend Selection key ([F8]) is on.
OVR	Overtype mode is on.
WPH	WordPerfect help is on.

Table 2.1
Status Bar Indicators with Conditions Indicated

Viewing Text in Different Ways

If you are writing an informal memo, it doesn't matter whether you see headers, footers, footnotes, and graphics because there are probably none to see. However, if you are creating an instruction book using advanced desktop publishing tools, you'll want to view each page in WYSIWYG (what-you-see-is-what-you-get, pronounced "wizzy-wig") format, which shows exactly how the printed page will look.

In this chapter, you've already used the **V**iew menu to turn on and off the Ruler and Toolbars. Next you'll use the **V**iew menu to choose to display your text in one of three different views: **N**ormal, **P**age Layout, and **O**utline.

Normal, the default, shows text as you have formatted it but does not display all page layout formats, such as headers, footers, page and line numbers, and footnotes. An example of **N**ormal view is shown in Figure 2.5. To display a document in **N**ormal view, click on the Normal button to the left of the horizontal scroll bar.

Page Layout shows how the body text, headers, footers, and footnotes appear on the printed page (see Figure 2.6). Page Layout view also shows the edges of the page, allowing you to see text relative to the page dimensions. Because all the formatting is displayed, this is the slowest view. To display a document in **P**age Layout view, click on the Page Layout button to the left of the horizontal scroll bar.

FYI
IDEAS

When working in a long document with headers, footers, special formats, and all the bells and whistles, it would be natural to think that you should work in **P**age Layout view. However, because **N**ormal view is faster than **P**age Layout view, it's a better idea to write and edit in **N**ormal view and occasionally look at your results in **P**age Layout view. Then when you get to the end of your editing, start working almost exclusively in **P**age Layout view.

Outline shows the heading levels of your document. To display a document in **O**utline view, click on the Outline button to the left of the horizontal scroll bar.

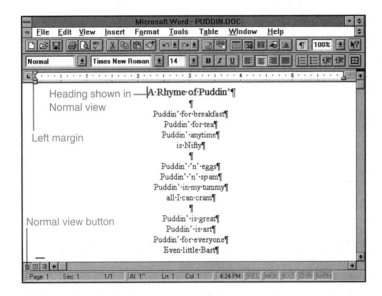

Figure 2.5
Normal view showing most formats.

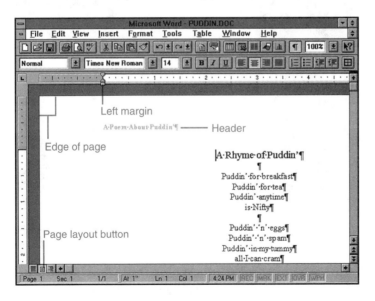

Figure 2.6
Page Layout view showing the placement of the text on the page and part of the header.

Viewing Text As It Will Print

In **N**ormal view, you can't see all the page formats. With **P**age Layout view, although the formats are there, you can't see the entire page on-screen. However, with the Print Preview command, Word gives you the chance to see one or two pages of your document on-screen as it will print. In this mode, text usually is illegible and cannot be edited, but you can print or adjust the margins of your document. Select the File menu and the Print Preview command (Alt), F , V)), and Word displays the first page of your document (see Figure 2.7). You can scroll through your entire document by pressing PgDn (to move down a page at a time) or PgUp (to move up a page at a time). You can also display your document two pages at a time by selecting Two Pages on the Print Preview screen drop-down editing view list.

Figure 2.7

The third page of a Word document in Print Preview.

Top margin   Left margin   Right margin

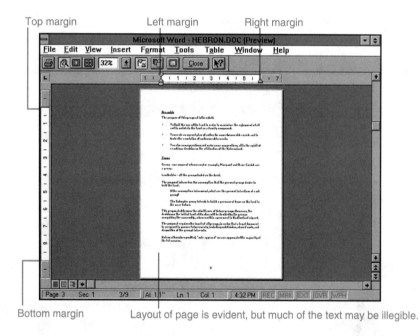

Bottom margin   Layout of page is evident, but much of the text may be illegible.

Before you print a document, use Print Preview to check the layout and look of the document. If you don't like what you see, it's easier to change things now. You'll learn more details of printing and Print Preview in Chapter 9.

The Basic Text Elements

Every document is unique—in size, in audience, and in purpose. The pattern of one document is small and plain, that of a second document is large and ornate, and so on. In order to change the appearance of each document, it is important for you to know which text elements are available to you and how you can work with them.

The smallest element used in Word is the character. A character is a letter, punctuation mark, number, blank space, or special symbol. Other text units are words, sentences, paragraphs, sections, and documents. Table 2.2 gives the definitions for the text elements discussed in this book.

Element	Description
Character	One alphabetic, numeric, or punctuation symbol
Word	One or more characters ending with a space or period
Sentence	One or more words ending with a period, a question mark, or an exclamation point
Paragraph	One or more characters ending with a paragraph mark
Section	One or more characters ending with a section mark
Document	A file containing any combination of text and graphics

Table 2.2
Elements of Text

As you start to manipulate the text elements of your document, you'll frequently use two Word formatting commands—**Fo**rmat **F**ont (Alt , O , F), which formats one or more characters up to and including your entire document, and **Fo**rmat **P**aragraph (Alt , O , P), which formats one or more paragraphs up to and including your entire document. In Chapter 3, you'll learn how to manipulate text elements, Chapter 5 details document wide and section formatting, Chapter 6 describes details of paragraph formatting, Chapter 7 covers character formatting, and Chapter 8 finishes the discussion with advanced formatting.

Unless you are an experienced graphics or document designer, plan to use the default formats for your first Word for

Windows documents. You can gradually develop your own styles over time.

Viewing Formatting Symbols

Every time you press Enter, the space bar, or Tab, and every time you create a new line or introduce an optional or nonbreaking hyphen, Word places a special mark in that location in the text. When you start your first Word session, you can't see these marks, but there are times at which it is important to see them. For example, if you want to see how many tab symbols start each item on a list or if you want to check that a single space follows each sentence, you'll want to see these special nonprinting marks. Table 2.3 shows the most common nonprinting symbols.

Table 2.3
Nonprinting
Symbols

Mark	Represents
↵Enter	New line mark
¶	Paragraph mark
→	Tab mark
Spacebar	Space mark
-	Optional hyphen
-	Nonbreaking hyphen

The Options dialog box for the View category, from the Tools menu, controls how a document looks on-screen, including whether nonprinting formatting marks are displayed. You not only can toggle the display of the scroll bars on-screen, but you can also turn the Status bar on and off. In the Nonprinting Characters group, you can control whether you will view formatting symbols. Note that **A**ll, the last entry in this box, is a counterpart to the Show/hide button, which was covered earlier in this chapter. The Show group allows you to control the display of other view options:

- The **D**raft Font check box controls the amount of formatting you view. Checking this check box shows underlined and bold formats, and shows picture placeholders rather than graphics.

- The condition of the **W**rap to Window check box indicates whether word wrap is turned on (a checked box) or off (a clear box).

- The **P**icture Placeholders check box controls whether you see a box or a graphic on the screen. If you choose to see a box instead of a graphic, you'll have faster processing time, because no time is devoted to drawing each graphic on the screen.

- The condition of the **F**ield Codes check box determines whether field codes or field results are displayed on the screen.

- The Boo**k**marks check box indicates whether you can see bookmarks in a Word document.

- The Fi**e**ld Shading drop-down list box indicates whether field results are highlighted at all times, only when se-lected, or not at all.

The following Quick Steps show you how to display nonprinting formatting symbols by using the Options dialog box for the View category.

Displaying Formatting Symbols

QUICK STEPS

1. From the **T**ools menu, select the Options com-mand (Alt , T , O).

   Word displays the Options dialog box.

2. Select the View category.

   Word displays the dialog box for view settings, which is shown in Figure 2.8. An X within a box indicates that an option is turned on.

3. Under Nonprinting Characters, select All.

   Word places an X in the box next to **A**ll.

4. Select OK or press ↵Enter .

   Word closes the dialog box and returns to the docu-ment.

Figure 2.8

The Options dialog box for the View category, which allows you to decide whether to display nonprinting options.

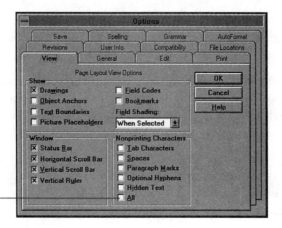

If you select this option you don't have to check any of the other options

TIP: To quickly turn on or off the display of formatting symbols within your document, click on the large paragraph mark on the Standard Toolbar.

Using the Mouse to Navigate a Document

Word offers three ways to move around a document: the mouse, the keyboard, and the Go To command. With the mouse or the keyboard, you can quickly scroll or jump around a document—from the top to the bottom or from the left margin to the right margin, or anywhere in between. If you know the specific page or section that you want to display, you can use the **Go** To command. This section explains how it's done with the mouse.

Using the Mouse in the Text Area

Using the mouse is an easy way to move around your document. You can either move the mouse pointer around the text area, or you can use the mouse with parts of the scroll bar.

To use the mouse in the text area, press the left mouse button, hold the button down, and drag the mouse along the desk. The mouse pointer moves in the direction the mouse moves. For example, to see the next page of a document, drag the mouse downward. As you drag the mouse, new parts of the document are displayed. The text that you drag over is highlighted, as in Figure 2.9 (that is, if text is normally displayed in black on a white background, it will now be displayed in reverse video, or white on a black background). Before making any changes to your document, make sure that you remove the highlight.

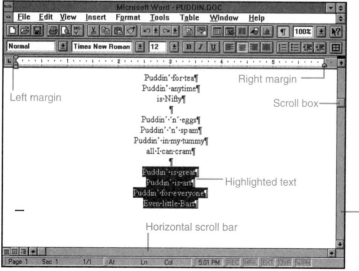

Figure 2.9

A screen showing highlighted or reverse video text. The scroll box indicates the specific location of the text on the screen within the document.

Using the Mouse with the Vertical Scroll Bar

There are three ways to move through a document by using the mouse and the vertical scroll bar: the scroll bar arrows, the scroll box (the small box within the scroll bar), and the area within the scroll bar. Since you'll be learning about both the vertical and horizontal scroll bars in this section and the next, make sure that both are displayed as shown in the following Quick Steps.

Turning On the Horizontal and Vertical Scroll Bars

1. Select the **T**ools menu and the **O**ptions command (Alt, T, O).

    Word displays an Option dialog box.

2. Click on the View tab.

    Word displays the Options dialog box for the View category (see Figure 2.8).

3. In the Window group, make sure that there are check marks on both the **V**ertical Scroll Bar and the Horizontal Scroll Bar.

    Word places Xs next to Horizontal Scroll Bar and the **V**ertical Scroll Bar, indicating that these options are both active.

4. Select OK or press ↵Enter.

    Word closes the dialog box and returns to the document.

You can use any combination of the three parts of a scroll bar to navigate your document:

Scroll bar arrows—Move through a document by dragging with the left mouse button on the arrows at either end of the scroll bar. As your document scrolls up and down the screen, notice that the thumb moves up and down the dark part of the bar to show you the part of the document currently displayed. If you click once on a scroll bar arrow, the document scrolls up or down one line.

Within the scroll bar—Click on the dark part of the scroll bar above or below the thumb. This entire area represents the length of your document. Every time you click, Word moves a screen minus two lines (you can use those lines to be aware of exactly where you are in the document). You won't see a change in the page number displayed in the Status bar until you click in the text area.

Thumb—Drag the thumb to a position on the scroll bar. When you release the left mouse button, you will move to a position in the document relative to the position of the thumb in the scroll bar. For example, if you move the thumb to the middle of the scroll bar, Word displays the middle of the document.

Using the Mouse with the Horizontal Scroll Bar

When your document is too wide to be completely displayed within the left and right margin of the screen, use horizontal scrolling to view the hidden portions. If you followed the preceding Quick Steps, the horizontal scroll bar is displayed.

The horizontal scroll bar is similar to the vertical scroll bar except that the dark area represents the width of the page (up to 22 inches) if you are in **P**age Layout view, or if you are in **N**ormal view. To display the edge of the document, drag the thumb to either end of the scroll bar. To alternately display the left and right edges of the document, click on the dark part of the scroll bar.

Using the Keyboard to Navigate a Document

When your fingers are on the keyboard, sometimes it's easier (and faster) to use keys to move around a document. That way you don't have to move your hand over to the mouse and then lose time finding your place on the keyboard again. Also, if you have to move the mouse and then press and hold a mouse button (when pressing one key can accomplish the same purpose), it might be more efficient to use the keyboard. As we pointed out in Chapter 1, you'll probably end up using both the mouse and the keyboard.

Table 2.4 lists the navigation keys and describes what happens to the insertion point when each key is pressed.

Table 2.4
Keyboard
Navigation
Commands

Press This Key	To Move the Insertion Point
↑	One item down a list or down one line of text
←	One character to the left
→	One character to the right
↑	One item up a list or up one line of text
Ctrl+↑	One paragraph down
Ctrl+←	One word to the left
Ctrl+→	One word to the right
Ctrl+↑	One paragraph up
Ctrl+Esc	To the end of the document
Ctrl+Home	To the beginning of the document
Ctrl+PgDn	To the bottom of a window
Ctrl+PgUp	To the top of a window
End	To the end of the current line
F5	To a specified location in the current document
Home	To the beginning of the current line
PgDn	Down one screen
PgUp	Up one screen

The Go To Command

In prior sections of this chapter, you learned two ways to navigate your document—with the mouse and with the keyboard. Word offers yet a third way to navigate your document: with the **G**o To command. When you know the number of the page that you want to jump to (especially if the document is very long), the **G**o To command on the **E**dit menu is a quick way of doing so.

Using the Go To Command

1. From the **E**dit menu, select the Go To command (Alt , E , G).

   Word opens the Go To dialog box, shown in Figure 2.9.

2. At the insertion point, enter a page number and select Go To or press ↵Enter .

   Word closes the dialog box and displays the top of the page that you requested.

3. To go forward or back a specific number of pages, type +n or −n (where *n* represents the number of pages), select Go To or press ↵Enter .

TIP: A shortcut for using the **G**o To command is double-clicking on the left part of the Status bar or pressing F5 . When Word displays the Go To dialog box, type the appropriate page number and press ↵Enter .

Figure 2.10

The Go To dialog box. Type the page number to which you want to jump.

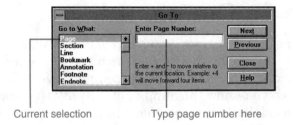

Current selection   Type page number here

Go To is a very powerful command, which you can also use to jump to sections, lines, bookmarks, footnotes, fields, tables, graphics, equations, objects, annotations, and so on.

Saving Your Work

In this chapter, you've learned the elements of a document and the basic steps to create it—entering and viewing text, and navigating a document. When you have completed your first document, it is time to save it. Word offers several ways to save your work.

- Use the **S**ave command from the **F**ile menu whenever you want to save a complete copy of a document.

- Use the Autosave feature to automatically save a document every few minutes as you are working on it. Simply tell Word that you want this feature turned on and then indicate the number of minutes between each save.

- Use the Fast Save feature to save only the changes that you have made since the last save, rather than saving the entire document.

- Use the **F**ile Save **A**s command to create a backup document as you save the original document or to save a copy of a document under a different name. In both cases, you will have two copies of the document.

You'll learn how to use each of these save commands in the following sections of this chapter.

Saving Your Document

Whether you have created a new document or changed an existing document, the only way to store a permanent copy on your hard drive is to use one of the save commands. Otherwise, when you turn off your computer or exit Word, the document will be lost forever.

 Click on the Save button to save the current document or template (see Chapter 12) or to open the Save As dialog box to save and name a new document.

To save a document, select the Save command from the **F**ile menu. Depending on whether you are saving a new document or an existing (previously saved) document, Word opens the Save As dialog box or automatically saves the document. If the document is a new document, Word opens the Save **A**s dialog box, shown in Figure 2.11. This dialog box looks complex but is easy to use. The parts of the Save As dialog box are:

File **N**ame—This section of the Save As dialog box lists all the documents in the current directory so you can avoid repeating a name. However, if you do type a duplicate name, Word asks if you want to replace the current file with this file, and you can answer Yes or No. For more information on naming documents, see the discussion following this list.

Figure 2.11

Save a new document using the Save As dialog box.

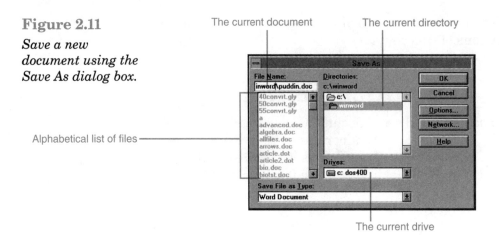

The current document

The current directory

Alphabetical list of files

The current drive

Save File as **Type**—This box allows you to convert a document to a different file type as it is saved. Use this feature when you edit a document using another word processor or another version of Word. Use it also when you need to transfer a document to another location—either to a mainframe computer at your office or to a remote site, using a communications service (such as CompuServe). You'll learn about file conversion later in this section.

Directories—The current directory is displayed at the top of this box, and all directories on the current drive, including the current directory and the root directory, are listed in the box. Directories listed in the **D**irectories box are aligned according to their relationship with the root directory and other directories: a subdirectory is shown below its parent directory, and is aligned farther to the right. This provides you with a visual illustration of the directory organization of your computer system.

NOTE: A computer's directory system resembles a family tree. The root directory is the ancestor from which all the parents and children come. A program directory such as winword is a parent; it is one level below the root directory. Winword has its own subdirectories, which are created during installation. As you create families of documents, you'll probably want to create other subdirectories under winword to help you organize your work.

Drives—This box displays the name of the current drive. If you click on the underlined down arrow at the right of the box, Word displays all the drives it sensed during installation. For many computer systems, c: represents the hard drive, and a: and b: indicate floppy disk drives. However, your computer might be set up with other disk-drive identifiers.

In addition to the standard OK and Cancel buttons, there are **N**etwork and **O**ptions buttons. Use **N**etwork to display the Connect Network dialog box (which is not covered in this book) and **O**ptions to go to the Options dialog box for the Save category (and any of the other Options dialog boxes).

TIP: Use the Save **A**s command to create a format for a new document. For example, if you create a standard cover letter, with margins and tabs carefully placed, save the original letter under a file name such as COVER. To use it again, retrieve COVER, type in the new name, address and other information, then use the Save As command to save it with a different name. COVER is saved without changes, ready for you to use as a pattern as often as you like.

Naming Your Document

When you save a document for the first time, Word asks you to provide a file name for the document. Recall that until you name your document, it has the default name of Document*n*, where *n* represents the number of this document for this Word session. Every time you start a new document, Word increases the document number by 1. When naming a document, follow these guidelines. File names are from one to eight characters in length, and valid file-name characters are alphanumeric (that is, letters or numbers) and the symbols ! @ # $ % &—( ) _ { } ~ ^. Try to give your documents file names that easily identify them. For example, name a letter LTR11281 (meaning that this is a letter created on November 28, 1991), or name a document about your company's inventory changes INVNCHGS. Start the names of a group of related files with the same combination of characters (W-CH01, W-CH02, W-CH03, and so on). When Word saves a document, it automatically adds a period (.) and the extension DOC to the file name (for example, W-CH01.DOC). When you save a new document, Word gives it a preliminary name of doc*n*.doc, where *n* represents the document number. Simply type a new file name right over the preliminary name.

Saving a New Document

When you save a document for the first time, Word gives you the opportunity to supply optional summary information in the Summary Info dialog box, shown in Figure 2.12. Enter anything you think will help to find this document in the future. Later in this chapter, you'll learn how to find files using the information you entered in the Summary Info dialog box. The name in the **A**uthor box is the name you typed during installation, but you can edit it. In the **K**eywords box, type unique or descriptive words pertaining to the document. Type any other sort of information in the Comments box. Select Statistics if you wish to see additional information about this document. Choose OK to save the information in the dialog box or Cancel to leave the dialog box without making any changes.

Figure 2.12

The Summary Information dialog box allows you to provide identification information for a new document.

Use the following Quick Steps to save a new document.

Saving a New Document

QUICK STEPS

1. With a new document to be saved for the first time displayed on the screen, select Save from the File menu, or press ⇧Shift + F12 .

   If this is a new unnamed document, Word opens the Save As dialog box, shown in Figure 2.11.

2. In the File **N**ame box, type a name up to eight characters long.

   Word will add the .DOC extension following the name you typed.

3. To save the file to another directory, click anywhere in the Directories box (or press Alt + D), which names the current directory.

   Word will place the document file in the directory you highlight.

4. To save the file to another drive, click anywhere in the Drives box (or press Alt + V) and select the drive you want.

   Word will place the document file on the drive you chose.

5. Select OK or press ↵Enter .

   Word opens the Summary Info dialog box (see Figure 2.12).

continues

continued

6. Select OK or press ⏎Enter, whether you entered summary information or not. You can also select Cancel to leave the Summary Info dialog box.

Word returns to the document and displays its new name in the Title bar.

From now on, when you save this document, either select the File menu and the Save command, then press ⇧Shift+ F12 or click on the Save button on the Toolbar, and Word automatically saves the document without displaying any dialog boxes.

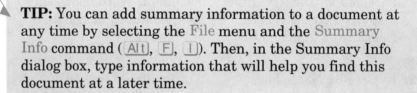

TIP: You can add summary information to a document at any time by selecting the File menu and the Summary Info command (Alt, F, I). Then, in the Summary Info dialog box, type information that will help you find this document at a later time.

TIP: If you do not want Word to display the Summary Info dialog box every time you save a new document or save using the Save **As** command, select the Tools menu and the Options command (Alt, T, O). Click on the Save tab. In the **O**ptions dialog box (see Figure 2.13), make sure that the Prompt for Summary **I**nfo check box is not checked.

Saving an Existing Document

When you saved the document the first time, you gave it a name and entered appropriate summary information. Because you have to provide this information only once, saving an existing document involves just one step, which follows.

Saving an Existing Document

1. With the document to be saved displayed on the screen, select Save from the **F**ile menu (Alt , F , S).

As Word saves the document, it displays status information in the Status bar. Then it returns to the current document.

Using the Autosave Feature

How much of your time are you willing to waste? Let's say that you've spent an hour working on a new document and suddenly there is an electrical blackout. When the lights come back on, you'll have to spend another hour re-creating the document unless you have saved it. Don't wait until you complete your work before you save it. Periodically use the **F**ile **S**ave command to save your document, or let Word automatically save your document at a regular time interval that you determine.

When you have Autosave turned on, Word counts the minutes (up to 120) since the last save. While this count goes on, you can continue working without interruption. When the count equals the number of minutes that you chose, the next time you stop typing or issuing commands, Word saves your document automatically. Then the cycle starts all over again.

Turn the Autosave feature on from the Options dialog box in the Save category. Open the dialog box by using Tools Options (Alt , T , O) or File Save As (Alt , F , A). The Options dialog box for the Save category provides four choices, all of which you will learn about in this section. You can choose:

Always Create **B**ackup Copy—When you select this option, Word saves both the new version of a document and the prior version.

Allow **F**ast Saves—This option, the default, requires Word to save only the most recent changes, not the entire document.

Prompt for Summary **I**nfo—This option, which is also a default, automatically displays the Summary Info dialog box when you first save a document.

Automatic **S**ave Every—When you select this option and set a time interval, Word automatically saves the current document every few minutes as you work on it. This means that your current copy will be no older than the interval you defined. To start the Autosave feature, use the following Quick Steps.

Using the Autosave Feature

1. Select Save As from the File menu (Alt, F, A).

   Word opens the Save As dialog box (see Figure 2.11).

2. Select the Options button.

   Word opens an Options dialog box.

3. Click on the Save tab.

   Word displays the Options dialog box for the Save category (Figure 2.13).

4. Click on the Automatic Save Every box.

   Word displays 10 in the Minutes box.

5. Choose the interval you want between saves (from 1 to 120 minutes). Select OK or press ↵Enter.

   Word returns to the Save As dialog box.

6. Select Close.

   Word returns to the document.

From now on, Word calculates the time and, if you have changed the document, saves the document automatically at the interval that you set. As an automatic save occurs, you'll see a message in the Status bar.

The Fast Save Feature

Fast Save, which is a Word default setting, saves only the changes made since the last save. This means that processing time is lessened because the computer does not have to save the entire document. However, Fast Save actually increases the size of a document because it doesn't change the document file; rather, it adds the changes to the end of the file. If this feature is turned off, Word saves the entire document.

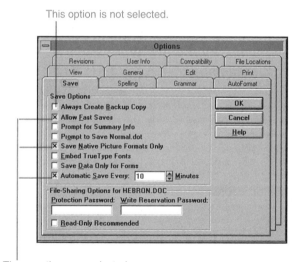

This option is not selected.

These options are selected.

Figure 2.13
The Options dialog box for the Save category, which allows you to define or change save options.

Note that Word occasionally consolidates all the changes you have made to your document since the last regular save by automatically performing a regular save. If you automatically create a backup copy of a document whenever you save, Word will not use the Fast Save feature, even if it has been turned on. Before using a feature that consumes a great deal of memory (for example, sorting or building an index), it's a good idea to do a regular save; otherwise, you may run out of memory during processing. This wastes time because you then have to start your task all over again.

Follow these Quick Steps to activate the Fast Save feature.

Setting the Fast Save Feature

1. Select Save As from the File menu (Alt , F , A).

   Word opens the Save As dialog box (see Figure 2.11).

2. Click on the Options button.

   Word opens an Options dialog box (see Figure 2.13).

3. If needed, click on the Save tab and optionally, click on the Allow Fast Saves box.

   If Word displays an X in the Allow Fast Saves box, the Fast Save feature is turned on. If there is no X, this feature is turned off.

4. Select OK or press ↵Enter .

   Word returns to the Save As dialog box.

5. Select Close or press ↵Enter .

   Word returns to the document.

Backing Up Your Files

What if you make many changes to a document and find that the original version is better? What if you discover that the most recent copy of a document has been saved to an unreadable part of your hard drive? In either case, if you are using Word's Always Create Backup Copy feature, you can recover the previous version of a document.

As you learned at the beginning of this section, when Word saves a document, it automatically adds the extension .DOC after the file name. If you activate the Always Create **B**ackup Copy feature, Word renames the prior saved version from .DOC to .BAK when you save the current version of a document. Each time you save this document, Word renames the previous .DOC file to .BAK, thus erasing the previous backup file. You can select either the Fast Save feature or the Always Create Backup Copy feature. You cannot select both. To create backup copies, follow these Quick Steps:

Creating Backup Copies

1. From the **F**ile menu select Save **A**s (Alt , F , A).

   Word opens the Save As dialog box (see Figure 2.11).

2. Click on the Options button.

   Word opens an Options dialog box (see Figure 2.13).

3. If needed, click on the Save tab, and then optionally click on the Always Create **B**ackup Copy box.

   If Word displays an X in this box, the last document saved becomes the backup document when a save occurs. The result is two documents with the same file name but different extensions.

4. Select OK or press ↵Enter .

   Word returns to the Save As dialog box.

5. Select Close.

   Word returns to the document.

Besides creating a backup, another way you can protect the original document is to use the Save **A**s command to give a different name to another copy of the document. For example, if the original document is named MEMO0822.DOC, save a "test" document as MEMOTEST.DOC.

Although regularly saving documents to the hard drive and using the Always Create **B**ackup Copy feature is important, it's equally important to back up, or copy, all your files to floppy disk (or tape backup) periodically. Backing up your documents and then storing the backup floppy disks away from your office may save you a great deal of work if there is a catastrophe at your workplace.

An additional security measure is to invest in a UL-approved electrical power strip containing a surge suppressor. Plug your computer system into the power strip rather than directly into a wall socket. Although this is not foolproof, the power strip helps to protect your computer system from power surges and brown-outs.

Retrieving a Document

Now you have created your first document, and you have also learned how easy it is to save a document. When you save a document to your hard drive or to floppy disk, you have a copy that you can use at a later time. But how do you move a copy of a document back to your computer screen? You won't always create a document from scratch. Many times, you will use Word to edit existing documents.

> Click on the Open button to display the Open dialog box from which you can retrieve an existing document.

To retrieve your document, select the Open command from the **F**ile menu. Word displays the Open dialog box, as shown in Figure 2.14. When you see this Open dialog box for the first time, it will look quite familiar. In fact, it's almost identical to the Save

As dialog box. The left side of this dialog box lists file names, directories, drives, and file types. On the right side, instead of Network and Options, you'll see the **F**ind File button, the **C**onfirm Conversions check box, and the **R**ead Only check box.

Find File allows you to view a document in a special window in the Find File dialog box. To see the contents of a document, click on the document name in the **L**isted Files list and the contents will appear (slightly shrunken but legible) in the window on the right. You'll get more information about the **F**ind File command later in this chapter.

Check the **C**onfirm Conversions check box to have Word prompt you to approve of the file converter that it uses to convert a file created in another word processing format to Word 6.0 format. Check the **R**ead Only box so that this document can be reviewed on-screen but not edited or saved. With this box checked you can, however, still save the file under a different name. The new document will not have the **R**ead Only restriction.

The following Quick Steps show you the simple procedures for retrieving a document from the hard drive.

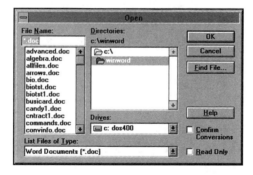

Figure 2.14
The Open dialog box with a list of the documents in the current directory and a list of other directories on your hard drive.

Retrieving a Document

1. From the **F**ile menu, select **O**pen (Alt, F, O), or press Ctrl+F12.

   Word displays the Open dialog box. The File **N**ame box lists the .DOC files in the current directory, and the **D**irectories box allows you to display a list of .DOC files in other directories and drives.

2. Select the name of the file you want to retrieve, and choose OK or press ↵Enter.

   Word displays the retrieved document on the screen.

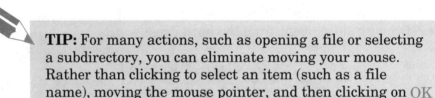

TIP: For many actions, such as opening a file or selecting a subdirectory, you can eliminate moving your mouse. Rather than clicking to select an item (such as a file name), moving the mouse pointer, and then clicking on OK or pressing ↵Enter, you can double-click on the item to take the action.

Shortcuts for Retrieving a Document

If you don't know either the name of the file that you want to retrieve, the extension of the file, or its location, Word provides alternate ways to retrieve a document from the Open dialog box. One way is to use an asterisk (*) as a wildcard to represent any group of characters in place of a file name and/or extension. If you type * in place of a file name, but type the .DOC extension, Word lists any files having the .DOC extension. If you type a specific file name and then type * instead of an extension, Word lists any files having that file name and any extension. Use the asterisk wildcard as follows:

- To retrieve a file whose name you don't know and with any extension, in the List Files of **T**ype box, select the arrow button (the underlined down arrow). When the list of types opens, select the type that you think is the most likely to be correct or select All files (*.*). Word displays all documents of that type in the File **N**ame box.

- To retrieve a file whose name you don't know but with a known extension other than .DOC, move the mouse pointer to the File **N**ame box and type *, then a period (.), then the desired extension.

- To retrieve a file when you remember part of its name, move the mouse pointer to the File **N**ame box and type as many characters as you remember followed by *, a period, and the extension. Word displays a list of all the files with that extension which start with the characters you typed.

- To display a complete list of files in the current directory, type *.* in the File **N**ame box.

Another Word wildcard character is the question mark (?), which represents a single character. For example, if you enter LTR?????.DOC, Word will list every file starting with LTR, followed by any five characters, and with a .DOC extension. So you will find LTR11110.DOC, LTRABCDE.DOC, but not LTRABCD.DOC, LTRGHIJK.BAK, or LTR0928.TXT.

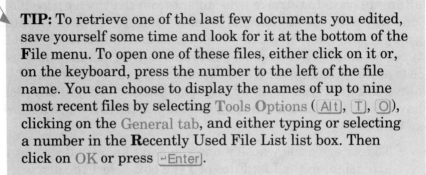

TIP: To retrieve one of the last few documents you edited, save yourself some time and look for it at the bottom of the **F**ile menu. To open one of these files, either click on it or, on the keyboard, press the number to the left of the file name. You can choose to display the names of up to nine most recent files by selecting Tools Options (Alt , T , O), clicking on the General tab, and either typing or selecting a number in the **R**ecently Used File List list box. Then click on OK or press ↵Enter .

Using the Find File Feature

Find File is an all-purpose command that allows you to copy, print, open and delete documents (in some cases, several documents at a time). In addition, you can search for specific documents using information from the Summary Info box, and you can view the contents of a file before opening it. In this book, we'll tell you about a few of the options that you can use to find Word files.

When you select the Find File command from the **F**ile menu or click on the Find File button in the Open dialog box (see Figure 2.14), Word displays the Find File dialog box (see Figure 2.15) as it appeared at the end of your last search. The Find File dialog box allows you to list the files in a particular directory or path, sort them in different ways, display the resulting list of files, and preview the document you are thinking of opening.

If you are looking for a particular file and remember only sketchy information about it (such as the approximate date it was created, its title, any keywords, or its author), click on the Search button in the Find File dialog box to narrow your choice of files. When you click on the Search button, Word displays the Search dialog box (shown in Figure 2.16), in which you can specify all or part of a file name and its location. When you click on OK, Word returns to the Find File dialog box and compiles a list of files that match the criteria that you set. Then you can preview the contents of a selected file, get information about a file, or read summary information.

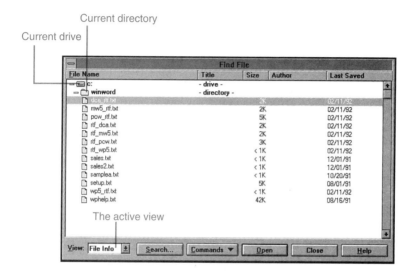

Current directory

Current drive

The active view

Figure 2.15
The Find File dialog box, showing the results of a search.

You can display different types of information about a file by selecting from the View drop-down list box. If you select Preview and select a file, Word displays part of the file in the Preview window. If you select File Info, Word displays a table that lists file names, titles, file size, authors, and the last date each file was saved. If you choose Summary, Word displays the list of file names and the summary information for the highlighted file.

When you choose a file, you can click on the Commands button to open, print, view the summary, delete, or copy it. You can also sort the list of files (by author, creation date, last saved by, last saved date, name, size). You can also use Find File to print a group of files at one time. To find out how to do this, read the next section of this chapter.

Figure 2.16

The Search dialog box in which you can define the next search for files.

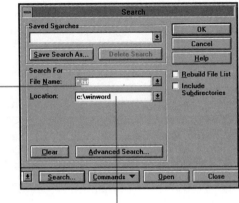

This entry indicates that you are searching for all files with the .txt extension.

The directory in which the search takes place.

Printing a Document

Now that you have created your first document, you are ready to print it. Word for Windows' printing options are so extensive that they warrant their own chapter, but, for now, just accept Word's default settings. Remember that earlier in this chapter, you were introduced to the Print Preview print option, which will be described more thoroughly in Chapter 9.

 Click on the Print button in the icon bar to print this document using the default print options.

When you start the print process, Word displays the Print dialog box, as shown in Figure 2.17. Here is an overview of the items in the Print dialog box. Chapter 9 will cover them in detail.

Printer—At the top of the dialog box, Word displays the name of the active printer and the port to which it is attached (for example, LPT1:, COM1:, etc.).

Print What—You can print the document, or you can print summary information, annotations, styles, AutoText entries, or key assignments for the document. Document is the default.

Copies—To print more than one copy of this document, enter a value (from 1 to 32767) in this box. The default number of copies is 1.

Curr**e**nt Page—Select this radio button to print the current page.

Selectio**n**—If you have selected any text in the document, you can select this radio button to print the selection. If no text is selected, this button is dimmed or unavailable.

Pa**g**es—You can print the entire document, the current page, or a range of pages by typing page numbers or ranges of page numbers in this text box.

Print—You can print the entire document, all odd pages, or all even pages by selecting from this drop-down list box.

Print to F**i**le—Check this box to print this document to a file rather than to the printer. This enables you to save the document with its print format in a file, and you can print it at a later time.

Collate Copies—If you are printing more than one copy of a document, check this box to print multiple copies from the first page to the last, or clear the box to print all the copies of the first page, then all the copies of the second page, and so on.

Figure 2.17

The Print dialog box with its default settings.

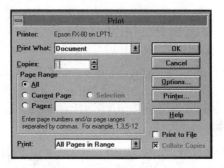

Select the Options button to display the Options dialog box for the Print category, which you'll learn about in Chapter 9. Select the Printer button to make another printer the active printer or to change any number of printer setup options.

Before you print a document, it's a good idea to preview it on-screen, so from the File menu, select Print Preview (Alt, F, V); then select Cancel to return to your document or print directly from Print Preview. Assuming that your document looks great, follow these Quick Steps to print it.

QUICK STEPS

Printing a Document

1. From the File menu select Print (Alt, F, P), or press Ctrl+⇧Shift+F12.

   Word opens the Print dialog box. Notice that the insertion point is in the Copies box.

2. Select OK or press ↵Enter.

   As Word prints the document, it advises you of its status. After printing, Word returns to the current document screen.

Word also enables you to print several files at once using the **F**ind File command. Follow these Quick Steps to print selected files:

Printing Several Files Simultaneously

1. From the **F**ile menu, select Find File (Alt , F , F)

   Word displays the Find File dialog box (see Figure 2.15) with the results of the last search.

2. To begin a new search, click on the Search button.

   Word displays the Search dialog box, as shown in Figure 2.16.

3. In the File **N**ame box either select a file type or type all or part of a file name. (Remember that you can use wild-cards.) In the Location drop-down list box, select a drive and then type directory and subdirectory names in the text box. It's a good idea to check the Include Subdirectories check box to automatically include subdirectories in the search. Then click on OK or press ↵Enter .

   Word closes the Search dialog box, returns to the Find File dialog box, and starts compiling a list of files.

4. Select files to be printed.

   Word highlights each file you select.

   continues

continued

5. Click on the Commands button. From the resulting list, select Print.

Word displays the Print dialog box.

6. Click on OK or press ⏎Enter.

Word begins to print.

TIP: You can choose one file by clicking on it. You can choose a contiguous list of files by clicking on the first file and then pressing and holding down the ⇧Shift key while clicking on the last file to be selected. You can choose several noncontiguous files by clicking on the first file and then pressing and holding down the Ctrl key while clicking on the files to be added to the list.

Selecting Text with the Mouse

- Selecting a word—Double-click anywhere in the word.
- Selecting a line—Click in the selection bar.
- Selecting a sentence—Hold down the Ctrl key and click anywhere in the sentence.
- Selecting a block of text—Click to start the selection, move the pointer to the other end of the selection, hold the ⇧Shift key down, and click.
- Selecting a document—Hold down the Ctrl key and click in the selection bar.
- Selecting a column of text—Press and hold down the right mouse button at one side of the selection, drag the pointer diagonally to the opposite corner of the selection, and release the mouse button.

Copying Text

To copy selected text, from the Edit menu, choose Copy (Ctrl+C, Ctrl+Ins, or Alt, E, C); or click on the Copy button (eighth from left) on the Standard toolbar.

Cutting Text

To cut selected text, from the Edit menu, choose Cut (Ctrl+X, ⇧Shift+Ins, or Alt, E, T); or click on the Cut button (seventh from left) on the Standard toolbar.

Pasting Text

To paste copied or cut text, from the Edit menu, choose Paste (Ctrl+V, ⇧Shift+Ins, or Alt, E, P); or click on the Paste button (ninth from the left) on the Standard toolbar.

Manipulating Text

Creating a document is only the first step in its evolution. Chances are you'll have to edit your document many times during its lifetime. For example, you might have to write a proposal that must be reviewed in order to get to its final form, or you might have to create a monthly report that must reflect the latest sales figures. In Chapter 2, you learned how to move around a document using both the mouse and the keyboard. In this chapter, you'll build on that knowledge by navigating a document in order to select text on one page and move or copy it to another. You'll also learn how to find text and replace it with other text.

Selecting Text

Selection is a key technique in Word for Windows. When you select text in your document, you identify for Word the particular unit of text, called a *block*, that you want a Word command to act on. The selected text appears highlighted on your screen. You can use either the mouse or the keyboard to select text; the upcoming sections will explain both techniques.

As you work on a document, you select blocks of text—words, sentences, lines, paragraphs, blocks, columns, even the entire document, so that you can perform an operation such as copying, moving, or deleting. For example, suppose your manager likes the contents of a document but doesn't like the order in which the information is presented. If you have to shuffle several sections around, simply select one section and move it to its new location, and then continue the process until your document is completely reorganized. On a smaller scale, you might be working on a letter with four paragraphs. To move the second paragraph after the third is an easy process using Word.

Word provides a special selection feature, column selection. You can use either the mouse or the keyboard to select a column. Regular text selection extends from the left margin to the right margin if you select one line or more of text. Although you can also use column selection from margin to margin, you'll probably use it to select a segment of a line (the width of the column) and then extend that selection up or down (the length of the column). For example, if you have a document with lines that have been indented by repeated pressing of the space bar, every line will start out with many spaces in front of the first character. If you need to edit that document, rather than taking the time to delete the spaces line by line, you can delete a column of excess spaces. You then can indent using tabs. You can also use the same method to remove the bullets preceding a list while keeping the list format. Just select the column of bullets and delete it.

Using the Mouse to Select Text

A beginner usually finds the mouse easier to use than the keyboard for selecting large sections of text. When you use the mouse, you can easily define and, at the same time, view the boundaries of your selection, and you don't have to learn special keys to do so.

To select a block of text, move the mouse pointer to either the beginning or the end of the block of text to be selected. Then press and hold down the left mouse button and drag the mouse pointer toward the other end of the block of text. (From here on, this book will refer to the procedure just described simply as *"dragging."*) As you move the mouse, Word highlights the selected block of text. When you reach the end of the selection, release the left mouse button. The highlight remains until you click the left mouse button or press a key.

When text is highlighted, be careful that you do not accidentally press a wrong key. Pressing any of the alphanumeric keys or keys such as the space bar, Tab, and Enter causes highlighted text to disappear and be replaced by the character or symbol that you typed. If this happens, immediately press Ctrl+Z to reverse your action and make the highlighted text reappear.

CAUTION

Use these Quick Steps to select any block of text, from one character to your entire document.

Selecting a Block of Text with the Mouse

1. Move the mouse pointer to the first character to be selected. Then press and hold down the left mouse button. (To select a column of text, press Alt and hold down the left mouse button.)

   The insertion point remains at the first character that you select.

2. Drag the mouse to the other end of the selection and release the mouse button.

   Word highlights the selected text.

Word also provides these mouse shortcuts for selecting specific text units:

To select a word—Move the mouse pointer to any character in the word and double-click the left mouse button. Word highlights both the word and the space immediately to the right of the word.

To select a line of text—Move the mouse pointer to the selection bar (see Figure 3.1), the invisible blank column located at the left edge of the text area. When the mouse pointer is in the selection bar, it changes shape from an I-beam to an arrow pointing up and to the right. Move the arrow to the left margin of the line you want to select and click the left mouse button. To select more than one line at a time, you can continue to hold the left mouse button down and drag the mouse up or down from the point at which you first clicked.

Figure 3.1

The mouse pointer within the selection bar.

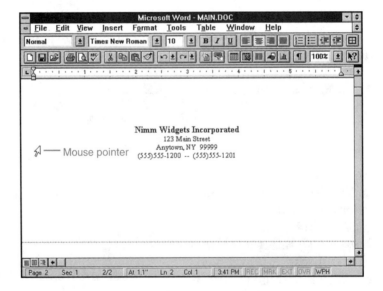

To select a sentence—Move the mouse pointer anywhere within the sentence, holding down the Ctrl key, and clicking the left mouse button.

To select a paragraph—Move the mouse pointer to the selection bar; move the mouse pointer in front of any line in the paragraph, and then double-click the left button.

To select multiple paragraphs—Move the mouse pointer to the selection bar in front of any one line in the first or last paragraph to be selected, double-click the left mouse button, and then drag the mouse pointer up or down within the selection bar.

To select text without dragging the mouse pointer—Move the mouse pointer to one end of the text to be selected and click the left mouse button. Then move the pointer to the other end of the text to be selected, hold the ⇧Shift key down, and click the left mouse button. This command is useful when the text you want to select extends beyond the boundaries of the computer screen.

To select the document—Move the mouse pointer to the left of the screen into the selection bar. Hold down the Ctrl key and click the left mouse button.

To select a column—Move the mouse pointer to the beginning of the column of text to be selected. Press Alt and click the left mouse button, and drag the pointer diagonally down to the opposite corner of the column. If any character is at least halfway in the selection area, Word considers it to be selected. When you've highlighted the area that you want to select, release the mouse button.

If you change your mind about the current text selection, just move the mouse pointer off the selected text and click. Word turns off the highlight. If you accidentally select too much text, you can "back up" by continuing to hold down the left mouse button and moving the mouse pointer to the left.

Using the Keyboard to Select Text

As you learned in Chapters 1 and 2, although the mouse is easier to use, utilizing the keyboard can be more efficient. For example, press F8 to begin a text selection at the insertion point. This action activates the EXT indicator in the Status bar, as shown in

Figure 3.2. EXT is an abbreviation for Extend Selection mode, which is the keyboard equivalent of pressing and holding the left mouse button. When Extend Selection mode is active, text selection is cumulative; each time you select text, the new selection is added to the text that you've already selected. Every time you press F8 , the next larger text unit is selected, from word, sentence, paragraph, section, to finally your entire document.

Figure 3.2

The EXT on the Status bar, which indicates that Word is in Extend Selection mode.

Active Indicator

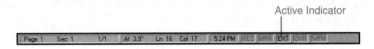

No matter how large a block you have selected, you can press a combination of arrow keys to adjust the characters selected. You can also deselect text in reverse order of selection. Press ⇧Shift + F8 and the highlight will back up in the reverse order that the text was selected. To turn off Extend Selection mode, either press the Esc key or perform an editing command.

When Extend Selection mode is active, you can extend your selection to a specific character to the right of your current selection by pressing that character (letter, number, or symbol) on the keyboard. For example, in the text The quick brown fox jumped over the lazy dog, move the insertion point in front of quick and press F8. If you type x, the selection will be extended to the end of the word fox.

To select text in Extend Selection mode with the keyboard, use the following Quick Steps.

Selecting a Block of Text in Extend Selection Mode with the Keyboard

1. Use any combination of arrow keys (↑ , ↓ , → , ←) to move the insertion point to either

Word turns on Extend Selection mode. The Status bar displays the text EXT, as shown in Figure 3.2, to

the beginning or the end of the area you want to select. Then press F8.

indicate that Extend Selection is active.

2. Keep pressing F8 until all the desired text is highlighted. Press ⇧Shift + F8 to deselect text in reverse order.

Word highlights the selected text.

Remember that Word remains in Extend Selection mode until you press Esc or perform an editing command.

CAUTION

You don't always have to enter Extend Selection mode to highlight text. For example, to start a selection at the insertion point, hold down the ⇧Shift key and use the arrow keys to define the block of text to be selected. Table 3.1 lists text selections and the keys used to make those selections.

Table 3.1
Text Selection Keys

To Select	Press
A document	Ctrl + F5 (on the numeric keypad)
To the end of a paragraph	Ctrl + ⇧Shift + ↓
To the beginning of a word	Ctrl + ⇧Shift + ←
To the end of a word	Ctrl + ⇧Shift + →
To the beginning of a paragraph	Ctrl + ⇧Shift + ↑
To the end of a document	Ctrl + ⇧Shift + End
To the beginning of a document	Ctrl + ⇧Shift + Home
One line down	⇧Shift + ↓
One character to the left	⇧Shift + ←
One character or graphic to the right	⇧Shift + →

continues

Table 3.1
Continued

To Select	Press
One line up	⬆Shift + ↑
To the end of a line	⬆Shift + End
To the beginning of a line	⬆Shift + Home
One screen down	⬆Shift + PgDn
One screen up	⬆Shift + PgUp

TIP: A shortcut for selecting a large block of text is to move the insertion point to one end of the text you want to select, press F8 (to start Extend Selection mode), press F5 (the Go To command), enter a page number in the dialog box, and press ⏎Enter. Then Word extends the selection to the top of the page that you just jumped to. If you change your mind about the selection, press ⬆Shift + F5; then Word places the insertion point back at the previous location.

You can also select a column of text using the keyboard. For example, you can use column selection to switch the positions of columns in a table. To select the first position in a column of text, usually starting at the top left of your selection, press Ctrl + ⬆Shift + F8. Press any combination of arrow keys to define the last position in the column, usually using a downward diagonal movement to the lower right corner. Word always lets you know the selected area by highlighting the column. To exit column selection, press Ctrl + ⬆Shift + F8 again or press Esc.

Moving, Copying, and Deleting Text

After you have selected text, use the **Cut, C**opy, and **P**aste commands on the **E**dit menu (see Figure 3.3) to copy or move the text to another location within your document. For example, to transpose two paragraphs, first select the paragraph to be moved and then use **Cut** and **P**aste to remove the paragraph from its original position in the document and place it in its new location. Note that if you try to use **Cut** or **Copy** without first selecting text, Word displays the **E**dit menu with these commands dimmed. This is a reminder that you must select text before using these commands.

Although **Cut** and **Copy** behave similarly, there is one important difference between the two commands: **Cut** actually deletes the selected text from its original location, while **Copy** makes a copy of the selected text AND the selected text remains in its original location.

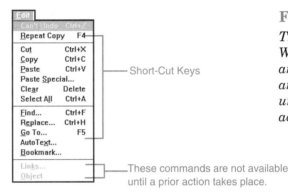

Figure 3.3

The Edit menu. When commands are dimmed, they are not accessible until another action takes place.

You can paste the same selected text as many times as you like by repeatedly executing the **P**aste command. For each copy to be pasted, execute the **P**aste command one time. Note that you can reposition the insertion point for each subsequent paste. Word remembers the pasted copy until you make another text selection.

Copying and Pasting Text

NOTE: To copy one section of a document to another position, select the text to be copied, and from the **E**dit menu, choose the Copy command (Ctrl+C, Ctrl+Ins, or Alt, E, C). Move the insertion point to the place the copied text should go. Then paste the text in its new location using the Paste command (Ctrl+V, ⇧Shift+Ins, or Alt, E, P). The original text remains in its original location in the document while a duplicate is in another location.

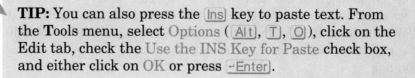

TIP: You can also press the ⌊Ins⌋ key to paste text. From the **Tools** menu, select Options (⌊Alt⌋, ⌊T⌋, ⌊O⌋), click on the Edit tab, check the Use the INS Key for Paste check box, and either click on OK or press ⌊↵Enter⌋.

Click on the Copy button to copy the specified text or graphics from the document and to place it in the Clipboard.

Click on the Paste button to insert the contents of the Clipboard at the location of the insertion point in the document.

Cutting and Pasting Text

To cut a section of a document and place it in another section, select the text to be cut, and from the **Edit** menu, choose the Cut command (⌊Ctrl⌋+⌊X⌋, ⌊⇧Shift⌋+⌊Del⌋, or ⌊Alt⌋, ⌊E⌋, ⌊T⌋). The selected text is deleted from its original location in the document. Then move the insertion point to the place where the deleted text should go, and paste the text in its new location using the Paste command (⌊Ins⌋, ⌊Ctrl⌋+⌊V⌋, ⌊⇧Shift⌋+⌊Ins⌋, or ⌊Alt⌋, ⌊E⌋, ⌊P⌋).

Click on the Cut button to delete the specified text or graphics from the document and to place it in the Clipboard.

Click on the Paste button to insert the contents of the Clipboard at the location of the insertion point in the document.

To quickly create multiple copies of a short form, open a document and enter the text. Place blank lines after the text by pressing ⏎Enter four or five times; then select the text and all the paragraph marks. Press Ctrl+C to copy the text, and move the insertion point to the bottom of the document. Repeatedly press Ctrl+V to paste the copied text until you have reached the end of the page or until you have created as many forms as you need. Then print and cut the forms apart. For example, teachers could use this technique to create permission slips for a school trip.

Moving Text with Drag and Drop

Word also provides a shortcut method, drag and drop, for moving text. The Quick Steps that follow show you how to move selected text from one location to another.

Moving Text with Drag and Drop

1. Select the text to be moved either with the mouse or with the keyboard.

Word highlights your selection.

continues

continued

2. Place the mouse pointer anywhere within your selection.

Notice that the mouse pointer outside the selection is an I-beam, but inside the selection is an arrow that points up and to the left.

3. Press and hold the left mouse button.

The mouse pointer changes shape (by adding a dimmed box to its tail) to indicate that it is holding the selected text.

4. Drag the selected text to its new location.

As you drag the selected text to its new location, a dim insertion point also moves along with the selected text.

5. When you reach the new location, release the left mouse button.

Word changes the mouse pointer back to its starting shape.

6. Click the left mouse button anywhere on the screen.

Word turns off the highlight.

TIP: To move selected text without changing the contents of the Clipboard, use drag and drop instead of selecting **E**dit **C**opy or **E**dit **C**ut. Using either command replaces the contents of the Clipboard with new contents. Using drag and drop does not place anything in the Clipboard.

Deleting Text

To delete characters, you can press the `◆Backspace` key to delete the character to the left of the insertion point or press the `Del` key to delete the character to the right of the insertion point. If you hold down either `◆Backspace` or `Del`, Word continues to delete characters until you release the key. To delete a block of text, select the text to be deleted and then press the `Del` key, or use the Cut command. If you use `◆Backspace` or `Del` to delete characters, the only way you can recover those deleted characters is to choose the Undo command (`Ctrl`+`Z`). You'll learn more about the Undo command shortly.

The Clipboard Versus the Spike

What happens to the selected text between the cutting and/or copying and the pasting? The text is stored in the Clipboard, which is a temporary storage facility that holds one piece of text (or graphics) at a time. Another storage facility is the Spike, a special AutoText entry that you use by pressing certain keys. (AutoText is an area in which you can store text or graphics that you plan to use often.) The Spike accumulates text and graphics, rather than holding just the last cut or copied text or graphics, as the Clipboard does. Later in this chapter, you'll learn about AutoText.

There are some important differences between the Clipboard and the Spike:

- The Spike doesn't keep just the last cut or copied text or graphics as the Clipboard does. The Spike accumulates all text and graphics until you choose to clear it.

- When you exit Windows, the contents of the Spike remains, but the contents of the Clipboard is lost.

- You can use both the mouse and the keyboard to cut, copy, and paste with the Clipboard, but the Spike uses only the keyboard (namely, Ctrl+F3, Ctrl+Shift+F3, and F3).

- While you can save the contents of the Clipboard to a file, you cannot save the contents of the Spike to a file.

- You can display the content of the Clipboard on its own small window (the Clipboard Viewer), but you cannot see the content of the Spike until you insert it into your document.

See Table 3.2 for a summary of the Clipboard and the Spike keys.

Table 3.2
Clipboard and Spike Keys

Press	To perform this task
Ctrl+Ins	Copies a selection from a windows application and puts it into the Clipboard
PrtSc	Copies the current screen into the Clipboard
Alt+PrtSc	Copies the active window into the Clipboard
Shift+Del	Cuts a selection from a Windows application and puts it into the Clipboard
Shift+Ins	Pastes the contents of the Clipboard into a Windows application
Del	Clears the contents of the Clipboard completely
Ctrl+F3	Cuts a selection from Word and puts it in the Spike
Ctrl+Shift+F3	Inserts the contents of the Spike into the Word document and empties the Spike
F3	Inserts the contents of the Spike into the Word document but does not empty the Spike. Be sure to type spike before you press F3.

Using the Clipboard

The Clipboard is actually a Windows program. Since Word for Windows runs under Windows, the Clipboard is available for

Word and other Windows applications or programs. Thus, you can use Clipboard to cut or copy text or graphics between Word and other Windows applications.

The Clipboard stores only one item at a time. Every time you store text or graphics, the last contents of the Clipboard are overwritten and are lost forever. If you exit Word but stay in Windows, the contents of the Clipboard remain. However, once you exit Windows, the Clipboard is emptied (unless you have saved the contents to a file, as you will see shortly).

One advantage of using the Clipboard is that you can easily see its contents from within Word. Once you have opened the Clipboard Viewer (see Figure 3.5), you can use its menus—**F**ile, **E**dit, **D**isplay, and **H**elp. Use the **F**ile menu to save the contents of the Clipboard to a file, which has a .CLP extension, or open that file to bring the contents back into the Clipboard. For example, if you are in the middle of an editing session and you have to leave the office quickly because of an emergency, just store the contents of the Clipboard. The next day, you can open the stored file and start where you left off. Use the **E**dit menu in the Clipboard window to delete the contents of the Clipboard, and use the **D**isplay menu to change the way you view the contents of the Clipboard. The **H**elp menu provides Clipboard-related help. To learn more about the Clipboard, refer to your Windows manuals.

The fastest way to get to the Clipboard Viewer is to press Ctrl+Esc to open the Task List (see Figure 3.4), double-click on the Program Manager line, and double-click on the Clipboard Viewer icon usually found in the Main group.

Figure 3.4

The Windows Task List from which you can select Program Manager or another active Windows application.

Figure 3.5
The Clipboard and
its contents—the
latest text that has
been copied or cut.

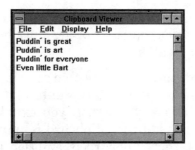

Using the Spike

The Spike is similar to the Clipboard, but while the Clipboard replaces its previous contents with the most recent text or graphics that you cut or copy, the Spike appends the cut text or graphics to the end of its current contents. You determine whether and/or when to clear the Spike. If you don't clear it, text and graphics continue to be added to the end of its current contents as you cut them from documents.

CAUTION   Because you have to cut text or graphics in order to insert them into the Spike, it's a good idea to finish your document, save it, and then make a copy from which you can cut.

Two ways to use the Spike to do your job more efficiently are:

Accumulate text from throughout a document and then insert it at the beginning of the document. This is a quick way to create a summary of your document.

Create portfolio or picture file of the graphics that you use in your documents and may want to reuse. Accumulate the graphics in the Spike, insert them into a new document, save, and then print.

These Quick Steps demonstrate how to use the Spike.

Using the Spike

1. Select some text and press Ctrl + F3.

The Spike cuts the text from the document.

2. Repeat step 1 until you have accumulated all the text you want in the Spike.

The Spike accumulates the text in order of deletion and separates each accumulated piece with a paragraph mark.

3. To insert the contents of the Spike into a document and empty the Spike at the same time, place the insertion point where you want to insert the contents and press Ctrl + ⇧Shift + F3.

The Spike empties its contents into the document.

4. To insert the contents of the Spike into a document without emptying it, move the insertion point where you want to insert the contents, type spike, and press F3.

The Spike copies its contents into the document over the word spike.

5. To reinsert the contents of the Spike, repeat step 4.

The Spike copies its contents into the document as many times as you repeat step 4.

Undoing and Repeating Actions

As you go through all the steps in editing your document, you'll inevitably make some mistakes along the way. Fortunately, Word provides the very important Undo command.

 Click on the Undo button to cancel the last action, if Word allows.

 Click on the Redo button to redo the last undo, if Word allows.

Undo is a context-sensitive command, which means that it adjusts itself to your last action. Examples of Undo commands are **Undo** Typing, **Undo** Paste, and **Undo** Cut. Select the Edit menu and the Undo command (Ctrl + Z or Alt , E , U) to perform this action. If Word can't undo the last action, the entry on the **E**dit menu is Can't Undo.

The **R**epeat command (F4 or Alt , E , R) is also context-sensitive. Like the **U**ndo command, the action to be repeated is displayed next to **R**epeat in the menu (for example, **R**epeat Typing or **R**epeat Paste). Press F4 to repeat an action. Editing and formatting actions are stored in a buffer, which is cleared when you move the insertion point and start typing or if you perform an editing command. At that point, the current action replaces the previous action in the buffer.

Finding and Replacing Text

Up to this point, you have edited your document one part at a time. You've selected text and moved it to another location, or you've duplicated text in another part of your document. However, when you are editing a document, you sometimes have to make the same change throughout a document. For example, if your company renames a product line from Mountain Lakes to Forest Pines, use Word's Find and Replace commands to search for every instance of the old text and then replace it with the new text.

You can use **F**ind and **R**eplace to search for and optionally change groups of characters, words, phrases, punctuation, and formatting. You'll learn about finding and replacing punctuation and formatting in Chapter 8.

Finding Text

Use the **F**ind command to move to a place in a document in which a certain word or phrase occurs. For example, you can look for the word printer, or you can look for the sentence I hate my printer; it doesn't work most of the time. The characters, words, or phrase that you are looking for is the search string.

You can enter any of the following information in the Find dialog box (see Figure 3.6) to help your search.

A search string

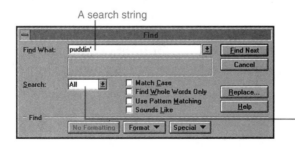

Search the complete document before and after the cursor location

Figure 3.6
The Find dialog box. Type a search string—the word or phrase that you want Word to find.

The Match **C**ase box allows you to base a search on upper- or lowercase text. For example, to look for White House and avoid all occurrences of white house, click on this box.

Search allows you to search from the insertion point toward the top (Up), the bottom (Down), or throughout the entire (All) document. Don't worry too much about choosing the direction, because once the search is at the beginning or end of the document, a small box (Figure 3.7) pops up to ask if you want to continue the search from the other end of the document.

Use the Find **W**hole Words Only box to refine your search by telling Word to find complete words rather than parts of words that match. Suppose that you are looking for all the occurrences of the word cap. If you simply click on OK or press Enter, Word will find cap and also caption, capitulate, cape, escape, etc. This is fine if you want to find all those words. However, if you want to find only the word cap, click on Find **W**hole Words Only.

The Use Pattern **M**atching box finds patterns of characters and operators, part of Word's ability to perform advanced searches.

TIP: To start a search at the top (or bottom) of a document, move the insertion point by pressing Ctrl+Home (or Ctrl+End).

At the bottom of the Find dialog box, there is a row of buttons used for finding certain formatting in a document. Use the **F**ormat and Sp**e**cial buttons to find special formats, such as fonts, paragraph formats, styles, page breaks, and special characters. Click on the No Formatting button to remove any formats that you have specified for searches and start with a "clean slate." Chapter 8 tells you how to search for formats and special characters, and Chapter 12 covers Styles. Use the following Quick Steps to find text.

Figure 3.7

When the search reaches the end of the Search direction that you have specified, Word displays this box.

Finding Text

QUICK STEPS

1. From the **E**dit menu, select Find (Alt , E , F).

Word displays the Find dialog box.

2. In the F**i**nd What box, type the search string— the word or phrase that you would like to find. Select **F**ind Next. Don't worry about the size of the search string—you can type up to 255 char- acters before you run out of space.

The F**i**nd What text box is filled with the search string.

3. Select the two check boxes —Find Whole Words Only and Match Case if you wish.

This narrows your search so you don't have to look at lots of words you don't want.

4. Select Find Next to have Word search your docu- ment for the search string.

If Word finds the search string, it displays the page on which it is located and highlights the search string. If Word does not find the search string it displays a message (Figure 3.7).

5. To search for the next occurrence of the string, repeat step 4.

Word continues the search. If you started searching below the top of the docu- ment, when Word reaches the end of the document, it asks if you want to con- tinue the search at the top.

continues

continued

6. To end the search, select Cancel.

Word closes the Find dialog box and returns to the current document.

FYI IDEAS

If you regularly use certain commands—especially those with no shortcut key or key combination, you'll find that using the shortcut key or key combination is much faster than using the mouse. For example, to perform a search, you can either select Find from the Edit menu or press Alt, E, F.

Searching with Wildcards

If you are not sure of the spelling of the word for which you are searching, fill in the questionable area of the word with question marks (?), inserting one question mark for each character that you are unsure of. For example, if you type p?t, Word looks for all three-letter words or parts of words starting with the letter p and ending with the letter t. If you are looking for a word or phrase that actually has a question mark in it, put a caret(^) in front of the question mark (for example, Do bears roam the woods^?).

Replacing Text

Finding text is easy, but most times you search for a search string to replace it with some other text. If you wanted to replace every instance of the word puddin' with the word cake, it could be a chore to find each puddin', cancel out of the dialog box, replace it with cake, and then repeat the process all over again. Word's Replace command searches for a string of characters and replaces that string of characters with another string.

The options in the Replace dialog box, shown in Figure 3.8, are very similar to those in the Find dialog box.

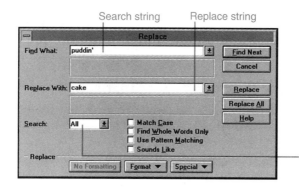

Search string   Replace string

Direction of the search from the current cursor location

Figure 3.8

The Replace dialog box. Type a search string and a replace string.

The Find **W**hole Words Only and Match **C**ase boxes have the same function as the boxes in the Find dialog box.

At the bottom of the Replace dialog box, there is the same row of No Forma**t**ting, **Fo**rmat, and Sp**e**cial buttons. However, in this case, you are replacing one format for another. Chapter 8 describes finding and replacing formats, and Chapter 12 talks about Styles.

Use the following Quick Steps to replace text.

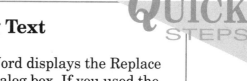

Replacing Text

1. From the **E**dit menu, select Replace (Alt, E, E).

Word displays the Replace dialog box. If you used the **F**ind command earlier in this Word session, your last search string will appear in the Fi**n**d What box; otherwise, the Replace dialog box is empty.

continues

continued

2. In the **Find** What box, type the search string that you would like to replace.

As you fill in the search string, notice that Word makes the **Find** Next and Replace **All** buttons available.

3. Select one of the two check boxes—Find Whole Words Only and Match Case— if you wish.

Your your search is narrowed according to what you entered.

4. In the Re**p**lace With box, type the replace string. You can type approximately 500 characters —don't worry about the size of a replace string.

As you fill the box, Word moves the first characters in the replace string beyond the left margin of the box to make room for additional characters.

5. To find the first occurrence of the search string after the insertion point, select Find Next.

Word highlights the search string but does not replace it.

6. To replace the highlighted search string, select Replace.

Word replaces the search string with the replace string and then highlights the next occurrence of the search string.

7. Repeat step 5 to replace the next highlighted search string.

When there are no more occurrences of the search string, Word issues a message.

8. To replace all occurrences of a search string at once, select Replace All.

Word replaces all occurrences of the search string and issues a message.

9. At any time, you can select Close to stop the

Word closes the Replace dialog box and returns to

find-and-replace process. You can select Cancel if you have not started a search, or Close if Word has performed a search.

the current document.

TIP: You can replace text with the contents of the Clipboard by typing ⌃ c in the **Replace With** box.

Checking Your Spelling

1. Select all or part of the document or let Word check all the document.
2. From the **T**ools menu, select Spelling ([Alt], [T], [S] or [F7]).

Creating a Custom Dictionary

1. From the**T**ools menu, select Options ([Alt], [T], [O]).
2. Click on the Spelling tab.
3. Select Add and name the dictionary.
4. Either click on OK or press [↵Enter].

Using the Thesaurus

1. From the **T**ools menu, select Thesaurus ([Alt], [T], [T] or [⇧Shift]+[F7]).
2. Select a word in the **M**eanings box to see its description.
3. To replace the selected word with the word in the **M**eanings box, click on **R**eplace.

Checking Grammar

1. From the **T**ools menu, select Grammar ([Alt], [T], [G]).
2. Reply to the prompts.
3. Either select OK or press [↵Enter] at the end of the grammar check.

Changing Grammar Rules

1. From the **T**ools menu, select Options ([Alt], [T], [O]).
2. Click on the Grammar tab.
3. In the Options dialog box for the Grammar category, choose another level of grammar and style rules.
4. Either select OK or press [↵Enter].

Chapter 4

Proofing Your Document

After you have created a document, it's important to review it. Unless the document is a note to yourself, others will see it and will evaluate its content. After you have edited one or two drafts of a document, consider using Word for Windows' proofing tools—the spell checker, the thesaurus, and the grammar checker.

Use the spell checker to correct misspelled words. Word uses the main dictionary as well as user-defined dictionaries that are unique to your occupation or business. It's a good idea to run the spell checker on every document you create.

While you're writing your document, use the thesaurus to find the best substitute for a selected word.

You can set the grammar checker to one of three levels and then customize the settings within the selected level. This means that you can use the grammar checker to polish a document or you can use it as a tool to improve your grammar and style. By using the readability statistics, you'll know whether the document is aimed at the appropriate audience.

Checking Your Spelling

Another step in editing your document is checking for spelling mistakes. No matter how beautifully your document is formatted and edited, a spelling error damages its image.

Word's spell checker is an invaluable writing tool. During a full installation of Word for Windows, two dictionaries are provided—the main dictionary, which cannot be modified or even viewed, and a custom dictionary, CUSTOM.DIC (a startup custom dictionary that you can rename). You can add words not found in the main dictionary to either of these custom dictionaries by using the **T**ools menu and the **S**pelling command or by editing it with Word. If the main or custom (or both) dictionaries are not installed on your computer system, you can use the SETUP program at any time to install them. Select Custom Installation and follow the prompts. See Appendix A for installation instructions.

> **ABC** Click on the Spelling button to run the spell checker
> for this document. If the spell checker finds any
> errors, it displays the Spelling dialog box.

You can use the standard dictionary with any document. If you work on a variety of documents, you might want to create a new custom dictionary for a certain type of document that you feel needs one. Suppose you are a pediatrician whose hobby is raising horses, and you write professional articles on children's medicine and horse raising. You'll probably have two custom dictionaries that contain the appropriate terminology. You don't need to enter every word in your lexicon into the custom dictionary because many words will already be in the main dictionary. When you use the spell checker, Word looks through the main dictionary and as many as ten custom dictionaries. Since the main dictionary contains hundreds of thousands of words, it also includes many abbreviations and acronyms. As you work with the spell checker and find gaps, simply add the words to a custom dictionary.

You can use the spell checker to review the entire document, part of a document, or a single word—depending on how much of the document you select. For example, in the process of creating your document, you can check the spelling of a single word by selecting that word, and using the **T**ools menu and the **S**pelling command (Alt, T, S).

The Spelling dialog box, shown in Figure 4.1, contains four options and ten buttons:

The Not in Dictionar**y** box displays a word that is not in the main dictionary or any active custom dictionary.

This word is not in any active dictionary.   Select this button to change to the suggested word.

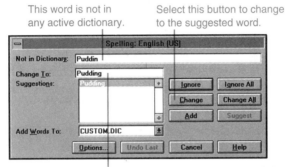

Figure 4.1
The Spelling dialog box.

The only word that Word found in any dictionary.

The Change **T**o box contains the first word in the Suggestions box. You can either accept one of the suggested words or type in a replacement word. If there are no suggestions, the word in the Not in Dictionar**y** box is displayed here. You can also delete a word from your document by deleting the word in the Change **T**o box. When you press Del to delete the word in the Change **T**o box, Word alters the **C**hange and Change A**l**l buttons to read **D**elete and Delete A**l**l, respectively. Then click on the **D**elete or Delete A**l**l button.

The Suggestio**n**s box lists potential replacement words that Word finds in the active dictionaries.

The Add **W**ords To box displays the name of the custom dictionary to which you can add a word. Press the list arrow to reveal the names of all active custom dictionaries.

The Spelling dialog box has several buttons, which provide a wide variety of functions. You can act either on a single word or on every occurrence of that word throughout your document.

Ignore/**Ig**nore All skips the selected word or all occurrences of the selected word and then moves to the next word not found in the active dictionaries.

Change/**Change** All changes the selected word or all occurrences of the selected word and then moves to the next word not found in the active dictionaries.

Delete/**Delete** All deletes the word or all occurrences of the selected word from your custom dictionary once you have deleted the word from the Change **T**o box. The **De**lete/**Delete** All buttons are only available if you have deleted all the text from the Change **T**o box. The spell checker then moves to the next word not found in the active dictionaries.

Add places the selected word in the custom dictionary named in the Add **W**ords To box.

TIP: To view and edit the words in your custom dictionary, open the dictionary just as you would another file. The extension is .DIC and it is located in the \windows\msapps\proof subdirectory. Then edit the dictionary as you would any document. When you have finished, save it.

Suggest, which is dimmed if you have checked the Always Suggest box in the Options dialog box for the Spelling category, allows you to type a word in the Change **T**o box so that you can see suggestions based on that word. If the Always Suggest box is cleared, you can select Suggest whenever the spell checker finds a word that is not in one of the active dictionaries, but you can also type a word in the Change **T**o box.

Undo Last changes the last word replaced back to the original word.

Cancel/Close cancels the dialog box without making any changes or closes it after making a change, which now cannot be undone.

Options displays the Options dialog box for the Spelling category, which is explained right after the following Quick Steps.

Now that you have some background about the Spelling dialog box, use these Quick Steps to check the spelling in a document.

> **TIP:** You can select the whole document, a single word, or anything in between. If you want Word to check the entire document, you don't have to select anything.

Checking the Spelling in a Document

1. Select the part of the current document that you want Word to check. Then select Spelling from the **T**ools menu (Alt , T , S or F7).

Word displays the Spelling dialog box and highlights the first word not found in either the main directory or an active custom dictionary or an active custom dictionary. The spell checker also suggests a replacement word and lists other replacement words.

continues

continued

2. To ignore or change the word using Word's suggestions, press one of the applicable buttons.

Word looks for the next word not found in a dictionary. If it finds another word, it highlights it and names replacement words.

3. To suggest a word to replace the highlighted word, type it in the Change **T**o box and select Suggest. This is a way to replace a word with a synonym and check its spelling in one step.

Word looks for the next word not found in a dictionary. If it finds another word, it highlights the word and names replacement words.

4. To add a word to the active custom dictionary, select the Add button.

Word reviews the remainder of the selected text. If it finds another word, it highlights the word and names replacement words.

5. Repeat step 2, 3, or 4 until Word has reviewed every word in the selected text.

If you started the spell check below the document top and Word finds no more words before the end of your selection, it displays a dialog box asking if you want the spell check to continue at the top of the document.

6. Answer Yes or No.

Word continues from the top of the document or not, depending on your answer. When the spell check is complete, Word displays an informational message.

7. Select OK or press ⏎Enter.

Word returns to the current document.

If the spell checker finds a word that is an odd combination of uppercase and lowercase letters, Not in Dictionary changes to Capitalization. You can fix the word, select Ignore, or add the word to your dictionary.

If the spell checker finds duplicate words (for example, the the), it informs you so that you can correct the error by pressing **D**elete. The Change button becomes **D**elete when this occurs.

NOTE: While the Spelling dialog box is displayed, Word allows you to return to your document to make manual changes.

Using the Spelling/Options Dialog Box

In Chapter 2, you were introduced to the Options dialog box for the View, Print, and Save categories. The spell checker has its own options dialog box, which allows you to define as many as four active custom dictionaries, to ignore certain words, and to determine whether the spell checker suggests replacement words. For example, if you are checking a document with a number of words that are all uppercase characters but you know that they are spelled correctly, check the Words in **UPPERCASE** check box. Then the spell checker will ignore the all-uppercase words. Suppose you are working with a report that contains a number of inventory codes that are combinations of letters and numbers. If you don't check the Words with Num**b**ers check box, you'll spend a great deal of time ignoring the inventory codes that the spell checker identifies.

If you check the A**l**ways Suggest check box, a list of suggested words for each "misspelled" word appears in the Spelling dialog box. If A**l**ways Suggest is clear, Word does not suggest replacement words. If you're working with a technical document containing words that are not likely to be in the dictionary, you're probably using the spell checker to "flag" the common words that are misspelled. In this case, clear the Always Suggest check box. You'll find that you save time, and if you want suggestions during a spell check, you can press **S**uggest in the Spelling dialog box.

You can display the Options dialog box for the Spelling category (see Figure 4.2) from within the Spelling dialog box or by choosing the **T**ools menu and the **O**ptions command (Alt, T, O).

Figure 4.2

The Options dialog box for the Spelling category.

Selecting this option means that Word always gives you a choice of words from which to select.

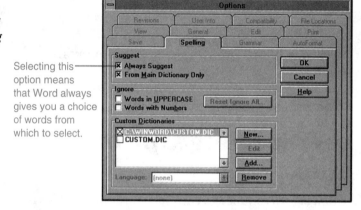

Creating a Custom Dictionary

If you are the pediatrician in the earlier example and, in addition to your horses, you dabble in the stock market and develop electronic equipment, you may need to create four different custom dictionaries. (Actually, you can create as many different custom dictionaries as you want, but you can use only ten at a time.)

To create your first custom dictionary, use the following Quick Steps.

QUICK STEPS

Creating a Custom Dictionary

1. From the **T**ools menu, select **O**ptions (Alt, T, O) and click on the Spelling tab.

Word opens the Options dialog box (Figure 4.2).

2. Select New.	Word displays the Add Dictionary dialog box (see Figure 4.3).
3. Enter the name you would like to give the dictionary.	Word reminds you to add a .DIC extension, however you can give your dictionary any extension or no extension. Word won't prompt you again.
4. Select OK or press ⏎Enter.	Word returns to the Options dialog box for the Spelling category and adds the new dictionary to the list in the Custom **D**ictionaries box.
5. Select OK or press ⏎Enter.	Word returns to your document.

TIP: You can also create a custom dictionary while checking spelling in your document. In the Spelling dialog box, click on the Options button, and Word opens the Options dialog box for the Spelling category.

Opening and Closing a Custom Dictionary

Before Word can use a custom dictionary to check spelling in the current document, the dictionary must be on the list of selected custom dictionaries in the Spelling Options dialog box. The dictionary must be opened before you run the spell check. The next set of Quick Steps explains how to open and close a custom dictionary.

Figure 4.3

You can create a new custom dictionary or open as many as ten custom dictionaries at a time from the Add Dictionary dialog box.

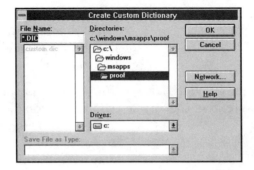

Opening and Closing a Custom Dictionary

1. From the **T**ools menu select **O**ptions (Alt), T, O).

   Word opens the last Options dialog box used during this session.

2. Click on the Spelling tab.

   Word opens the Options dialog box for the Spelling category.

3. If you use the mouse, move the mouse pointer to the name of a custom dictionary in the Custom **D**ictionaries box. Then click to open or close that dictionary.

   Word indicates that a custom dictionary is open by highlighting it; otherwise, there is no highlight.

4. If you use the keyboard, press the Tab⇆ key to

   Word surrounds your choice with a dotted border.

move to the Custom
Dictionaries box. Then
press any combination of
⬆ or ⬇ to highlight a
custom dictionary.

5. Press the Spacebar to open or close that dictionary.

Word indicates that a custom dictionary is open by highlighting it; otherwise, there is no highlight.

6. Select OK or press ↵Enter.

Word returns to the current document.

Adding Words to a Custom Dictionary

The simplest way to add words to a custom dictionary is during a spell checker session. Make sure that you have chosen the custom dictionary to which you want to add words. Then check one or more documents and add words where needed.

If you want to add many words to the custom dictionary at one time, you can create a special document containing the words, separated by spaces. Then run the spell checker against this document. When Word finds a word that is not in either the standard or the custom dictionary, you can add it.

Identifying Selected Text to the Spell Check

Word allows you to identify words that should be checked by another language dictionary or should be excluded from the spell check altogether. For example, if you are writing an instruction booklet in four languages, it doesn't make much sense to check the French section of the book against the English (US) dictionary. If your instruction book includes your company name, technical terms, product names, and other words that you think will not appear in the main dictionary it's best to bypass those words.

> **NOTE:** In order to spell check in a language other than your default language, you must have a copy of the appropriate dictionary. Otherwise, Word attempts to find the closest match to that dictionary.

To run special spell checks with another language dictionary, select the appropriate text, and from the **Tools** menu, select Language (Alt , T , L). In the **M**ark Selected Text As scroll box of the Language dialog box (see Figure 4.4), select the desired language. Click on OK or press ↵Enter .

To create a list of excluded words, select a word to be bypassed, and from the **Tools** menu, select Language (Alt , T , L). In the **M**ark Selected Text As scroll box of the Language dialog box, select (no proofing), the first entry on the list. When you click on OK or press ↵Enter , Word adds the selected word to the current dictionary.

Figure 4.4

The Language dialog box, in which you can identify a new dictionary or exclude words from the spell check.

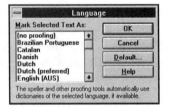

Using the Thesaurus

The next step in refining your document is to use the thesaurus. A thesaurus adds spice to your documents by letting you choose words with similar meanings instead of using the same word repeatedly. You can also use the thesaurus to choose a word that is slightly closer to what you mean in a sentence. For example, does the word improve mean advance or repair? Does loud mean deafening or powerful? In both examples, the groups of words are synonyms but the meanings are not identical.

Word's Thesaurus command allows you to replace a word with a synonym from a list. The Thesaurus dialog box (see Figure 4.5) includes these options:

Lo**ok**ed Up displays the word or phrase that you selected before you displayed this dialog box. If there is no synonym for a selected word, the box is labeled Not Found.

Replace With **S**ynonym displays the suggested replacement word or phrase. If you're starting a new document and use the Thesaurus command, this box is labeled Ins**e**rt. If you select **A**ntonyms from the Meanings box, this box is labeled Replace with **A**ntonym. **M**eanings displays definitions of recently displayed words or phrases so that you can make an informed decision. If there is no meaning, this box is labeled **A**lphabetical List and the thesaurus displays words or phrases that are in the same area alphabetically as the selected word but are not synonyms of the selected word or phrase.

Selected word   Current replacement

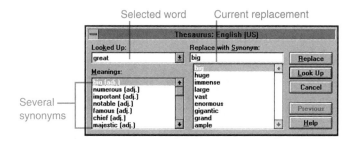

Several synonyms

Figure 4.5
The Thesaurus window displays words from which you can choose.

You can either select the L**o**ok Up button to display synonyms for the suggested replacement word or phrase or select **R**eplace/Ins**e**rt to replace the selected word or phrase with the word or phrase in the Replace With **S**ynonym box. To use the thesaurus, follow these steps:

Using the Thesaurus

1. Position the insertion point anywhere in a word or to its immediate right, and select the Tools and Thesaurus ([Alt], [T], [T] or [⇧Shift]+[F7]).

   Word displays the Thesaurus window with the selected word in the Looked Up box.

2. Highlight an appropriate word in the **M**eanings box.

   For the highlighted word in the **M**eanings box, Word displays synonyms (and sometimes antonyms) in the Replace with **S**ynonym (or Replace with **A**ntonym) box.

3. Highlight an appropriate word in the Replace with **S**ynonym or Replace with **A**ntonym box.

   Word places the selected word in the Replace with **S**ynonym or Replace with **A**ntonym box.

4. To further investigate the word in the Replace With **S**ynonyms or Replace with **A**ntonyms box, click on the Look Up button.

   Word displays meanings and synonyms from which you can select.

5. To replace the original word with the selected word, click on the **Re**-place button.

   Word replaces the original word with the replacement word and returns to the current document.

Checking Your Grammar

The final step in perfecting the content of your document is to check the grammar and readability of your document with the grammar checker.

Select the Tools menu and the Grammar command
(Alt), T, G) to display the Grammar dialog box, shown in Figure 4.6, with these options:

The suggested replacement   The word in question

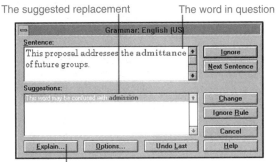

For an explanation, select explain.

Figure 4.6

When the grammar checker finds problems with your document, Word opens the Grammar dialog box.

Sentence—In this box, the grammar checker displays a
sentence that you should evaluate and perhaps correct.

Suggestions—In this box, the grammar checker either
describes the problem or offers one or more corrections.

Ignore—Press this button to skip to the next error in a
sentence or to the next incorrect sentence without changing the sentence.

Next Sentence—Press this button to ignore the errors in a
sentence and find the next incorrect sentence.

Change—Press this button to have the grammar checker
correct a sentence with its suggestion. If the button is not
available, move the insertion point to the document and
make the change.

Ignore **R**ule—Press this button to ignore the errors in a
sentence and similar errors in other sentences. The grammar checker then finds the next incorrect sentence.

Explain—Press this button to display a small window
expanding the explanation in the Su**gg**estions box.

Options—Press this button to open the Grammar/Options
dialog box (see Figure 4.7), which allows you to select

specific grammar and style rules, show readability statistics, and customize settings.

Figure 4.7

The Options dialog box for the Grammar category allows you to specify the grammar and style rules to be used.

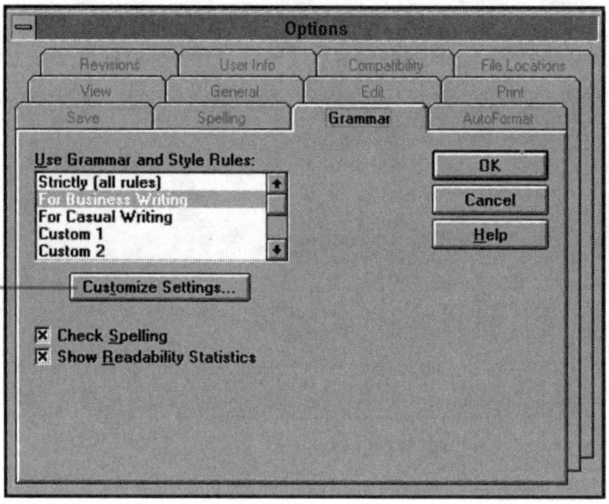

You can change the settings for the grammar and style rules by selecting Customize settings.

The Options dialog box for the Grammar category enables you to customize the grammar and style rules that the grammar checker uses. You can choose from and customize Strictly (all rules), For Business Writing, For Casual Writing, and for up to three Custom rules that you specify. You can also indicate whether you want to Show **R**eadability Statistics or Check **S**pelling after proofing.

To set your own grammar and style rules, select Cus**t**omize Settings. The grammar checker then displays the Customize Grammar Settings dialog box (see Figure 4.8). Select Strictly (All Rules), For Business Writing, or For Casual Writing from the top of the screen (you could have also selected one of these from the previous screen). Click on or clear the **G**rammar and **S**tyle radio buttons to display check boxes in which you can adjust the rules to fit your strengths and weaknesses. To learn about individual grammar and style rules, select Explain. In the Catch group, you can set triggering levels for Split **I**nfinitives, Consecutive **N**ouns, and Prepositional **P**hrases. To return to the grammar checker's original settings, select Reset All. When you have finished customizing the rules, select another level of severity and repeat the process just described. When you have finally completed customization, select OK or Cancel.

Checking Your Grammar

Quick Steps

1. Select the part of the document that you want Word to check. To check the entire document, you don't have to select anything. Then, select Tools Grammar (Alt , T , G).

   The grammar checker evaluates your document or the selected text. If the grammar checker finds a sentence that is grammatically incorrect, Word opens the Grammar dialog box.

2. Correct your document or ignore the suggestions using the options described previously.

   When the grammar checker finds a misspelled word, Word opens the Spelling dialog box. If it finds a spelling error first and opens the Spelling dialog box, don't think Word has forgotten to check GRAMMAR.

3. To switch from the Grammar dialog box to your document, move the insertion point outside the dialog box and click.

   Word dims the dialog box.

4. To switch back to the dialog box, select Start in the dialog box.

   Word activates the dialog box.

5. Continue correcting your document.

   When the grammar checker has completed its evaluation of selected text, Word displays a message that it has finished checking. However, if you chose to display readability statistics, Word now displays those instead of the message.

continues

continued

6. Select OK or press ⏎Enter.   Word returns you to the current document.

Figure 4.8

The Customize Grammar Settings dialog box for the Grammar category, which allows you to change grammar and style rules.

Selecting and Customizing Grammar Rules

The grammar checker has three preset levels of severity for grammar and style. This means that you can change grammar rules to fit your environment. For example, suppose you are writing a letter to your grade-school English teacher. If you apply the strictest grammar rules, chances are you'll get that A+ you always wanted. On the other hand, if you're writing an informal note to your best friend, you can loosen the rules somewhat.

Word offers three sets of grammar or style rules:

Strictly (all rules) enforces most grammar and style rules in the grammar checker.

For Business Writing enforces most grammar rules and some style rules.

For Casual Writing enforces most grammar rules and eight style rules.

Depending on the type of document you are writing, you can select from and/or customize any of the three sets of grammar rules using the following Quick Steps.

Selecting and Customizing Grammar Rules

1. With a document open, select Tools Options ([Alt], [T], [O]) and click on the Grammar tab if necessary.

   Word opens the Options dialog box for the Grammar category.

2. If the selection within the scroll list box is not your choice, choose another level of grammar and style rules.

3. To display or customize settings for grammar and style rules, select Customize Settings.

   Word opens the Customize Grammar Settings dialog box (see Figure 4.8).

4. Select settings in the **G**rammar and/or **S**tyle boxes to ease or tighten the rules. In the Catch box, you can adjust the settings.

   Word displays the new setting.

5. If you don't understand the selected Grammar or Style entry, select Explain.

   Word opens a Grammar Explanation window (see Figure 4.9), which contains a brief explanation. Note that you can adjust the size of this window by moving the mouse pointer to a border and dragging it until you like its new size.

continues

continued

	To close the window and return to the dialog box, either press Alt + F4 or click on the Control Menu button, and select Close from the menu.
6. If you want to reset the rules to Word's default settings, select **R**eset All.	Word displays the default settings.
7. When you have completed customizing the rules, Select OK or press ⏎Enter.	Word returns to the Grammar/Options dialog box.
8. Select OK or press ⏎Enter.	Word returns to the Grammar dialog box.
9. Click on Close or Cancel.	Word returns to your document.

TIP: You can also change grammar rules while checking grammar in your document. In the Grammar dialog box, click on the Options button, and Word opens the Options dialog box for the Grammar category.

To improve your writing skills or to learn more about grammar and style, set the Grammar Settings to Strictly (All Rules) and run the grammar checker for most of your documents.

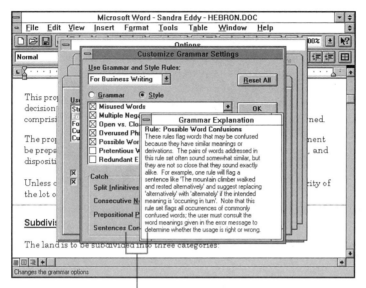

Figure 4.9

*Open the
Grammar
Explanation
window to see a
brief explanation
about a rule.*

You can drag any border to
expand this box to see all the
text at one time.

Grammar Statistics

At the end of a grammar check, Word displays the Readability
Statistics window, shown in Figure 4.10. (If you don't want to see
Readability Statistics after every grammar check, clear the Show
Readability Statistics box in the Options dialog box for the
Grammar category.) It is up to you to evaluate the statistics for
your document, and if you have any questions, press the Help key.

Some of the basic aspects of the readability evaluation are:

• Don't use passive voice if you can avoid it (for example,
  "the patient was revived by Mike" instead of "Mike revived
  the patient"). Keep your passive voice score as low as
  possible.

• The Flesch Reading Ease score decreases as the difficulty
  of the document increases.

• The Bormuth Grade Level and Flesch-Kincaid Grade
  Level scores both measure the school grade level.

Figure 4.10

The Readability Statistics window displays statistical information about the document that was just checked.

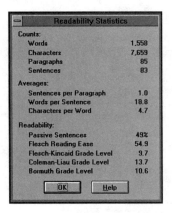

Readability Statistics	
Counts:	
Words	1,558
Characters	7,659
Paragraphs	85
Sentences	83
Averages:	
Sentences per Paragraph	1.0
Words per Sentence	18.8
Characters per Word	4.7
Readability:	
Passive Sentences	49%
Flesch Reading Ease	54.9
Flesch-Kincaid Grade Level	9.7
Coleman-Liau Grade Level	13.7
Bormuth Grade Level	10.6

OK   Help

Document Statistics

As you worked through Chapter 2, when you saved your first document, you might have filled in the Summary Info box. From that box, you could view document statistics. There is another way to access statistics for your document. After thoroughly checking your document for spelling, word usage, grammar, and style, you may wish to check your document statistics again.

Document statistics include the name of this document file, the directory in which it is located, its title, the creation date, the date you last saved it, and the name of the person who last saved the file. Word also tells you the number of times you've saved the document and the time you have spent editing it. Probably the most important statistics are the number of pages, number of words, and number of characters.

To see information about your document, including a count of words, when it was created, and other information, follow these Quick Steps.

QUICK STEPS

Displaying Statistics About a Document

1. From the File menu, select Summary Info (Alt, F, I).

Word opens the Summary Info dialog box (see Figure 4.11).

2. Select Statistics.

Word opens the Document Statistics dialog box (see Figure 4.12).

3. After you have reviewed the statistics, select Close or press ⏎Enter.

Word returns to the Summary Info dialog box.

4. Select OK or press ⏎Enter or Cancel.

Word returns to the current document.

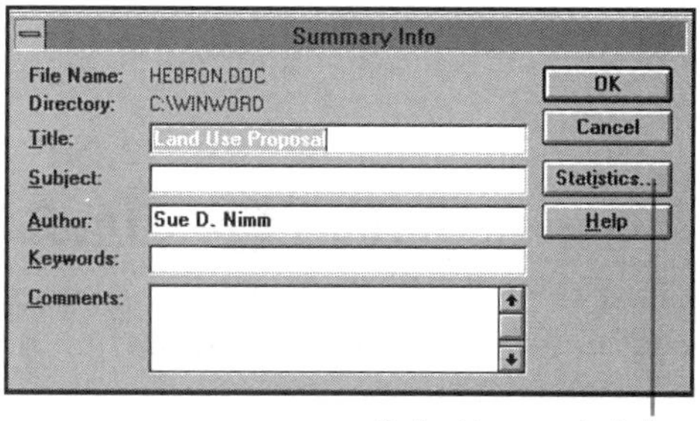

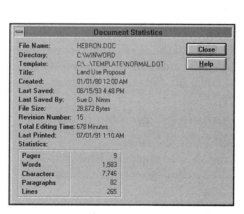

Select to see statistics about this document.

Figure 4.11
The Summary Info dialog box displays information about the current document and allows you to add more.

Figure 4.12
The Document Statistics dialog box provides extensive information about the current document.

Changing the Unit of Measure in Word

Select Tools Options (Alt, T, O), click on the General tab, open the Measurement Units box, and select the unit of measurement. Either select OK or press ⏎Enter.

Changing Margins Using the File Page Setup Command

Select File Page Setup (Alt, F, U). Click on the Margins tab, and set any combination of margins. Select OK or press ⏎Enter.

Changing Margins Using the Ruler

Select the left margin marker and drag it to its new location, and select the right margin marker and drag it to its new location.

Changing Paper Size

Select File Page Setup (Alt, F, U). Click on the Paper Size tab. Either select from the Paper Size drop-down list, or type dimensions in the Width box, the Height box, or both. Select OK or press ⏎Enter.

Changing Page Orientation

Select File Page Setup (Alt, F, U). Click on the Paper Size tab, and click on either the Portrait or Landscape radio button. Select OK or press ⏎Enter.

Creating a Header or Footer

Select View Header and Footer (Alt, V, H). Type the text for your header within the border on the screen. To create a footer, move to the bottom of the page and type the text for your footer within the border on the screen. To close the header and footer toolbar and return to your document, click on the Close button.

Defining Document-Wide and Section Formats

Formatting in Word for Windows

Once you have finished organizing your document and editing its text, you can enhance its appearance through formatting. Formatting can make the difference between an indifferent and an enthusiastic reception on the part of your reader.

Word for Windows handles formatting through the **File**, **Format**, and **Tools** menus. Word has four basic format levels: document, section, paragraph, and character. Document-wide formatting encompasses the entire document; section formatting defines major changes (such as page orientation, paper dimension, and page numbering) within the document; paragraph formatting changes the appearance of one or more selected paragraphs; and character formatting determines the appearance of words and characters.

Because these formatting concepts and the associated commands play such a large role in Word, it's important for you to understand them thoroughly.

Document-wide formatting controls the size of margins on a page, the dimensions of the paper on which you will print, and other measures of the printed page. Document-wide formatting applies to every page of your document-from the title page to the index. Although the text on individual pages in the document might look very different (for example, compare body text with the table of contents), you'll print your document on the same size paper, and the page numbers will appear in the same spot on every page.

Section formatting controls major changes within your document. For example, in a sales brochure, most of the text will be oriented across the shorter page dimension, from the left to the right margin. However, there might be one or two pages of tables containing long lines of text that stretch between the top and the bottom margins. You have to create a new section whenever you change the orientation of text in a document. You can also use section formatting to create breaks between chapters, to change the content of headers and footers, or to place endnotes after each chapter. Section formatting sends a strong signal to Word that a major change must take place in order to start the next part of the document.

Paragraph formatting controls strings of text that end with a paragraph mark. You can determine how text is aligned between the margins, whether there are indented or block paragraphs, and how many blank lines are placed between paragraphs. Paragraph formatting also determines where a headline or graphic appears on a page. Paragraph formatting is covered in Chapter 6.

Character formatting changes the appearance of text, changes spacing between characters, and creates special characters. For example, you can use character formatting to create the appropriate text type and size for a headline or footnote. Chapter 7 explains character formatting.

Word provides automatic formatting for documents. AutoFormat applies paragraph and character formats throughout a document using default Word styles. Chapter 12 explains AutoFormat and styles.

The best way to format a document is to start at the largest level (that is, document-wide) and work your way down to the smallest level (or character). The first thing to do is to decide whether you want to change the unit of measure used for formatting.

Changing Units of Measure in Word

Some people are used to measuring with inches, and others are more comfortable with centimeters. A person who is experienced in the printing industry or who requires fine gradations between measurements might want to use picas or points. Word allows you to choose from a list of units of measure so that you can use the one with which you are most comfortable and which suits your purpose best. Table 5.1 shows which measurement units are available and the abbreviation that you type for each.

To Use This Unit	You Type
Centimeters	cm
Inches	in or "
Picas	pi
Points	pt
Lines	li

Table 5.1
Units of Measure in Word for Windows

All units of measure in Word are set by default to inches. It is an easy matter to change to centimeters, lines, picas, or points. From the Tools menu, select the Options command (Alt), T , O) and click on the General tab to display the Options dialog box for the General category (shown in Figure 5.1). Open the Measurement Units list box in the dialog box by clicking on the underlined ↓ at the right side of the box or repeatedly pressing the Tab key until you have highlighted the Measurement Units box or press Alt + M . Press ↓ to show the contents of the box, shown in Figure 5.2. Select the unit that you want and click on OK or press ↵Enter . The unit of measure on the Ruler will change to reflect your choice (see Figure 5.3). For the rest of this book, you will use the default unit of measure, inches.

Figure 5.1
The Options dialog box for the General category.

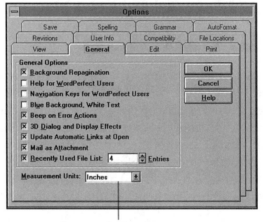

Current unit of measure

Figure 5.2

The Measurement Units list box.

Default tab stops

Left margin   Right margin

Tab alignment button

Figure 5.3

The Ruler as it looks with points as the default unit of measure.

Use the following Quick Steps to define a new default unit of measure and to change the unit shown on the Ruler.

Changing the Default Unit of Measure

1. From **T**ools, select **O**ptions (Alt , T , O).

   Word displays the last Options dialog box you used in this Word session.

2. Click on the General tab.

   Word changes the display in the Options dialog box (see Figure 5.1).

3. Select the underlined arrow in the **Measure**ment Units box (see Figure 5.2).

   Word displays the available units of measurement. The current default is highlighted on the list of choices and also appears in the arrow box.

4. Select the unit of measurement. Choose OK or press ↵Enter .

   Word changes the measurement type on the Ruler and in all boxes containing measurements.

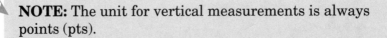

NOTE: The unit for vertical measurements is always points (pts).

Whenever you open a dialog box that requires a measurement, you don't have to add an abbreviation if you type a value that is measured in the same units as the current unit of measure. For example, if the default value is inches, you can type 5 and Word knows that you mean "5 inches." However, if you want to temporarily use another unit of measure, type the number and then the abbreviation of the unit type (for example, 64 pt or 75 cm).

NOTE: You have to use decimal equivalents for fractions (for example, .75 instead of 3/4 or .5 rather than 1/2) because you cannot enter fractions.

Document-Wide Formatting

Once you have chosen your default unit of measure, you can put it to work in determining document-wide formats. You can accept Word's defaults, which are a good starting point for a beginner, or you can define your own. For example, if you are creating a business letter, using Word's top, bottom, left, and right margins certainly makes sense. However, if you are preparing a one-page advertisement with plenty of white space, you'll want to make those margins larger. For a legal document, you may change the margins as well as the paper size.

Document-wide formats control the overall appearance of your document on a page-by-page basis. These formats include:

- The size of margins; left, right, top, bottom, gutter, and mirror. A gutter margin allows for binding or hole-punching on the left side of a page printed on a single side. A mirror margin allows for binding or hole-punching of a page printed on both sides; the inside margins "mirror" each other.

- The size of the paper on which your document prints, for example, 8 1/2 by 11 inches.

- The orientation of text on a page, either the way memos and books (such as this one) are oriented, with the page longer than it is wide; or the way some spreadsheets are oriented, with the page wider than it is long.

To set or change document-wide formats, use the **Page Setup** command on the **File** menu (Alt), F , U). Word displays the Page Setup dialog box shown in Figure 5.4. At the top of this box, you will see four tabs representing the attributes that you can modify: **M**argins, Paper **S**ize, **P**aper Source, and **L**ayout. You can choose only one at a time. Word will display a different dialog box for each attribute.

The Page Setup dialog box for Margins (Figure 5.4) includes boxes into which you can type settings for the top, bottom, left, and right margins. You can also determine the size of the gutter and mirror margins.

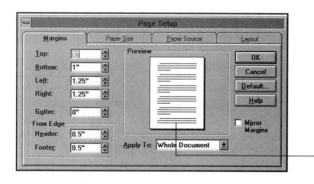

Figure 5.4

The Page Setup dialog box for Margins with its default settings.

Illustration of a page with the current settings.

In the **A**pply To box, you have several choices. You can change the page setup for the entire document or from the location of the insertion point forward (whether or not there is text after the insertion point). To change the margins for a piece of text, select the text and then choose the Selected Text option. When you select text, the This Point Forward option is not available. In the Default button, you can also select the new margins as your default measurements for all new documents that you create until you select a new set of default measurements.

Changing Margins

The first step in choosing document-wide formats is to set the margins for your document.

Page margin settings control the space between the edge of the page and the text on the page. For example, the top margin is the space from the top of the page to the first line of text. Word's initial top and bottom margins are 1 inch, and the left and right margins are 1.25 inches. As the margin measurements increase in size, the amount of text printed on a page decreases. Word's default text area is 6 by 9 inches; the default page dimensions are 8 1/2 by 11 inches.

The margins that you set determine the appearance of your document. With narrow margins, your text looks more dense. It's more difficult for some people to read because the number of characters on a line increases. To some readers, a page with a large amount of text and a small amount of white space looks forbidding. Conversely, a page with a great deal of white space and less text area is easier to read and "friendlier" in appearance.

You can change the margins of a block of text by first selecting the text, and then following the Quick Steps below. You can also establish new margins which begin at the insertion point and remain in effect to the end of your document. To do this, set the insertion point at the place where you want the new margins to begin and follow the same Quick Steps.

NOTE: You can change margins whether or not there is a document in the text area.

Use these Quick Steps to change all document-wide margins:

Changing Margins

1. Select the appropriate text or set the insertion point where you want the new margin. Then select Page Setup from the **F**ile menu (Alt , F , U).

Word opens the Page Setup dialog box.

2. Click on the Margins tab, if needed.

The Page Setup box appears with the **Margins** options displayed (Figure 5.5).

3. To set any combination of **T**op, **B**ottom, **L**eft, or **Ri**ght margins: With the keyboard, move the insertion point to the number in a box and type a measurement.

The new settings are shown in the Preview box.

OR

With the mouse, move the pointer to the arrow button in the box, then press and hold the left mouse button. A list of numbers scrolls through the window. Release the button when the desired number is displayed.

continues

---

continued

4. To change the **Gu**tter margin, move the insertion point to the number in the **Gu**tter box and type a replacement (between 0 and 22 inches). Or move the mouse pointer to the arrow button to the right of the Gutter box, press and hold the left mouse button while the numbers scroll, and release it when the desired number is displayed.

Word shows the gutter margin. Word adds the gutter (in this case, mirror) margin measurement to the left margin of single pages, as shown in Figure 5.6.

5. To select the part of the document for the margin changes, select the list arrow next to **A**pply To and select Whole Document or Selected Text (if you have selected text) or This Point Forward (if you have not selected text).

Depending on your choice, Word changes the margins of the entire current document, selected text, or all text beyond the insertion point.

6. To use the new margin settings as the default measurements for every Word document you create from now on, click on Default.

The new margins now apply to documents using the default template, NORMAL.DOT. The margins of other templates are not changed.

7. Word asks if you want to use the new settings as the default (Figure 5.7). Select Yes (change all new documents based on the NORMAL.DOT template) or No (just this document).

If you select Yes, Word returns to the current document or to the screen from which you selected the command. If you select No, Word returns to the box.

8. If you have completed filling in the dialog box, select OK or press ⏎Enter.

Word returns to the current document or the screen from which you selected the command.

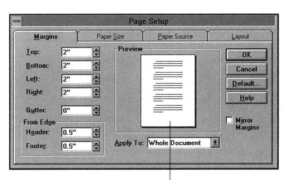

A sample page with wider margins

Figure 5.5

The Page Setup dialog box with the Sample document reflecting the new margin settings.

NOTE: The measurements for the top and bottom margins must be between 00 and 22. The measurements for the right and left margins must be between 0 and 22. Word changes margins on the page illustrated in the Sample box (Figure 5.5).

Figure 5.6

The Page Setup dialog box with the Sample document showing the addition of a gutter.

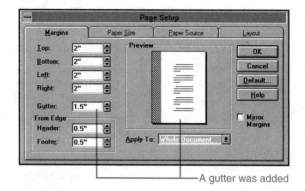

A gutter was added

NOTE: Templates are guidelines to the overall look and content of a Word document. They are described in Chapter 12.

Figure 5.7

Word displays a prompt box when you click on the Default button.

If you have a document on-screen, you can see how margins change by using the **R**uler, shown in Figure 5.8, to set the left and right margins. For example, if you have just heard that your resume must be on a prospective employer's desk by tomorrow morning, you can adjust formatting "on the fly" by viewing your changes as you make them.

Figure 5.8

The Ruler showing its default width across the text area.

Left margin   Right margin

On the **R**uler, a single pointer represents the right margin. All text ends at or before the right margin, depending on paragraph alignment. Two pointers indicate the left margin. The top pointer controls the location of the first character in the paragraph's first line; the bottom pointer controls the left margin of the remaining lines in the paragraph.

The following Quick Steps show how to set margins with the **R**uler in Page Layout view.

Using the Ruler to Set Margins in Page Layout View

QUICK STEPS

1. Select both **R**uler and Page Layout from the **V**iew menu, or press `Alt`, `V`, `R` and `Alt`, `V`, `P`.

   Word displays the **R**uler across the top of the document, and a second ruler down the left side.

2. To change the left margin move the mouse pointer either to the small rectangle below the left margin pointers or to the place at which the two pointers meet. The mouse pointer changes to a double-headed arrow (see Figure 5.9) which you drag to its new location.

   Word adjusts the left margin of the current document. Figure 5.10 shows the changed margins.

3. To change the right margin, move the mouse pointer to the margin pointer at the right of the **R**uler and drag it to its new location. If you can't see the pointer, drag the scroll box on the horizontal bar to the right.

   Word adjusts the right margin of the document on the screen.

TIP: If you adjust the margins using the Ruler in **P**age Layout view, you can adjust all margins—top, bottom, left, and right. If you use the Ruler in Normal view, you can adjust only the side margins.

Figure 5.9

The Ruler show-ing the left margin ready to be adjusted.

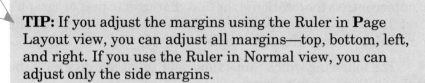

When the mouse pointer turns to a double-headed arrow, you can move the left margin.

Drag this rectangle to change the left margin.

Drag to change the right margin.

Figure 5.10

The document window as margins are being changed.

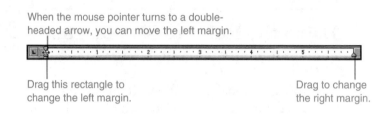

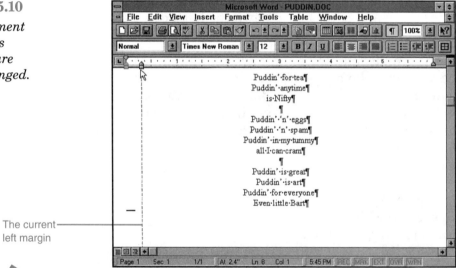

The current left margin

TIP: To display measurements as you set margins by dragging within the **R**uler, press and hold down the Alt key. For example, if you are working in the horizontal **R**uler and use this technique, Word displays the width of the margins and the text between the margins.

Word also provides another way to change margins. In Chapter 9, you'll learn how to change margins within Print Preview.

Changing Paper Size

You won't always use 8 1/2-by-11-inch paper for your documents. If you work in a law office, you'll use 8 1/2-by-14-inch paper much of the time. Or you might use Word to print envelopes, create advertising flyers, or even design notepaper and greeting cards.

As you learned earlier, there are four Page Setup dialog boxes. You have just finished learning about the Page Setup dialog box for **M**argins. Next you'll learn about the Page Setup dialog box for Paper **S**ize, shown in Figure 5.11. Use this dialog box to change paper dimensions and orientation. The Paper **S**ize box provides options for changing the height and width of the paper on which the text is printed. The options are dependent on the printer that is active. For example, the Hewlett-Packard LaserJet III provides nine options, including Custom Size, and an Epson FX86E provides six options, including Custom Size. You can adjust both the height and width of Custom Size from 0 to 22 inches.

The Orientation group allows you to determine the direction in which the text prints, either across the narrower dimension (like a memo) or across the wider dimension of a page (like a spreadsheet). Use the **A**pply To drop-down list box to apply these changes to the entire document or to the remaining part of the document either after the insertion point or just to the text selection. In the Default button, you can make the new settings the new Word default measurements for the documents (based on NORMAL.DOT) that you create from now on.

Figure 5.11

*The Page Setup
dialog box for
Paper Size.*

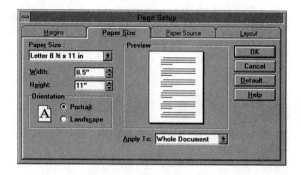

It's a simple process to change the paper dimensions for the
active printer. Select the File menu and the Page Set**u**p command
(Alt, F, U). When the Page Setup dialog box opens, click on the
Paper Size tab. When you select the list button (the underlined
down arrow) on the right side of the Pape**r** Size box, Word displays
the paper sizes available for the active printer.

The following Quick Steps lead you through the procedures
required to change paper size.

Changing Paper Size

1. Either select some text
or move the insertion
point to the position
where you want the
change to begin. Then
select Page Setup from
the **File** menu (Alt,
F, U).

Word opens the Page Setup
dialog box.

2. Click on the Paper Size
tab, if needed.

Word changes the Page
Setup dialog box to display
page size and orientation
options (Figure 5.11).

3. You can choose from the Paper Size drop-down list, or type dimensions in the **W**idth box, the **He**ight box, or both. Or, you can move the mouse pointer to the arrows in either box and press and hold the mouse button to scroll through the range of valid dimensions (from 0 to 22 inches).

Word changes the illustration in the Sample box.

4. You can select the underlined down arrow next to **A**pply To and select Whole Document, Selected Text (if you have selected text), or This Point Forward (if you have not selected text).

Depending on your choice, Word changes the margins of the entire current document, selected text, or all text beyond the insertion point.

5. You can click on the Default button.

Word asks you if you want to use the new settings as the default.

6. Select Yes (change all new documents based on NORMAL.DOT) or No (just this document).

If you select **Y**es, Word returns to the current document or the screen from which you selected the command. If you select **N**o, Word returns to the Page Setup dialog box.

7. When you finish using the dialog box, select OK or press ⏎Enter.

Word returns to the current document or the screen from which you selected the command.

Portrait Versus Landscape Orientation

A typical document is printed with the text oriented to the smaller dimension of the page. For example, with paper that is 8 1/2 by 11 inches, the text is printed across the 8 1/2-inch dimension. This is called portrait orientation, which is used for the majority of documents. The main reason that portrait orientation is so popular is that the eye can easily scan across the text that can fit on a line.

If you want to present a great deal of information on a page and that information does not have to be read line by line, use landscape orientation, in which the text is printed across the 11-inch dimension of an 8 1/2-by-11-inch page. Probably the most popular use of landscape orientation is for spreadsheets, which contain cells of information rather than lines of text. You don't scan across a spreadsheet; you jump around from cell to cell. Two other examples are time lines and large tables.

To switch between portrait and landscape orientation, use the following Quick Steps.

Changing Page Orientation

1. Either select text or move the insertion point to the position after which you want orientation to change. Then select Page Setup from the **F**ile menu (Alt, F, U).

Word opens the Page Setup dialog box.

2. Click on the Paper Size tab, if needed.

Word changes the Page Setup dialog box to display page size and orientation options.

3. In the Orientation group, you can choose either Portrait or Landscape.

Word changes the illustration in the Preview box.

4. You can select the list arrow (the underlined down arrow) next to **A**pply To and select Whole Document, Selected Text (if you have selected text), or This Point Forward (if you have not selected text).

Depending on your choice, Word changes the margins of the current document, selected text, or all text beyond the insertion point.

5. You can click on the Default button.

Word asks you if you want to use the new settings as the default.

6. Select Yes (change all new documents based on NORMAL.DOT) or No (just this document).

If you select **Y**es, Word returns to the current document or the screen from which you selected the command. If you select **N**o, Word returns to the Page Setup dialog box.

7. If you have completed filling in the dialog box, select OK or press ↵Enter.

Word returns to the current document or the screen from which you selected the command.

Viewing Formatting Changes

As you apply document-wide formatting to a document, you might want to see the changes before you continue formatting. As you learned in Chapter 2, you can use **F**ile Print Pre**v**iew (Alt, F, V) so that Word displays the first page of your document as shown in Figure 5.12. You can scroll through the document on the screen by using the scroll bar or the PgUp and PgDn keys.

Figure 5.12

A one-page Print Preview showing Multiple Pages button.

Show multiple pages button

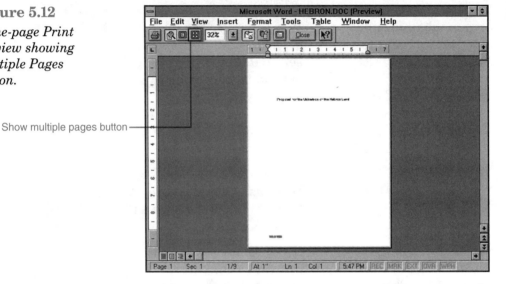

You can click on the Multiple Pages button at the top of the Print Preview screen. Then you'll see how multiple pages work together.

Remember that you'll learn a great deal more about all the printing options in Chapter 9.

Creating Headers and Footers

Up to this point in the chapter, you have learned how to apply document-wide formats to an entire page—margins, paper size, and orientation. Now you'll see how to format parts of each page in your document by using headers and footers, which are the lines of text within the top and bottom margins, respectively. One key to a professional looking document is the use of headers and footers.

In this book, the headers on the even-numbered pages iden-tify the chapter number, and the odd-numbered pages display the chapter title. When you flip through the pages of this book, you can quickly find a topic in which you are interested.

Headers and footers are used extensively in technical books, how-to books, dictionaries, and encyclopedias. By using headers and footers in your documents, you can give readers quick infor-mation about a document. This information often includes the page number, date of preparation of the document, the author, and the document or section title. However, you can include whatever information is appropriate for your document.

You can't see either headers or footers in **N**ormal view, but you can see them using the Print Pre**v**iew feature or **P**age Layout view. You can control where headers and footers appear—on every page, odd-numbered pages, even-numbered pages, every page but the first, and so on.

Use the **F**ile menu and the Page Set**u**p command (Alt, F, U) to open the Page Setup dialog box. Then click on the **L**ayout tab, if needed, to display the Page Setup dialog box with the layout options (see Figure 5.13). In this dialog box, you will see the Headers and Footers group, which displays the types of headers and footers that are available to use. To display different headers and footers on the first page of a document, check the Different **F**irst Page check box. To display different headers and footers on odd-numbered and even-numbered pages, check the Different

Odd and Even pages check box. The maximum number of headers and footers that can be displayed if both boxes are checked is six: First Page Header, First Page Footer, Even Page Header, Even Page Footer, Odd Page Header, and Odd Page Footer.

Figure 5.13
A document displayed with facing pages.

Facing pages aid in laying out a double-sided document with even and odd-numbered pages.

When you select **H**eader and Footer from the **V**iew menu, Word changes your document to **P**age Layout view and displays areas in which you can type headers and footers as well as a small toolbar (see Figure 5.14).

From left to right, the buttons are:

Switch Between Header and Footer—Click on this button to jump between the header and footer.

Show Previous—Click on this button to jump to the header or footer in the previous section if there is one.

Show Next—Click on this button to jump to the next header or footer in the next section if there is one.

Same As Previous—Click on this button to change the current header or footer to the header or footer in the previous section

Page Number—Click on this button to insert a page number field in this header or footer.

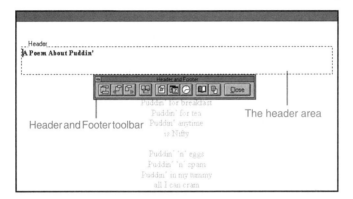

Figure 5.14
A standard header with the Header and Footer toolbar.

TIP: Insert the current page number into a document by moving the mouse pointer to the location where you want the page number and then press ⒜Alt⒝+⒨Shift⒩+⒫P⒭.

Date— Click on this button to insert a date field in this header or footer.

Time— Click on this button to insert a time field in this header or footer.

Page Setup— Click on this button to display the Page Setup dialog box for **L**ayout so that you can change layout attributes for a header or footer.

Show/Hide Document Text—Click on this button to display or hide the text in the document.

Close—Click on this button to close the Header and Footer toolbar.

TIP: Double-click anywhere in a header or footer to display the Header and Footer toolbar.

QUICK STEPS — Defining Headers and Footers

1. From the **File** menu, select Page Setup (Alt, F, U).	Word displays the Page Setup dialog box.
2. Click on the Layout tab, if needed.	Word displays the Page Setup dialog box for Layout (Figure 5.13).
3. To be able to place a different header and footer on the first page, place a check in the Different **F**irst Page check box.	Word adds First Page Header and First Page Footer to the choices for your document.
4. To be able to place a different header and footer on odd and even numbered pages, place a check in the Different **O**dd and Even box.	Word adds Even Page Header, Even Page Footer, Odd Page Header, and Odd Page Footer to the choices for your document.
5. Either click on OK or press ↵Enter.	Word returns to the current document.

6. From the **V**iew menu, select Header and Footer (Alt , V , H), or double-click in an existing header or footer.

Word switches to **P**age Layout view, displays areas in which you can type header or footer text, and opens the Header and Footer toolbar (Figure 5.14).

7. Type the text for your header or footer using the same methods you use for any Word document.

Word moves the insertion point and end mark as it does in any document.

8. You can move from header to header (or footer to footer) by clicking on toolbar buttons. You can insert a page number, system date (the date to which your computer is set), system time (the time to which your computer is set) by clicking on toolbar buttons.

Word inserts the appropriate information in the header/footer text.

9. Whether or not the header/footer pane is open, you can change the position of the header (or footer) from the default setting of 1/2 inch from the top (or bottom) of the page by selecting Page Setup from the **F**ile menu (Alt , F , U) and clicking on the Margins tab.

Word returns to the current document and the header/footer pane.

continues

continued

In the From Edge group (Figure 5.4), adjust the value in the **H**eader or **F**ooter box by moving to the arrow in one of the boxes, and pressing and holding the mouse button down until the value that you want is displayed. You can also type a value ranging from 0 to 22 inches. Then select OK or press ⏎Enter.

10. After you finish defining the header/footer, click on the Close button.

Word closes the Header and Footer toolbar and displays the current document.

Figure 5.15

A footer with the system time, the system date, and a page number.

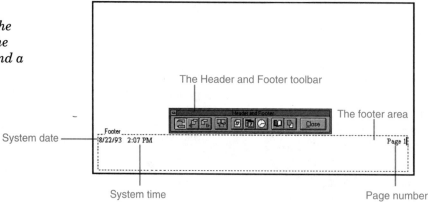

If your company distributes confidential documents and you want to be sure that there is no confusion about the importance of maintaining confidentiality, clearly mark Company Confidential in a footer. You can either use a large, bold font or even WordArt to make a highly noticeable statement.

TIP: To customize page numbers (for example, "Page 1"), type the word Page in the header or footer and then insert the page number by selecting the page number icon in the Header and Footer toolbar.

TIP: In longer documents, you can provide a great deal of information in the headers and footers. For example, you can display the chapter number on every even page and the chapter title on every odd page (see the headers in this book). For a document in which date and time are important, "stamp" this information on every page.

Creating Page Breaks

Word automatically specifies page breaks by using the measurements for page height and the top and bottom margins. However, there are times when you want to manually determine where to start a new page. For example, you should have a page break between the end of a title page and the beginning of body text or between major sections. Or you may want a list to appear on one page or an entire paragraph (rather than a fragment) to end a page.

To embed a break in your text, select the Insert menu and the Break command (Alt , I , B). The Break dialog box, shown in Figure 5.16, is small and simple. You can select either a Page Break, a Column Break, or a Section Break. (You'll learn about section breaks later in this chapter.) After selecting the type of break, select OK or press ↵Enter . Word places a horizontal dotted line across the page at the location of the page break. To learn about placing and removing page breaks in a document, use the Quick Steps that follow.

Placing and Removing Page Breaks in a Document

1. Move the insertion point in front of the line that you want to start the new page and select Break from the Insert menu (Alt , I , B).

Word displays the Break dialog box (Figure 5.16).

2. Select Page Break and select OK or press ↵Enter .

Word returns to the current document, places a dotted line at the insertion point (Figure 5.17), and changes the page number in the status bar.

3. To remove a page break that you have created, move the insertion point to the beginning of the line below the break and press the ←Backspace key.

Word removes the page break line. At the bottom of the screen, the number of the page is displayed.

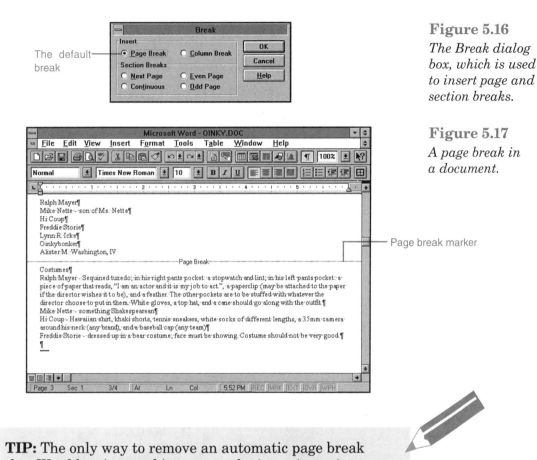

The default break

Figure 5.16
The Break dialog box, which is used to insert page and section breaks.

Figure 5.17
A page break in a document.

Page break marker

TIP: The only way to remove an automatic page break that Word has inserted is to move the insertion point to a line that is above the page break and then to insert a page break by pressing the shortcut keys Ctrl+↵Enter.

Sometimes you will want to turn off automatic page breaking altogether. For example, long documents with automatic pagination cause Word to process very slowly. Or, if you are creating a document and want total control of format, you'll want to make sure that you, and not Word, determines every page break.

Use the following Quick Steps to turn off automatic pagination.

Turning Off Automatic Pagination

1. Select Options from the Tools menu (Alt , T , O).

    Word displays the Options dialog box.

2. Click on the General tab, if needed.

    Word changes the dialog box options to general settings (see Figure 5.18).

3. If the **Background** Repagination box is checked, clear it and select OK or press ↵Enter .

    You must be in **Normal** view to make changes. Word returns to the current document.

Figure 5.18

The Options dialog box for the General category.

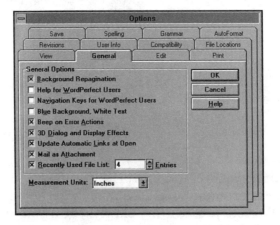

Controlling Orphan and Widow Lines

An automatic page break sometimes splits a paragraph between two pages. A single line of a paragraph ending a page is called an orphan line; a single line starting a page is a widow line. In most cases, you don't want a single line at the beginning or end of a page. The Word default ensures that at least two lines of a paragraph remain at the beginning or end of a page.

To check the status of widow and orphan lines, select the Format menu and the Paragraph command (Alt, O, P). Click on the Text Flow tab. When Word displays the Paragraph dialog box for Text Flow (see Figure 5.19), see whether the **W**idow/ Orphan Control check box is checked or clear.

In Chapter 6, you'll learn how to ensure that a paragraph starts a new page, how to keep a paragraph on the same page with the following paragraph, and how to keep the paragraph intact on the same page using the same dialog box.

NOTE: If a paragraph is only one line long, Word does not consider it either an orphan or widow.

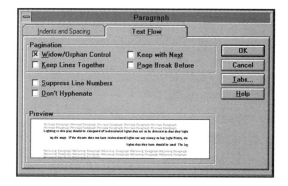

Figure 5.19
The Paragraph dialog box for the Text Flow category.

Customizing Page Numbering

Sometimes, you create a document that is made up of several files. With Word's customized page numbering, you have the ability to define the starting page number for each new file. When you are writing a book in which each file begins a new chapter, this is a handy feature to have. Some books are numbered sequentially from the first page to the last. Other books start numbering at the beginning of each chapter (for example, Page 3 in Chapter 4 of the book you are reading is 4-3). Either way, Word can help you set your page numbers quite easily.

When you add a page number to a header or footer, Word starts counting page numbers. You can control where Word starts counting page numbers by selecting the Insert menu and the Page Numbers command (Alt, I, U). When Word displays the Page Numbers dialog box, shown in Figure 5.20, click on the Format button. In the Page Number Format dialog box, shown in Figure 5.21, select a number format and determine whether your pages continue from the last page number or start at a specific number that you designate.

Figure 5.20

The Page Numbers dialog box, which is used to control the position and alignment of page numbers.

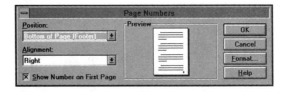

Figure 5.21

The Page Number Format dialog box, in which you customize page numbering.

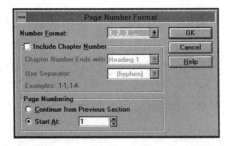

To customize the format of page numbers and set the page numbers themselves, use the Quick Steps in the following page.

Customizing Page Numbering

QUICK STEPS

1. Select Page Numbers from the **I**nsert menu, (Alt I, U).

Word displays the Page Numbers dialog box (Figure 5.20).

2. Click on the Format button.

Word displays the Page Number Format dialog box (see Figure 5.21). The default starting page number appears in the text box next to the Start **A**t radio button.

3. Type the starting page number in the box, or move to one of the arrows to the right of the box and press and hold the mouse button down until the value that you want is displayed. For example, to start the numbering on page three, type a 3 in the box.

Word keeps the insertion point in the Start **A**t box in case you want to change the number.

4. Move to the Number **F**ormat drop-down list box to show page number formats. Select the underlined down arrow to display all the choices and then select one.

When you make your selection, Word displays the page number format in the Number **F**ormat box and closes the list.

5. Select OK or press ↵Enter.

Word returns to the Page Numbers dialog box (Figure 5.20).

6. Select OK or Close or press ↵Enter.

Word returns to the current document.

If you want to add page numbers to your document without defining headers or footers, select the Insert menu and the Page Numbers command (Alt), (I), (U)), open the Position drop-down list box, and select Bottom of Page (Footer) or Top of Page (Header). Then from the Alignment drop-down list box choose Left, Center, Right, Inside, or Outside. Then you can select Format to start or format page numbering. Select OK or press (↵Enter) repeatedly until you return to the current document.

Section Formatting

Use section formatting when there is a major change in your document—starting a two-column layout, placing a headline, or beginning new or reformatted page numbers. Other uses of section breaks are to change the content of headers and footers, or to place endnotes after each chapter.

One example of a section break in some documents is the change between the first part (from the front cover through the table of contents, known as the front matter) and the body of the document. In the front matter, page numbers are usually lower-case roman numerals. When the body of the document begins, numbers change to Arabic and start at 1. To make this change, insert a section break at the location of the page numbering change.

Another example is a sales brochure in which most of the text is oriented across the shorter page dimension, from the left to the right margin, with one or two pages of tables containing long lines of text that stretch between the top and the bottom margins. Insert a section break at the location of the change in page orientation.

Although the default is for Word to start a new page at a section break, you can start (and even end) a new section on the same page as the previous (or following) section. A section can be as small as a paragraph or as large as your entire document. Because sections are so important, you'll read more about them throughout this book.

Creating a Section Break

Creating a section break is very similar to creating a page break, as shown in the following Quick Steps.

Creating a Section Break

QUICK STEPS

1. Place the insertion point where you would like to place a section break. Then select the Insert menu and the Break command (Alt , I , B).

   Word displays the Break dialog box (Figure 5.16). The section break controls are located at the bottom of the box.

2. Select a section break option and select OK or press ↵Enter. Table 5.3 describes section break options.

   Word returns to the current document, places a double-dotted line at the insertion point (in Normal view), and changes the page and section numbers in the Status bar (Figure 5.22).

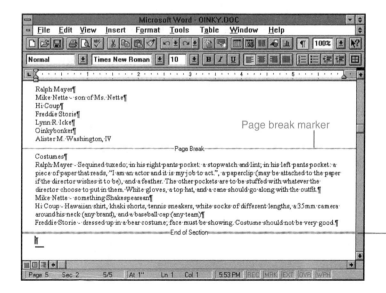

Figure 5.22

A section break and a page break displayed in a document. Notice that Word displays a double-dotted line at the section break and changes the page and section numbers in the Status bar.

Table 5.3
Section Break
Insertion Options

Option	Starts the Next Section
Next Page	At the top of the next page
Continuous	On the same page as the previous section
Even Page	At the top of the next even-numbered page
Odd Page	At the top of the next odd-numbered page

The section break mark is a double-dotted line that extends across the document window. As you will learn about the paragraph mark, the section break mark contains all the formatting information of the section that precedes it.

You can edit (selecting, copying, pasting, and deleting) the section break mark like any character. If you delete the section break mark, the text preceding the deleted section mark assumes the format of the following section.

The status bar shows you the section in which the insertion point is located (for example, Sec 1, Sec 2, or Sec 100).

To control page numbering after a section break, move the insertion point anyplace within the section and select Page Numbers from the **I**nsert menu (Alt, I, U). Word displays the Page Numbers dialog box shown in Figure 5.20. Click on Format, and when the Page Number Format dialog box (See Figure 5.21) appears, select from the Page Numbering group. You should have already selected whether this section follows the preceding section on the same page, the next page, the next odd page, or the next even page.

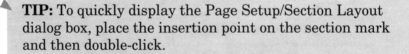

TIP: To quickly display the Page Setup/Section Layout dialog box, place the insertion point on the section mark and then double-click.

Select one or more paragraphs and:

- Click on an alignment button in the Formatting toolbar.
- Press Ctrl + L (left), Ctrl + R (right), Ctrl + E (center), or Ctrl + J (justify).
- Select Format Paragraph (Alt, O, P). From the Alignment drop down list box, select an alignment.

Changing Line Spacing

Select one or more paragraphs and then select Format Paragraph (Alt, O, P), make a selection from the Line Spacing drop down list box, and select OK or press ↵Enter. For single spacing, press Ctrl + 1, for one and one half spacing, press Ctrl + 5, and for double spacing, press Ctrl + 2.

Changing Spacing Before and After Paragraphs

Select paragraphs; then select Format Paragraph (Alt, O, P). Type or select a value in the **B**efore box or the **A**fter box. Select OK or press ↵Enter.

Indenting Paragraphs Using Format Paragraph

Select paragraphs; select Format Paragraph (Alt, O, P). Select the Indents and Spacing dialog box tab if necessary. Make a selection from the **S**pecial drop down list box, type in or select a value from the **B**y box, the **L**eft box, or the **R**ight box, or all. Select OK or press ↵Enter.

Indenting Paragraphs Using the Ruler

Select paragraphs and then drag the left margin marker, the first line marker, or the right margin marker to the desired locations.

Chapter

6

Formatting Paragraphs

Chapter 5 explained the first two of Word for Windows'
four formatting levels: document-wide and section formatting.
Document wide formatting affects the overall appearance of a
document—the margins, paper size, page orientation, and headers and footers. Section formatting defines the appearance of a
particular section within a document.

This chapter will explain the next formatting level: paragraph formatting. As you might suspect, paragraph formatting
affects the text within a paragraph—a string of text that ends with
a paragraph mark. Paragraph formatting defines six different
aspects of a paragraph:

Alignment of text between the left and right margins

The space between the lines of text in the paragraph

The space before and after the paragraph

The page breaks involving the paragraph

The indentations in the paragraph, and

Paragraph enhancements (borders, lines, and shading).

In the discussion of section formatting in Chapter 5, you were introduced to both the section mark and the paragraph mark, which end a section and a paragraph, respectively. Like the section mark, which contains all the formatting information of the section that precedes it, the paragraph mark (_) contains all the formatting information of the paragraph that precedes it. To display the paragraph mark and other nonprinting formatting symbols, select the Show/Hide button on the Standard toolbar.

Figure 6.1

The Formatting toolbar contains four paragraph alignment buttons.

Paragraph alignment buttons

To format a single paragraph, place the insertion point anywhere in the paragraph that you want to change. To format multiple paragraphs, select the paragraphs by using the mouse or the keyboard. Word provides several methods for applying paragraph formats: the Ruler, the Standard toolbar, the Formatting toolbar (Figure 6.1), the Borders toolbar, keyboard shortcuts, or the Format menu and the Paragraph command. This chapter will explain each method and point out its advantages.

You can also format documents, including paragraphs and characters, by using the AutoFormat feature, which is explained in Chapter 12. However, some paragraph formatting features (such as line spacing, and adding white space above and below paragraphs) are available only via the Format menu and the Paragraph command.

Aligning Paragraphs

Paragraph alignment is the first of Word's paragraph formats featured in this chapter. You can align paragraph text so that it is flush with either the left or the right margin, centered between the margins, or flush with both the left and the right margins.

Word's options for these paragraph alignments are left, right, centered, and justified, respectively. Figure 6.2 shows you a sample of each type of paragraph alignment.

Left alignment

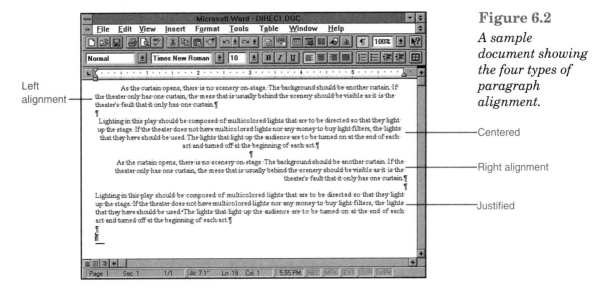

Figure 6.2

A sample document showing the four types of paragraph alignment.

Centered

Right alignment

Justified

Paragraph alignment is one way to emphasize a paragraph or to differentiate it from the rest of the document. For example, if you write a term paper or thesis that contains extensive quotations, you can center the quotations within the margins. (You can further enhance the quotation by indenting it, which is covered later in this chapter, or by changing the appearance of its text format, which you'll learn in Chapter 7.) Another example of a change in alignment is a poem which has verses that are left aligned, centered, and right aligned successively. Newspapers and magazines use justified alignment to create neat, clean looking columns. However, the disadvantage of justified text is that the spacing between words can appear uneven and therefore distracting to the eye.

If you want a document with paragraphs aligned with the left margin, you don't have to do a thing. This Word's default. To change paragraph alignment to right, centered, or justified, use either the **Fo**rmat **P**aragraph command or the Formatting toolbar.

Using the Format Paragraph Command to Align Paragraphs

Use the Format Paragraph command to change paragraph align-ment and then to format your paragraph in other ways. The following Quick Steps show how:

Aligning Paragraphs

1. Select one or more paragraphs to align.	Word highlights the selected text.
2. Select Paragraph from the Format menu, (Alt, O, P).	Word opens the Paragraph Indents and Spacing dialog box (Figure 6.3).
3. In the Alignment drop down list box, select the list arrow (the underlined down arrow).	Word displays your choices—Left, Centered, Right, and Justified. See Table 6.1 for a description of the alignment types and keyboard shortcuts for each.
4. Select one of the alignments.	Word changes the align-ment in the highlighted paragraph in the Preview box of the Indents and Spacing dialog box (Fig-ure 6.3).
5. Select OK or press ↵Enter.	Word returns to the current document and aligns the text in the selected paragraphs as you specified and as you saw in the Preview box.

If you wish to change back to the previous paragraph alignment, select Edit Undo (Alt , E , U) or press Ctrl + Z before you perform another action. You can learn more about the Undo command in Chapter 3.

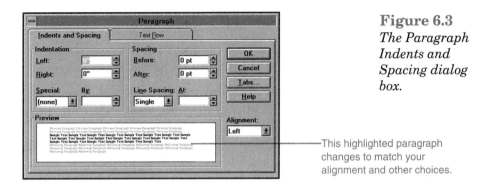

Figure 6.3
The Paragraph Indents and Spacing dialog box.

This highlighted paragraph changes to match your alignment and other choices.

Table 6.1 sums up the types of paragraph alignment and provides shortcut keys for each type. Just select one or more paragraphs in a document and press the shortcut keys. Word changes the alignment.

Alignment Type	Keys	Description
Left	Ctrl + L	Text aligns with the left margin. The right margin is ragged.
Right	Ctrl + R	Text aligns with the right margin. The left margin is ragged.
Center	Ctrl + E	Text is centered between the margins.
Justified	Ctrl + J	Text aligns with both the left and right margins by adding extra spaces between words.

Table 6.1
Types of paragraph alignment.

Using the Formatting Toolbar to Align Paragraphs

When you use the Formatting toolbar, you don't have to spend time in a dialog box so you can make changes more quickly. To change alignment with the Formatting toolbar, either move the insertion point to a paragraph or select one or more paragraphs. Then move the mouse pointer to the Formatting toolbar and select one of the paragraph alignment buttons.

If you are starting out with a new document or have not changed paragraph alignment in the current document, notice that the Left Alignment button appears to be pressed in to indicate that the paragraph is left aligned. To change the alignment press another paragraph alignment button on the Formatting toolbar.

 Click on the Left Alignment button to align the selected paragraph to the left margin.

 Click on the Center Alignment button to center the selected paragraph between the left and right margins.

 Click on the Right Alignment button to align the selected paragraph to the right margin.

 Click on the Justify Alignment button to align the selected paragraph to both the left indent and the right margin.

Adjusting Line Spacing

In the last section, you learned how to emphasize a paragraph by changing its alignment. Next you'll see how to adjust the leading, which is the spacing between the lines within a paragraph. Two common examples of line spacing are found in business letters, normally single spaced, and term papers, usually double spaced. You can also vary the line spacing settings within a document to emphasize particular paragraphs (for example, to set off quotations). Don't confuse line spacing with paragraph spacing, which adjusts spacing before and after paragraphs.

Word's default line spacing setting is single spacing, which is the measurement between the bottom of one line of text and the bottom of the next line. This measurement includes the text as well as the white space between the lines of text. As the size of the type in a document increases, Word increases the white space measurement as well. You'll learn more about selecting text types (fonts) and size (points) in the next chapter.

Use Format Paragraph (Alt, O, P) and select the Indents and Spacing dialog box if necessary to choose line spacing. Then open the list in the Line Spacing box to view the available options. You can select either fixed or adjustable spaces between lines (see Figure 6.4). Fixed spacing options are:

Single, 1.5 (1.5 times Single)

Double (twice the measurement of Single)

Exactly, which enables you to choose line spacing ranging from 0 to 1584 points

Multiple, which allows you to select line spacing ranging from 0 to 132 lines

If you choose Exactly, you can type the measurement in the At box, or use the arrow button at the right side of the At box to cycle through the range of measurements. Spacing between lines always remains the same, regardless of changes in point size. Exactly remains at the measurement you set, even if adjacent text lines overlap. This is in contrast with Single, 1.5, and Double line spacing; Word adjusts line spacing automatically when you increase or decrease line spacing. Therefore succeeding lines cannot overlap preceding lines.

TIP: You can use keyboard shortcuts to set single, one-and-a-half, and double line spacing. Ctrl+1 sets single spacing, Ctrl+5 sets one-and-a-half spacing, and Ctrl+2 sets double spacing. To remove one or add one line space, before a paragraph, press Ctrl+0.

Figure 6.4
The Paragraph Indents and Spacing dialog box with the Double spacing option chosen. Notice that the highlighted paragraph in the Preview box reflects the chosen settings.

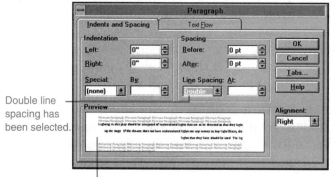

Double line spacing has been selected.

The sample paragraph is double spaced.

Word also provides two adjustable spacing options: Auto and At Least. Auto measures the tallest ascender, the part of a letter above the body of the letter (for example, h, b, d, f, and h are letters with ascenders) to determine the line spacing measurement. At Least requires you to enter a minimum measurement or cycle through the measurements in the **At** box (from 0 to 1584 points) but adjusts line spacing when it encounters a large character. Table 6.2 summarizes Word's line spacing options.

Option	Key Shortcut	Option Type	Description
Auto	–	Adjustable	Automatic spacing. Word selects the spacing for you based on the tallest ascender in a line of text.
Single	Ctrl+1	Fixed	Single spacing, based on a single line of text.
1.5	Ctrl+5	Fixed	One-and-one-half spacing, based on 1 1/2 lines of text.
Double	Ctrl+2	Fixed	Double spacing, based on two lines of text.
At Least	–	Adjustable	A specific minimum measurement that you decide but that Word can increase, if needed.
Exactly	–	Fixed	A specific measurement that you decide, and that Word will not change.
Multiple	–	Fixed	A specific measurement that you decide, and that is a multiple of its previous setting.

Table 6.2
Line spacing options.

The following Quick Steps show you how to adjust the line spacing in a paragraph.

Adjusting Line Spacing

1. After selecting one or more paragraphs, select the Format menu and the Paragraph command (Alt, O, P).

Word opens the Paragraph *Indents and Spacing* dialog box (Figure 6.3).

continues

continued

2. On the right side of the Line Spacing box, select the list arrow (the underlined down arrow).

Word displays the line spacing options (see Table 6.2).

3. To set your own line spacing measurement, select At Least or Exactly and in the **At** box, either type the number of points (from 0 through 1584) or move to one of the arrows to the right of the box, pressing and holding the left mouse button down until the value that you want is displayed.

As you select an option, the Preview document in the dialog box changes.

4. To let Word select the line spacing measurement, select Single, 1.5, Double, Auto, or Multiple.

As you select an option, the Preview document in the dialog box changes.

5. Select OK or press ⏎Enter.

Word returns to the current document and adjusts the line spacing of the selected paragraphs as you just saw in the Preview box.

To return to the previous line spacing setting if you haven't performed any other actions, select Edit Undo (Alt, E, U) or press Ctrl+Z. Chapter 3 explains the **Undo** command in greater detail.

Setting Paragraph Spacing

In the last section, you learned about line spacing, which adjusts spacing within a paragraph. Next you'll see how to use paragraph spacing to adjust spacing above and below a paragraph. Word's default paragraph spacing is no lines between paragraphs, however if you add a space between each paragraph in a letter, each will stand out and be easier to read.

You can use either **F**ormat **P**aragraph (Alt, O, P) or keyboard shortcuts to adjust spacing between paragraphs. Using the **F**ormat **P**aragraph command provides more flexibility than using keyboard shortcuts because you can adjust in increments of half a line and you have more spacing options before and after a paragraph. Word's default settings are 0 lines before and after each paragraph. To create an extra line before one or more selected paragraphs, press the keyboard shortcut Ctrl+0. Then press Ctrl+0 to remove the extra line. There is no keyboard shortcut for adding line spacing after a paragraph.

The following Quick Steps show you how to use the Format Paragraph command to adjust paragraph spacing.

Adjusting Paragraph Spacing

1. Select one or more paragraphs and then select the Format menu and the Paragraph command (Alt, O, P).

   Word displays the Paragraph Indents and Spacing dialog box (Figure 6.3).

2. Either type a value in the **B**efore box, or press and hold down the left mouse button on the up or the down arrow (in the right of the box) until the desired value (ranging from 0 to 1584 points) is displayed.

   As you change the settings, Word changes the sample document in the Preview box (Figure 6.5).

continues

continued

Enter a value in the After box in the same way.

3. Select OK or press
⏎Enter.

Word returns to the current document and changes its paragraph formatting.

Figure 6.5

The Paragraph Indents and Spacing dialog box showing paragraph spacing options.

Line spacing group —

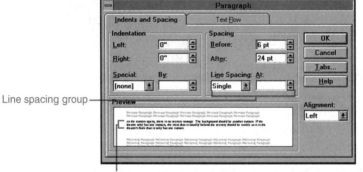

The sample paragraph shows spacing before and after.

Press Ctrl + Z or choose Edit Undo to change back to the previous paragraph spacing format before you perform another action. See Chapter 3 for an explanation of the Undo command.

It's a good idea to apply spacing with either **B**efore or Aft**e**r but not both so that you'll have better control over your entire document. For example, suppose a document consists of four paragraphs. If you use the Aft**e**r option to change spacing for the second paragraph and **B**efore for the third paragraph, you'll have extra space between paragraphs two and three but not enough space between paragraphs one and two as well as paragraphs three and four.

Controlling Page Breaks for Paragraphs

In Chapter 5, you learned about inserting page breaks and preventing widow and orphan lines in your document. The page breaks that you insert are called hard page breaks. They remain where you put them regardless of the addition or deletion of text throughout the document. These are different from the automatic page breaks (or soft page breaks) which Word inserts as you create a document. The locations for Word's automatic page breaks are calculated based on the amount of text that fits on a page. When you add or delete text, Word recalculates and automatically moves the page break. Then it recalculates the remaining pages in the document and places page breaks where needed. Both types of page breaks are displayed as dotted lines that extend between the left and right margins. However, the hard page break symbol, which displays more densely packed dots, also includes the text Page Break centered between the margins (see Figure 6.6).

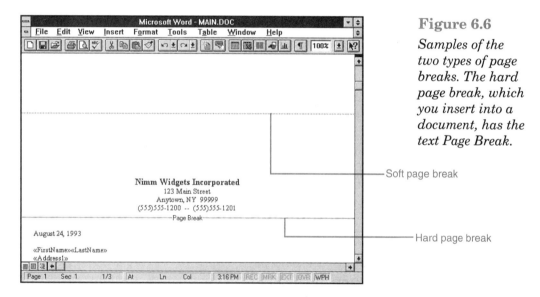

Figure 6.6

Samples of the two types of page breaks. The hard page break, which you insert into a document, has the text Page Break.

Soft page break

Hard page break

Next you'll learn how to insert a hard page break before a paragraph. This is a way of ensuring that the paragraph starts a new page. For example, for a document consisting of a memo and an attachment, you can place a hard page break before the first paragraph of the attachment. You can insert a page break using **I**nsert **B**reak, as you learned in Chapter 5, but if you're formatting the paragraph using the Paragraph dialog boxes, you can insert the page break from the Text Flow dialog box as you change formats. It is best to select only one paragraph when you use this option. Otherwise, Word places a page break before every paragraph that you select.

Figure 6.7

The Text Flow Paragraph dialog box from which you select the location for hard page breaks.

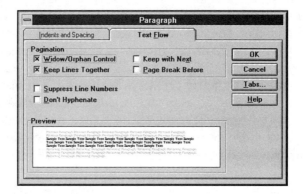

Word allows you to keep a paragraph on the same page with the following paragraph by providing the Keep with Next option in the Text Flow dialog box. For example, suppose you write a term paper containing quoted material. Each quotation is preceded by a paragraph giving background information about the quotation. You'll probably want to keep the introductory paragraph on the same page with the quotation that it introduces. You can also use this option if you have a list consisting of separate paragraphs and you want to print the list on one page.

As you learned in Chapter 5, controlling widow and orphan lines prevents single lines of a paragraph from printing separately from the rest of the paragraph. However, a paragraph can still print with two or three lines on one page and two or three lines on the next. To force a paragraph to print on one page, select Keep Lines Together. In our term paper example, you may want to make sure that each line of a quotation prints on the same page. Table 6.3 summarizes Word's pagination options for paragraphs.

Text Flow Option	Description
Page Break Before	Inserts a page break before each of the selected paragraphs.
Keep with Next	Prevents a page break between the selected paragraphs and the following paragraph.
Keep Lines Together	Prevents a page break within the selected paragraphs.
Widow/Orphan Control	Prevents a single line at the top of a new page or a single word in the last line of a paragraph.

Table 6.3
Text Flow options for paragraphs from Text Flow dialog box.

The following Quick Steps describe how to control page breaks for paragraphs.

Controlling Page Breaks for Paragraphs

1. Select one or more paragraphs. From the **F**ormat menu, select the Paragraph command (Alt , O , P).

   Word displays either the Paragraph Indents and Spacing dialog box (Figure 6.3) or the Paragraph Text Flow dialog box (Figure 6.7).

2. If the Text Flow dialog box is not displayed, select its tab.

   Word displays the Paragraph Text Flow dialog box (Figure 6.7).

3. In the Pagination group, you can check any combination of the four options.

   For an explanation of each, see Table 6.3.

4. Select OK or press ↵Enter .

   Word returns to the current document and changes its paragraph formatting.

Indenting Paragraphs

Early in this chapter, you learned about aligning paragraphs against the left and right margins. Another paragraph formatting option that uses margins as a guide is indentation, which moves either the entire paragraph or the first line away from the left and/ or right margin.

There are four ways to indent paragraphs—the Formatting toolbar, the Ruler, the Format Paragraph command, and shortcut keys. Use the **F**ormat **P**aragraph command to indent using precise measurements with any of Word's units of measurements; use the Ruler and the Formatting toolbar to indent quickly using the current unit of measurement; and use shortcut keys to indent using tab positions.

There are five types of indents:

First line indent—Start the first character in the first line of a paragraph several spaces after the left margin but align succeeding lines with the left margin. Use the first line indent for letters or for documents where there is minimal spacing between paragraphs but you want to show where a new paragraph begins. The right margin can be either justified or ragged, depending on the paragraph alignment you have set for this paragraph.

Hanging indent—Start the first line in a paragraph either at the left margin or close to it. Then, following lines are further indented from the left margin. The right margin can be either justified or ragged, depending on the paragraph alignment you have set for this paragraph. Hanging indents are ideal for bulleted and numbered lists.

Left or right indent—Indent all the lines of a paragraph from either margin. This is also known as a *block indent*.

Centered indent—Indent all the lines of a paragraph from both margins. This emphasizes the text in the paragraph and makes it stand out from the rest of the text. This is also known as a *block indent*.

Tabbed indent—You can press the Tab key to indent the first line of a paragraph or to indent within a paragraph. The last topic in this chapter explains the use of tabs in Word.

Click on the Unindent button to align the selected paragraph or paragraphs with the previous tab position (to the left). The current indentation format (hanging, first line indent, etc.) remains.

Click on the Indent button to align the selected paragraph or paragraphs with the next tab position (to the right). The current indentation format (hanging, first line indent, etc.) remains.

Using the Ruler to Indent

The quickest way to indent paragraphs and lines is by using the small markers on the Ruler. The left margin markers on the Ruler are two pointers; the top pointer is the first line indent marker, and the bottom pointer is the left margin marker. To indent paragraphs from the left, simply move the bottom pointer with the mouse pointer. To create first line or hanging indents, move the top pointer. The right margin marker on the Ruler is represented by a single pointer. To indent paragraphs from the right, move the right margin marker. When you use the Ruler to indent paragraphs, you see the result instantly.

Using the Format Paragraph Command to Indent

Another way to indent paragraphs is by using the Format Paragraph command. When the Paragraph dialog box is displayed, either type values in the **L**eft or **R**ight text boxes, or move the mouse pointer to the arrow keys and press and hold down the left mouse button until the value that you want is displayed. To specify a particular indentation for the first line of a paragraph, open the Special drop down list box and select from the list and either type in or select a value from the By box. You can indent selected paragraphs by a value ranging from –0 inches through 22 inches. However, Word won't allow a line of text in a document to be narrower than 1 inch or allow the first line indent to be closer than .1 inch from the right margin (see Figure 6.8).

Figure 6.8

You can indent paragraphs using the Indentation boxes in the Paragraph Indents and Spacing option.

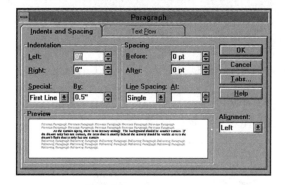

Use the **Fo**rmat **P**aragraph command when you must set an indent based on a unit of measurement that is not your regular one. For example, if you normally use inches, and you need to indent a certain number of centimeters, it's easy to display the Paragraph *Indents and Spacing* dialog box and enter the measurement in the appropriate box.

To create a first line indent, select First Line from the **S**pecial drop down list box, and then in the **By** box type a value that represents the amount of indentation of the first line in the paragraph. The value in the By box can be any positive number from 0 to 22 inches. Word uses the value in the **L**eft box as the left margin, and indents the paragraph by the amount in the By box from the left margin. If you type a negative number in the By box, you are attempting to create a hanging indent, which you'll learn about shortly. Word changes the sample in the Paragraph dialog box to match the indent (see Figure 6.9).

To create a hanging indent, type the value of the left margin in the **L**eft box, if needed. In the **S**pecial drop down list box, select Hanging, and in the B**y** box, type a value (from 0 to 22 inches) that moves the first line back toward the left margin. Word changes the sample in the Preview box to match the indent (see Figure 6.9).

A good use for hanging indents is in creating a simple business memo with To:, From:, Date:, and Subject: paragraphs. Highlight all four paragraphs and create a hanging indent that is wide enough to allow a small tab after the Subject: paragraph.

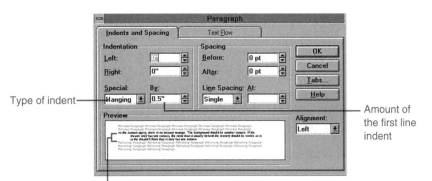

Type of indent

Indented sample paragraph

Amount of the first line indent

Figure 6.9
A hanging indent. The entire paragraph is indented except for the first line, which is moved back toward the left margin.

To indent selected paragraphs from both margins, enter values that represent the indentation from the left and right margins in the **L**eft and **R**ight boxes. To indent both margins equally, type the same value in each box. Word changes the sample in the Paragraph Indents and Spacing dialog box to match the indent (see Figure 6.10). To indent selected paragraphs from the left margin, enter a value in the **L**eft box; to indent from the right margin, enter a value in the **R**ight box.

The following Quick Steps show you how to create a first line indent.

Creating a First Line Indent

1. Select one or more paragraphs.

   Word highlights the selected paragraphs.

2. Select the Format menu and the Paragraph command (Alt, O, P), and the Indents and Spacing dialog box if necessary.

   Word displays the Paragraph Indents and Spacing dialog box.

3. From the Special drop down list box, select First Line, and in the By box, type any positive number from 0 to 22. In the Left box, type a value that represents the left margin. Word indents the first line in the paragraph by the value in the First Line box.

   Word changes the illustration in the Preview box.

4. Select OK or press ↵Enter.

   Word returns to the current document and changes its paragraph formatting.

Figure 6.10

A left and right indent. The text indents from both left and right margins.

Type of indent

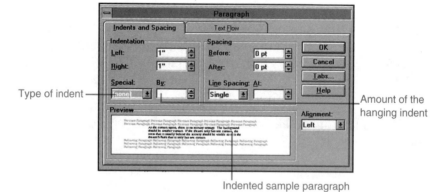

Amount of the hanging indent

Indented sample paragraph

Indenting Paragraphs with the Keyboard

Word also provides shortcut keys for paragraph indentation. Select one or more paragraphs and the paragraph is indented to the next or preceding tab stop, depending on the shortcut key you press. Table 6.4 presents a synopsis of the keys along with a description of each.

Key	Type of Indent	Description
Ctrl+T	Hanging Indent	Indents all but the first line of selected paragraphs. Press repeatedly to increase the indent by moving to the next tab stop.
Ctrl+M	Indent	Indents all the selected paragraphs from the left margin, one tab stop at a time.
Ctrl+Shift+M	Remove an indent	Removes the indent from a selected paragraph.
Ctrl+Q	Remove all indents and formats	Removes all indents and paragraph and character formatting from the selected paragraphs.
Ctrl+Shift+T	Remove hanging indent.	

Table 6.4
Indenting paragraphs with the keyboard.

To change from indented paragraphs to paragraphs that are aligned with the left margin, press Ctrl+5 (on the numeric keypad) to select the entire document; then press Ctrl+Q.

Enhancing Paragraphs

Up to this point in the chapter, you have formatted paragraphs for emphasis by aligning, indenting, and adding space. However, if there are paragraphs that you want to stand out from the rest in a distinctive way, consider adding borders, lines, and/or shading with the Format Borders and Shading command.

For example, you can use borders to call attention to one or two paragraphs in a document. Perhaps they warn the reader or emphasize an important step in a set of instructions. You can also use a combination of text and border to quickly make a poster. If you select several paragraphs, Word places borders or lines around the entire selection. When you choose the Format Borders and Shading command, Word displays the Paragraph Borders and Shading dialog box with the Shading dialog box tab visible as shown in Figure 6.11. Together the two boxes provide these options:

- The Border dialog box shows illustrations of the options you selected.

- The From Text box allows you to specify the amount of white space (from 0 pt to 31 pt) between the text and the border.

- The Presets box presents three types of borders: None, which represents no border; Box, which is a standard border; and Shadow, which is a drop shadow border.

- The Line group provides a variety of single and double lines from which you can select. None, which means no line, is the default.

- The Color drop down list box gives you a choice of 17 border colors to use on a color monitor or a color plotter or printer.

- If you click on the **S**hading tab, the Paragraph Shading dialog box is displayed. You'll learn about shading later in this chapter.

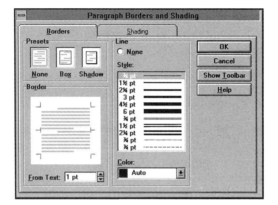

Figure 6.11

The Paragraph Borders and Shading dialog box, for Borders, which allows you to define or change borders around paragraphs.

Placing Borders Around Paragraphs

The easiest way to emphasize a paragraph is to surround it with a border. There are two ways to place a border around a paragraph: either use the Format Borders and Shading command (Alt, O, B) or open the Borders toolbar. To create a border using the Format Borders and Shading command, in the Borders dialog box select Box, select a Style in the Line group, and press OK. To use the Borders toolbar, open it and then click on the buttons and drop down list boxes. Suppose you are writing instructions for installing a light fixture or switch. You'll want to warn your customers to turn off the electricity when they are working with bare wires. These Quick Steps describe how to apply a border using the Format Borders and Shading command.

Applying a Border to a Paragraph using the Menu Bar

1. Select one or more paragraphs, and from the **Fo**rmat menu, select the Borders and Shading command (Alt, O, B) and the Borders tab

   Word displays the Paragraph **B**orders dialog box.

2. Select Box and then from the **St**yle box, select the appropriate border box.

   Word displays your selection in the Bo**r**der box (Figure 6.13).

3. In the Bo**r**der group, select From Text to define the space between the text and the border.

   Word changes the illustration in the Bo**r**der group (Figure 6.12).

4. To display or print in color (if you have a color monitor, printer or plotter), open the Color drop down list box to display a list of colors from which you can choose.

   Word displays a list of colors and their names.

5. You can select the type of border—None, Box, or Shadow—in the Presets box.

   Word changes the illustration in the box in the Border group (Figure 6.13).

6. When you have completed selecting your options, select OK or press ↵Enter.

   Word returns to the current document and applies the border to the selected paragraph.

The current selection

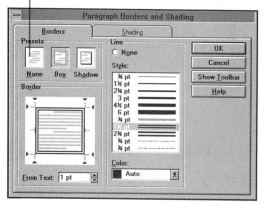

Figure 6.12
When you select a border, Word changes the illustration in the Border box.

The current selection

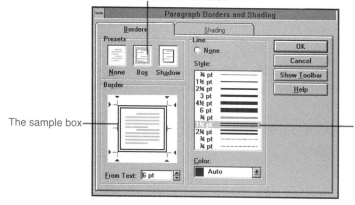

The sample box

The selected line style

Figure 6.13
The Border Paragraphs dialog box, with more white space added between text and the border.

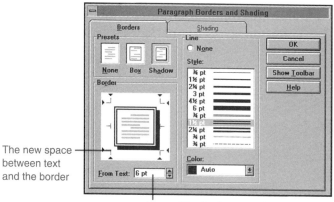

The new space between text and the border

The setting for the space between text and the border

Figure 6.14
The Border Paragraphs dialog box. When you select the type of border, Word adds to the illustration in the Border box.

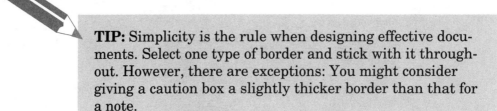

TIP: Simplicity is the rule when designing effective documents. Select one type of border and stick with it throughout. However, there are exceptions: You might consider giving a caution box a slightly thicker border than that for a note.

Emphasizing Paragraphs with Lines

Another way of emphasizing a paragraph is to place lines against one, two, three, or four sides. (Of course, lines around four sides of a paragraph are a border.) Remember that in earlier sections of this chapter, we used a term paper with extensive quotations as an example. Another way to emphasize each quotation is to put lines above and below it. To emphasize a list, you could place a vertical line to the left and a horizontal line below. This emphasizes the paragraph but also demonstrates that this paragraph has different content than the paragraph surrounded by a border.

The next set of Quick Steps describes how to add lines around a selected paragraph.

Adding Lines Around a Paragraph

1. First select one or more paragraphs. Then select the Format menu and the Border and Shading command (Alt, O, B) the Borders tab if necessary.

   Word displays the Paragraph Borders dialog box.

2. In the Presets box, select None, which indicates that you want no border.

Word deletes any borders Border box (Figure 6.15).

3. In the Border box, click one of the sides of the illustration to which you want to apply a line.

Word changes the illustration in the Border box (Figure 6.16). The triangles at the corners of the illustration are the points between which any line or border is drawn.

4. In the Line box, select the Style of line or None (to remove lines).

Word changes the illustration once again.

5. To add a line to more than one side, hold down ⬆Shift after you select the first line, and then select the additional sides. Or, press Alt+R and any arrow key to cycle through the available line combinations until you find what you want.

Word changes the illustration in the Border box (Figure 6.17).

6. When you have completed your selection, press OK.

Word returns to the current document and applies the specified lines to the selected paragraph (Figure 6.18).

Note that you can only select one line type at a time to emphasize the selected paragraph.

Figure 6.15

The Border Paragraphs dialog box with no border selected.

The current selection

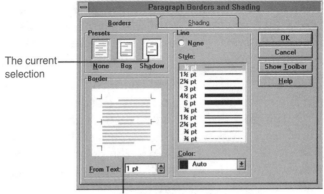

A border with a shadow

Shading Paragraphs

Another way to emphasize selected paragraphs, whether or not you have selected borders or lines, is to apply shading. For example, you can make a sign advertising a sale or a school play, surround it with a border, and then shade it. Another example is creating screen illustrations for computer software documentation. First, type the appropriate text and format it to match the screen image; then add a shadow box border and light shading. This differentiates the screen images from the rest of the text.

Figure 6.16

The Paragraph Borders dialog box. At this point, a line would be drawn between the arrows at the top of the selected paragraph.

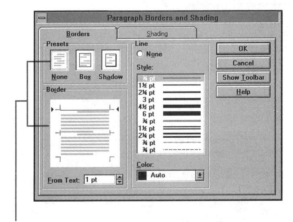

Starting with no border

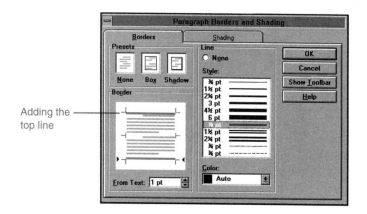

Adding the
top line

Figure 6.17
*The Paragraph
Borders dialog
box. If you select
OK or press Enter,
lines will be
drawn at the top
and bottom of
the selected
paragraph.*

Note: Before you do any electrical work, make
sure that the electricity is shut off, and
remember not to fish for wires with a metal coat
hanger.

Figure 6.18
*A paragraph with
double lines above
and below.*

Select Format Borders and Shading (Alt , O , B) and, when
Word displays the Paragraph Borders and Shading dialog boxes,
click on the Shading tab. The Paragraph **S**hading dialog box,
shown in Figure 6.19, allows you to select either no shading or
coloring (the default) or **C**ustom, from which you can choose a
pattern and foreground or background colors. You don't need to
have a color printer, plotter, or monitor to select colors. If you have
selected colors, you can use a color printer, plotter, or monitor
anytime later.

To shade selected paragraphs, use the following Quick Steps.

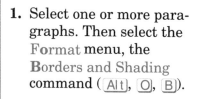

Shading Paragraphs

1. Select one or more paragraphs. Then select the
   Format menu, the
   Borders and Shading
   command (Alt , O , B).

   The Paragraph Borders
   dialog box is displayed.

   continues

continued

2. If needed, add a border or lines.

Word changes the illustration in the Border box.

3. Click on the Shading tab.

Word displays the Paragraph Shading dialog box.

4. Click on the Custom radio button.

If you selected **None** instead of **Custom**, Word cleared the previous pattern from the Preview box.

5. Move the mouse pointer to the list arrow on the right side of the Shading box. Or press `Tab↹` repeatedly until you highlight Clear in the Shading box. Then press `↓` repeatedly to find the desired pattern. Or press `Alt`+`D`.

Word shows the pattern in the Preview box.

6. To add colors to the selected paragraph, choose Foreground or Background.

Word opens a list of colors from which you can choose. Auto, the default color, uses your monitor's, printer's, or plotter's default colors.

7. Select a foreground and background color.

Word closes each list and displays your choices.

8. Select OK or press `↵Enter`.

Word returns to the current document and applies the pattern within the border of the paragraph (Figure 6.20).

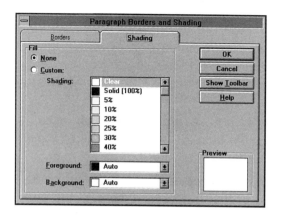

Figure 6.19

To add shading or color to a paragraph with a border, choose from the options in the Paragraph Shading dialog box.

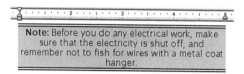

Figure 6.20

Word adds the pattern to the selected paragraph.

 Click on the Borders button to display or hide the Borders toolbar.

Using the Borders Toolbar to Apply Borders and Shading

To apply borders and shading to selected paragraphs using the Borders toolbar, use the following Quick Steps.

Shading Paragraphs

1. Select one or more paragraphs, and then select the View menu and the Toolbars command

   Word opens the Borders toolbar, as shown in Figure 6.21.

   continues

continued

([Alt], [V], [T]). Check the Borders check box and select OK.	
2. Open the Line Style drop down list box, and click on a line.	Word changes the toolbar to show your selection.
3. Click on one or more of the line or border buttons.	Word applies the formats to the selected paragraphs.
4. To choose a pattern, open the Shading Pattern drop down list box, and click on your selection.	Word applies the pattern to the selected paragraphs.
5. To close the Borders tool-bar, select the View menu and the Toolbars command ([Alt], [V], [T]). Toggle the Borders check box off.	Word closes the Borders toolbar.

Figure 6.21
The Borders toolbar from which you can select lines styles, lines, borders, and shading.

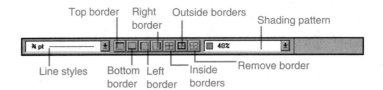

Using Tabs

Earlier in this chapter, you learned about paragraph indentation and specifically about first line indents. In this section, you'll be given information about using tabs—how to set tabs at regular intervals or at specific locations, how to clear some or all tabs, and how to use some other tab options.

Tabs indent paragraphs more quickly than when you use Format **P**aragraph. Move the insertion point to the beginning of the paragraph you want to indent and press Tab⇄. On screen, the tab symbol appears as a right pointing arrow if Word is set to display hidden characters.

Use tabs to indent text within a line or paragraph. For example, to format a computer program, you may need to place parts of each command line at specific tab positions or indent some lines using the same tab positions. Either accept Word's default tab positions (every 1/2 inch) on the Ruler or change the tab settings. Then, in your document, press Tab⇄ to start text at the next tab position. On the Ruler, the default tab positions appear as small vertical lines on the bar just below the Ruler scale line.

Another use for tabs is to create tables. Although you should probably use the **T**able menu to create most tables, occasionally you can use tabs for small tables. See Chapter 11 for a complete description of how to create tables using Word.

Use the Ruler to set and clear tab positions and to change tab alignment: Left, Right, Decimal, or Center. Use the F**o**rmat Tabs command to define tab positions at either regular intervals or specific locations, to clear some or all tab positions, to determine the type of leader (the dotted lines between a title and a page number in some tables of contents—not to be confused with leading, which is related to line spacing) to use, and to set or change five types of tab alignments (including Bar alignment). Table 6.5 lists each tab alignment setting and provides a description for each.

Setting	Description
Left	The leftmost character aligns with the tab position. The rest of the text flows to the right.
Right	The rightmost character aligns with the tab position. The rest of the text flows to the left.
Decimal	Any decimal point is aligned with the tab position. The remaining digits flow left and right from the decimal point. If there is no decimal point, this setting behaves like a right tab.
Center	The text is centered on the tab position.
Bar	Word draws a vertical line through the selected text at a specific tab position.

Table 6.5
Tab alignment types.

Setting Tabs

Use the Format Tabs command to set tabs at regular or varying intervals. To set tabs at regular intervals (for example, every .75 inch), type a value in or select a value from the Default Tab Stops box in the Tabs dialog box (see Figure 6.22). To set tabs at varying intervals (for example, .5", 1.5", 3.3") for tabs, type measurements between .01 and 22, one at a time, in the Tab Stop Position box. (A negative number can be used for tabs within hanging indents.)

Word allows you to set tab alignment in the Tabs dialog box in five ways: Left, Right, Center, Decimal, and Bar. To set left aligned tab positions (the default) at regular intervals using the Format Tabs command, use the following Quick Steps.

Figure 6.22

The Tabs dialog box enables you to set tabs and define their alignment.

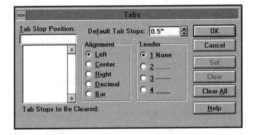

QUICK STEPS

Defining Tab Positions at Regular Intervals Using the Format Tabs Command

1. From the Format menu, select the Tabs command (Alt, O, T).

   Word displays the Tabs dialog box.

2. In the Default Tab Stops box, type a new tab setting (from .01 to 22 inches). Ten select **OK** or press ↵Enter.

TIP: To find out the relative location of a tab stop along the width of a document, move the mouse pointer to the tab stop you wish to check, press Alt and click the mouse button. Word displays the measurements of the tab stop to the left margin and to the right margin.

Word sets new tab positions at the intervals you have defined. So if you enter .25 in the box and select OK or press ⏎Enter, the new default tabs on your page will start at a quarter of an inch from the left side of the edge of your page and then appear every .25 inch.

To find the exact location of a tab setting in a document, select a paragraph with that tab setting, display the Tabs dialog box, and write down the measurement.

TIP: To quickly display the Tabs dialog box, double-click on any tab mark on the ruler.

Many times, you will want to set specific tab positions at varying intervals. Use either the Ruler or the Format Tabs command to set varying tab positions and alignment. There is a set of Quick Steps for each method. Before starting the Quick Steps, make sure that the Ruler is displayed by choosing the View menu and then making sure that there is a check mark next to Ruler (Alt, V, R). If the Formatting toolbar is not on your screen, select View Toolbars (Alt, V, T) and check the Formatting check box.

To define varying tab positions using the Ruler, follow these Quick Steps:

Defining Tab Positions at Varying Intervals Using the Ruler

1. Select the text for which you want to define tab positions.

Word highlights your selection.

2. Select one of the tab alignment buttons on the Ruler by clicking on the Tab alignment button until the correct one appears, shown in Figure 6.23.

Word changes the tab symbol on the ruler.

3. On the Ruler, click where you want a tab position. Or, drag an existing tab symbol to a new location and release the mouse button.

When you insert a tab mark, it causes all of the default tab marks to the left of the one you just inserted to disappear.

4. Repeat steps 2 and 3 until you have placed all the tab positions you want.

If the highlighted paragraph includes any tab marks that are affected by the new tab positions, Word changes the format.

TIP: To delete a tab symbol, just drag it off the Ruler and release the mouse button.

Figure 6.23
This Ruler illustrates all types of tab settings.

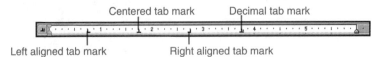

A feature that is not available when you use the Ruler is defining a leader, typically a dotted line that extends from the last character or space in the text before the tab and the tab itself (see Figure 6.24). Leaders are used in many tables of contents. The following Quick Steps show how to define tab positions at specific locations.

Defining Tab Positions at Varying Intervals Using the Format Tabs Command

1. Select the text for which you want to define tab positions.

Word highlights your selection.

2. Select the Format menu and the Tabs command (⎡Alt⎤, ⎡O⎤, ⎡T⎤).

Word displays the Tabs dialog box.

3. In the Tab Stop Position box, enter a number representing the tab position. Valid values for tab positions range from −0 inches to 22 inches.

Word informs you if you enter a number outside the valid range.

4. Select the type of alignment (Left, Center, Right, Decimal, or Bar) for the tab position.

Word fills in the appropriate button.

5. To select a leader, choose one of the four leader types.

Word places a border around the leader that you have selected.

6. Select Set.

Word highlights the contents of the Tab Stop Position box.

continues

continued

7. To add more tab positions, repeat steps 3 through 6 until you have finished.	Word adds each position to the list in the **T**ab Stop Position box. You can set a maximum of 50 tab positions.
8. Select OK or press ↵Enter.	Word returns to your document and places the new tab setting on the Ruler.

Clearing Tabs

You can clear one specific tab position or all tab positions. From the Format menu, select the Tab command (Alt, O, T). Word displays the Tabs dialog box. To clear one specific tab position, first select a tab position from the list in the Tab Stop Position box and then click on the Clear button. Select OK or press ↵Enter. To clear all tab positions, just click on the Clear All button. Select OK or press ↵Enter. To clear a tab position using the Ruler, select a tab position and drag it off the Ruler.

Figure 6.24

An example of leaders in a document table of contents.

Table of Contents

Preamble..3
Terms..3
Subdivision..4
Land Use..5
Ownership and Disposition of Land..6
Costs..7

NOTE: Once you have cleared a tab position, there is no way to undo this action other than setting the tab again.

Font

A family of characters in different sizes and enhancements but having the same overall design.

Point Size

The vertical size of a character measured from the top of a character such as d to the bottom of a character such as p.

Emphasizing Characters with Boldface, Italics, and Underlines

Select the text to be enhanced, and then enhance it:

- Select Format Font ([Alt], [O], [F]), select from the Font Style text/list box, and select OK or press [↵Enter].
- Click on the Bold, Italic, or Underline button on the Formatting toolbar.
- Press [Ctrl]+[B] (bold), [Ctrl]+[I] (italics), or [Ctrl]+[U] (underline). To return to regular text, press [Ctrl]+[Scroll Lock].

Adjusting Character Spacing

Select characters to be adjusted, select Format Font ([Alt], [O], [F]), click on the Character Spacing tab, select from the **S**pacing drop-down list box, and adjust the amount in the **B**y box. Select OK or press [↵Enter].

Hiding Text

Select the text to be hidden, and then select Format Font ([Alt], [O], [F]). Click on the Font tab. Place a check mark in the **H**idden check box, and either select OK or press [↵Enter].

Formatting Characters

Up to this point, you have learned about Word for Windows formats which define large parts of a document. You've created formats for the entire document and for individual paragraphs. There is a smaller text element that you can format, the character.

A character is the smallest unit of text in Word. A character is any letter, number, or special symbol. Special symbols are characters like hyphens, punctuation marks, or those symbols that are displayed on the number keys of your keyboard.

Formatting characters lets you emphasize text in a document. For example, a newspaper uses character formatting to emphasize the headlines for its articles. Newspaper headlines are displayed in larger, bolder letters than the text in the articles.

There are two main types of character formatting. The first type of formatting has to do with the design of the characters, or font. Characters that have the same font share similarities in their design. For example, if the characters h, k, d, and l are in the same font, the straight vertical line that is part of these letters should look the same and have the same point size (the vertical size of a character measured from top to bottom). You can differentiate between headlines and normal text by different fonts and point sizes.

The second type of character formatting concerns the appearance of a character. Keeping the same font and point size, you can change the appearance of a character to give it greater emphasis. You can underline it, slant it, make its lines thicker, move it above or below other characters, or even change its color.

Word for Windows provides three ways of formatting characters. You can use the Formatting toolbar, the Format Font command, or keyboard shortcuts.

You can either format existing characters or set new formats for characters you are about to type. To format existing characters, select the text to be changed and then use the Formatting toolbar or the Format Font command. When you apply a different character format for new text, the new format starts at the insertion point and doesn't change until you change to another character format. Unless you change the character format, text that you type has the same format as the text before it. Word starts out with normal, unemphasized text as the default.

You can also format documents, including paragraphs and characters, by using the AutoFormat feature, which is explained in Chapter 12.

When you use the Format Font command, Word displays the Font dialog box. All its options are explained in this chapter.

Emphasizing Characters with the Formatting Toolbar

The easiest way to format characters is to use the Formatting toolbar, shown in Figure 7.1. The Formatting toolbar not only enables you to manipulate characters but also shows you how the characters are formatted. The second drop-down list box from the left on the Formatting toolbar shows you the current font. Moving to the right, the next box shows the point size of the current text. The next three buttons allow you to set bold, italic, and underlined text, respectively. You can press any combination of these buttons to enhance text.

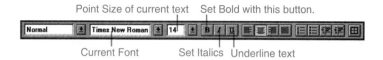

Point Size of current text   Set Bold with this button.

Current Font   Set Italics   Underline text

Figure 7.1
The Formatting toolbar. When a button is selected on the Formatting toolbar, it looks as though it has been pressed.

Use the following Quick Steps to enhance text using the Formatting toolbar.

Emphasizing Characters Using the Formatting toolbar

QUICK STEPS

1. To use the Formatting toolbar, it must be displayed. If the Formatting toolbar is not displayed on-screen, select the View menu and the Toolbars commands (Alt, V, T).

   Word opens the Toolbars dialog box.

2. Place a check mark in the Formatting check box, and click on OK or press Enter.

   Word returns to the current document and displays the Formatting toolbar.

3. To enhance text already in your document, select it. Then select one or more buttons on the Formatting toolbar.

   When a button is selected, it appears to be pressed. Word also changes the appearance of the selected text (Figure 7.2).

4. To enhance text that you have not yet typed, move the insertion point to the place at which you want to start typing. Then select a button on the Formatting toolbar.

   Word changes the appearance of the Formatting toolbar to reflect the format at the insertion point.

continues

continued

5. To turn off or undo a character enhancement, click on the button or buttons that control that enhancement.

The buttons that you click on no longer appear to be pressed. If text is selected, it changes to the new format. Any future text assumes the new format.

Figure 7.2

A document showing text formatted for boldface and italics.

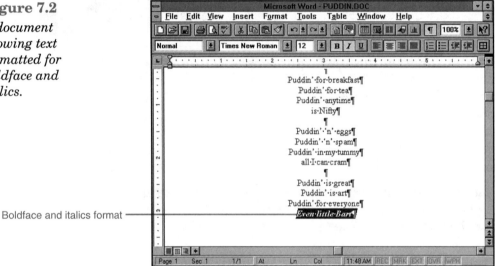

Boldface and italics format

Using the Format Painter

 Click on the Format Painter button to copy format of the selected text to other text.

Use the Format Painter button to quickly copy formats from selected text to other text in a document. Simply select text with the desired format, double-click on the Format Painter button on the Standard toolbar, and "brush" over text to be changed.

Emphasizing Characters with the Format Font Command

Although using the Formatting toolbar is the easiest way to change character formats, it doesn't cover all formatting options. For example, if you have a color monitor, you can display text in different colors, or if you have installed and configured a color printer or plotter, you can print files in color. To use the **Fo**rmat **F**ont command to apply additional character formatting, follow these Quick Steps.

Emphasizing Characters Using the Format Font Command

1. Select existing text to be formatted or move the insertion point to the location at which you want to type formatted text.

   Word highlights the selected text or displays the insertion point in its new location.

2. From the **Fo**rmat menu, select the **F**ont command (⌨Alt⌨, ⌨O⌨, ⌨F⌨).

   Word displays the Font dialog box (Figure 7.3).

3. Select one or more choices from the **F**ont **S**tyle text/list box (see Table 7.1 for a list of styles along with their shortcut keys).

   In the Preview box, Word displays the format that you selected.

4. If you have a color monitor, printer, or plotter, select **C**olor and select a color from the list of colors.

   In the Preview box, Word displays the color that you selected.

5. To change additional character formats, repeat steps 2 and 3.

   Word changes the Preview text accordingly.

continues

continued

6. When you have completed your selections, select OK or press ⏎Enter.

Word returns to your document and either emphasizes the text that you selected or will emphasize the text that you enter at the insertion point. Note that the appearance of the enhancement buttons on the Formatting toolbar also change, depending on your selections.

TIP: If you move the mouse pointer anywhere on the Formatting toolbar buttons or boxes and double-click, Word displays the toolbar in the work area. You can change its size by dragging its border. To return the toolbar to its original location, double-click on it.

Table 7.1 describes each of the formatting options in the **Font** Style box of the **Font** dialog box, and names shortcut keys for these formats.

Table 7.1
*Font Dialog Box
Formats*

Style	Shortcut Key	Description
Bold	Ctrl+B	Applies boldface to selected text
Italic	Ctrl+I	Applies italics to selected text
Hidden	None	Hides selected text
Small Caps	None	Changes selected text to small capitals
Underline	None	N/A
Single	Ctrl+U	Underlines all selected text, including spaces between words
Words Only	None	Underlines all selected text, excluding spaces between words

Style	Shortcut Key	Description
Double	None	Applies double underline
Superscript	Ctrl+	Moves selected text
	⇧Shift+=	Higher relative to other text on the line
Subscript	Ctrl+=	Moves selected text lower relative to other text on the line
Regular	Ctrl+Scroll Lock	Removes character
		Formatting from the selected text

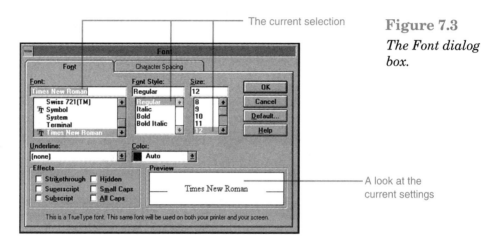

Figure 7.3

The Font dialog box.

It's easy to add an initial dropped cap to the beginning of a paragraph. Highlight the first character in a paragraph, and select Format Drop Cap (Alt, O, D). In the Drop Cap dialog box, select the position of the drop cap, and either select OK or press ⏎Enter.

TIP: To change the case of selected text, select Format Change Case (Alt, O, E). In the Change Case dialog box, click on one of the radio buttons, and select OK or press Enter. You can also cycle through a list of cases from which to choose. Just press ⇧Shift + F3 until the selected text is formatted the way you want.

Using Superscripts and Subscripts

Up to this point, you have used character formatting to change the way characters look, but you have not changed their size or location. The superscript/subscript format in the Font dialog box is a way to change the location of characters above or below the normal line of text. Use this format primarily for mathematical formulas and other technical material. Suppose you typed the equation $Z=x^2+y^2$. In order to show that each number is an exponent, you need to raise it above the other characters in the formula. To format the number as a superscript, first select the number; then choose Format Font (Alt, O, F), and check either the Superscript check box or the Subscript check box. Use the following Quick Steps to apply superscript or subscript formats.

Using Superscript and Subscript Styles

1. Select the text to be formatted.

   Word highlights your selection.

2. Select the Format menu and the Font command (Alt, O, F).

   Word displays the Font dialog box.

3. To apply Superscript to the selected text, check the Superscript check box. Select OK or press ⏎Enter.

   Word closes the dialog box and applies the changes to the selected text (Figure 7.4).

4. To apply Subscript to the selected text, check the Subscript check box. Either select OK or press ⏎Enter.

   Word closes the dialog box and applies the changes to the selected text (Figure 7.4).

1) $x_2 + 4x + 12 = 8$ ————— Subscript

2) $x_0 x^2 - x_0 + 5x = 25$ ————— Superscript

where $x_0 = 5$

Figure 7.4
Text formatted with subscript and superscript styles.

To remove all character formatting (including any changes to the font and point size), select the text and press Ctrl + Scroll Lock . If you change your mind about removing character formatting, select Edit Undo (or press Ctrl + Z).

Adjusting Spacing Between Characters

You can adjust the space between characters to subtly change their appearance. Reducing or tightening the space between letters is called *kerning*. Kerning is particularly important for text with a large point size, such as headlines. An unkerned headline can look like a series of letters rather than words. When you tighten the space between letters, the letters become a related group—a word. If you select more than two characters at a time for kerning, it's difficult to fine-tune the separation between letters, but if all the letters need to be moved, you can get a start that way; then you can adjust pairs of letters. Often you'll find that some letters don't need to be moved at all. When you use the Format Font command for kerning, be aware that the spaces are compressed between selected characters and after the last character. For examples of kerned and unkerned text, see Figure 7.5.

Figure 7.5
These two headlines are examples of kerned and unkerned text. In all three words of the second headline, the space between characters has been tightened, and then pairs of letters were kerned where needed. The effect is subtle but effective.

Unkerned text ——— **Away from Home**

Kerned text ——— **Away from Home**

To adjust the spacing between characters, follow these Quick Steps.

Adjusting Character Spacing

1. Select characters to be kerned.

   Word highlights the selected letters.

2. Select the Format menu and the Font command ([Alt], [O], [F]).

   Word opens the Font dialog box.

3. Click on the Character Spacing tab, if needed.

   Word displays the Font dialog box for Character Spacing (see Figure 7.6)

4. Open the Spacing drop-down list box. The **By** box lets you adjust the amount by which you can expand (up to 14 points) or condense (down to .25 points) the text.

   As you adjust the spacing, Word changes the Preview text accordingly, as shown in Figure 7.7.

5. Select OK or press [↵Enter].

   Word returns to your document and adjusts the text that you selected.

Repeat these Quick Steps to adjust the rest of the headline.

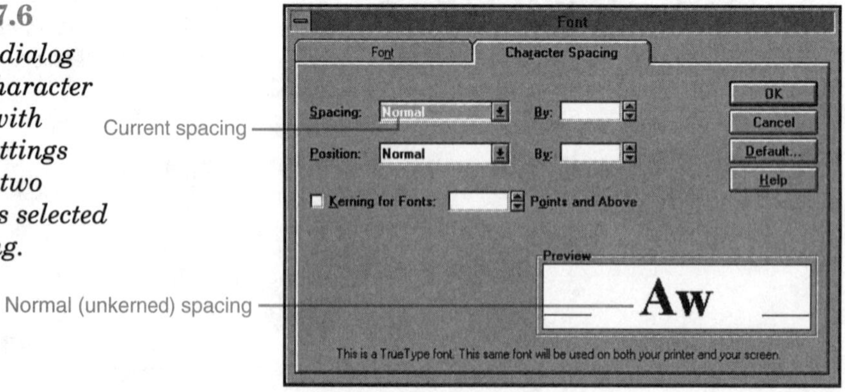

Figure 7.6

The Font dialog box for Character Spacing with default settings and with two characters selected for kerning.

Current spacing

Normal (unkerned) spacing

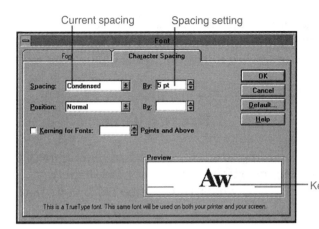

Current spacing   Spacing setting

Figure 7.7
As you adjust the spacing, Word changes the text in the Preview box accordingly.

Kerned text with condensed spacing

TIP: Use kerning to reformat a paragraph when the last line of the paragraph consists of only one word. Kern the letters and words in the preceding line of the paragraph so that Word moves the single word up from the last line.

As you get to be an expert in document creation, you'll start to notice rivers, which are spaces between words occurring at approximately the same point on successive lines. These spaces are called *rivers* because they flow vertically down the page. Often, rivers are caused by justification and the extra spaces placed between words. Use kerning to adjust spaces between words so that rivers are eliminated.

Hiding Text

Up to this point, all character formatting described in this chapter has changed the appearance or position of characters in a document in order to emphasize the selected characters. Using the **Format Font** command, you can also hide text. Use hidden text to make notes to yourself or to others throughout a document. At a later time, you can print these hidden notes for your records. Before hiding text or typing hidden text, be sure to turn on the

Show/Hide button on the Formatting toolbar so that you can see all the characters and symbols in your document, whether they are hidden or not. To hide text, use the following Quick Steps.

QUICK STEPS

Hiding Text

1. Select existing text, or move the insertion point to the place at which you want to type hidden text.

   Word highlights the selected text or displays the insertion point in its new location.

2. Select the Format menu and the Font command (Alt), O, F).

   Word displays the Font dialog box.

3. If needed, click on the Font tab.

   Word displays the Font dialog box for Font.

4. In the Effects box, place a check mark next to Hidden. Then select OK or press Enter.

   Word returns to the current document and either hides the selected text or hides the text that you type at the insertion point. As you type hidden text, Word underlines it (Figure 7.8).

5. To switch back to normal text, repeat steps 1, 2, and 3, clear the Hidden check box, and then select OK or press Enter.

   Word returns to the current document and either reveals the selected text or returns to normal text at the insertion point.

TIP: To hide text, select it, and press Ctrl+⇧Shift+H.

Displaying or Concealing Hidden Text

When you use the Show/Hide button on the Formatting toolbar, all hidden text and nonprinting symbols are affected. As a way to selectively display or conceal hidden text, tabs, spaces, paragraph marks, and optional hyphens, use the **T**ools **O**ptions command. Use the following Quick Steps to display or conceal hidden text using **T**ools **O**ptions.

Hidden text

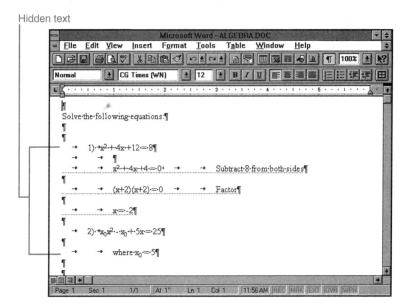

Figure 7.8
A document with hidden text. Notice that the hidden text is underlined with a dotted line.

Displaying or Concealing Hidden Text

1. Select the Tools menu and the Options command (Alt, T, O).

   Word displays the Options dialog box.

2. Click on the View tab.

   Word displays the Options dialog box for the View category (Figure 7.9).

continues

continued

3. To display hidden text, under Nonprinting Characters, place a check in the Hidden Text check box and select OK or press ⏎Enter.

Word returns to the current document and displays all hidden text.

4. To conceal hidden text, remove the check from the **Hid**den check box and select OK or press ⏎Enter.

Word returns to the current document and conceals all hidden text.

Figure 7.9

The Options dialog box for the View category.

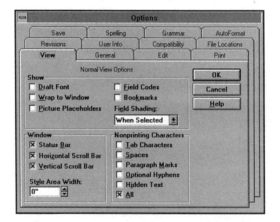

Printing Hidden Text

Your document can serve two purposes: to inform its ultimate audience and to provide a printed record of the changes it has gone through. Suppose that a document has gone through extensive review by your co-workers, and each reviewer has typed comments that have resulted in a series of changes to the document. The recipients of the document don't need to see the notes, so you have hidden them and printed the final document for distribution. To keep a file copy of the finished document including your co-workers' comments, reveal the hidden text and then print. Note that when you print hidden text, the page breaks and page numbering are affected. The following Quick Steps describe how to print a document with and without its hidden text.

Printing a Document with and without Hidden Text

1. Select the Tools menu and the Options command (Alt, T, O).

   Word displays the last Options dialog box you used in this session of Word.

2. Click on the Print tab.

   Word displays the Options dialog box for the Print category (Figure 7.10). You'll learn all about this dialog box in Chapter 9.

3. To print hidden text, place a check in the Hidden Text check box in the Include with Document group. To exclude hidden text from being printed, remove the check from the Hidden Text check box.

   Word places a dotted line around the Hidden Text box, indicating that this option is your last selection.

4. Select OK or press ↵Enter.

   Word returns to the current document.

5. Select the File menu and the Print command (Alt, F, P).

   Word opens the Print dialog box (Figure 7.11).

6. Select OK or press ↵Enter.

   Word prints your document with or without hidden text, as you choose. You'll learn more about printing options in Chapter 9.

Figure 7.10

The Options dialog box for the Print category.

Check to print hidden text.

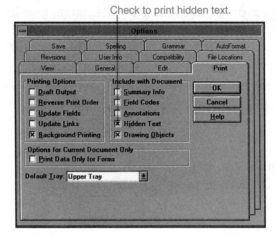

TIP: You can use Print Preview to check whether you have chosen to print hidden text. Remember that whether you are displaying or concealing hidden text on-screen, Word can print or not print hidden text.

When you want to print your document without hidden text affecting page numbering, use the Tools Options dialog boxes to clear the Hidden Text check boxes in both the Print category and the View category. Also, be sure that you have not accidentally formatted page or section breaks as hidden text, which negatively affects pagination.

Figure 7.11

The Print dialog box.

Teachers and those involved in employee training can use hidden text to advantage when constructing tests and quizzes. The test questions can be in regular text and the answers in hidden text. On the student version, the hidden text is not printed.

Using Fonts

Earlier in this chapter, you learned about enhancing words in a document. The rest of the chapter describes setting the overall tone of a document with another type of character formatting.

Font choice can add character to a document. By selecting fonts carefully, you can help identify your document as serious or comic, technical or informal.

Introducing Fonts and Points

Fonts are families of typeface designs. For example, two pages of text from different documents (for example, a typewritten letter versus a page from a book) will look different because the sets of characters used for the text probably have different designs. This means each set of characters comes from a different font. For example, the most common typewriter font is Courier. However, typeset technical manuals quite often use a combination of Times Roman for the regular text and Helvetica for headlines, and many textbooks use Century Schoolbook.

Fonts can be either serif or sans serif. Serif fonts have decorative lines at the ends of letter strokes, and sans serif fonts are simple and undecorated. Font and typeface experts consider serif fonts easier to read, so most body text falls into the serif category.

You can also divide fonts into proportional and monospace or nonproportional fonts. Proportional fonts use different widths for each letter. For example, the space for the letter I is much narrower than the space used for W. Every character in a monospace (or nonproportional) font has the same width, which is very useful when you have to align text vertically or at specific column locations.

As you become more accustomed to using fonts in your documents, you'll find that the variety of fonts is almost endless. See Table 7.2 for a list of common fonts and descriptions of each.

Table 7.2
Commonly Used Fonts

Font	Usage	Description	
Times Roman	Standard body text	Serif	Proportional
Optima	Standard body text	Serif	Proportional
Courier	Letters	Serif	Monospace
Line Printer	Tables	Serif	Monospace
Century Schoolbook	Textbooks	Serif	Proportional
Bookman	Textbooks	Serif	Proportional
Avante Garde	Headlines	Serif	Proportional
Helvetica	Headlines	Sans serif	Proportional
Zapf Chancery	Invitations	Serif	Proportional
Palatino	Invitations	Serif	Proportional

Fonts can differ not only in style, but also in size. The size of a character is measured in points. The higher the point number, the larger the character. A point is 1/72 of an inch, so a 72-point character measures one inch from top to bottom. When you are planning a document and deciding upon font, point size, and the length of a line of text, a general rule is that a line should contain no more than 1 1/2 alphabets—about 40 characters. See Table 7.3 for the point sizes and formats of typical text elements.

Document Element	Point Size	Format
Body text	8–12	Normal
Subheadings	10–14	Bold or Bold Italic
Headings	14–28	Bold
Headers/Footers	8–12	Italic
Captions	8–12	Italic
Page numbers	10–14	Bold or Bold Italic

Table 7.3
Point Size and Format of Typical Text Elements

Changing Fonts and Point Sizes

When you start Word, a default font and point size are assigned to the new document. You may decide that the default font isn't appropriate for a particular document. For example, to subtly encourage people to read a report, select a font with round, easy-to-read characters. However, if you're trying to fool all of the people all of the time, select a font with condensed type and a tiny point size. You can change fonts and point sizes by using either the Format Font command or the Formatting toolbar.

Changing the Font and Point Size with the Format Font Command

The Format Font command is more versatile than the Formatting toolbar. Both allow you to change the font and point size, but the Format Font command provides formatting options not available with the Formatting toolbar. For example, you can only apply the strikethrough format with the Format Font command. Thus, if you wish to do more than define fonts and point sizes, the Format Font command is probably the better choice.

Selecting a Font and Point Size Using the Format Font Command

1. Select your entire document by pressing Ctrl + F5 (on the numeric keypad).

Word highlights the document.

2. From the Format menu, select the Font command (Alt, O, F).

Word displays the Font dialog box.

3. If you don't know the name of the font you want to select, scroll through the list in the Font list box.

Word displays a list of fonts associated with Windows and the active printer and displays the highlighted font in the Preview box (Figure 7.12). The symbols next to some fonts represent either a Windows TrueType font or a printer font (a font that is associated with your printer).

4. Either select a font name or type one in the Font text box.

Word displays sample text from the font in the Preview box.

5. If you happen to know the point sizes available for the selected font, type the one you want in the Size text/list box. Otherwise, select the list arrow next to the Size text/list box.

Word displays a list of point sizes. If this is a scalable font (such as a TrueType font), you'll see a long list of numbers that increase by one. (A *scalable* font is a mathematically defined font that can be expanded or contracted to achieve a wide range of sizes.)

6. Select a point size.	In the Preview box, Word displays a sample of the font in the selected point size.
7. Select **OK** or press ⏎Enter.	Word returns to the current document and applies the new font to the selected text.

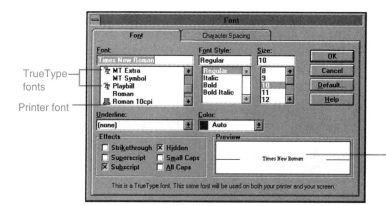

TrueType fonts

Printer font

Figure 7.12
The Font dialog box showing the Font list.

The current font, style, and point size

TIP: To get information about the formatting for both paragraphs and characters, click on the Help button on the Standard toolbar. Then move the help icon to the area of your document you want to check. Click and Word displays a box of information. Click again to close the box.

Changing the Font and Point Size with the Formatting Toolbar

If all you want to do is change font and/or point size, use the Formatting toolbar (shown earlier in Figure 7.1). In the Font drop-down list box, either type the name of a font that has been installed on your computer system or printer or open the list of fonts and click on your choice. At this point, Word changes the name in the Font drop-down list box and closes the list. To select a point size, use the same procedures. Type a number in the Points drop-down list box or click on the list arrow to its right and select a point size from the list. Word changes the number in the Points box and closes the list. Then when you start entering new text, Word uses the newly defined font and point size. To specify a font and point size for existing text, select the text to be changed and edit the values on the Formatting toolbar.

TIP: Press [Ctrl]+ [] to increase the point size of selected text by one point. Press [Ctrl]+ [] to decrease the point size of selected text by one point.

More About Fonts and Points

Be aware of the fact that Word uses two basic sets of fonts— TrueType fonts (which are Windows screen and printer fonts) and printer fonts, which come from the active printer attached to your computer system. In addition, there are a few more fonts that Windows uses for dialog boxes and messages. If you select a printer font that does not have a TrueType font counterpart, Word tries to substitute the most closely related TrueType font. In this way, the printed page will not differ too much from the page on-screen.

For a beginner, an easy solution to the font selection dilemma is to use the same font throughout a document. For example, select the easy-to-read Times Roman 10-point size because it is a good font for body text. Then use 14-point bold Times Roman for headers. Select 12-point bold italic Times Roman for page numbers and 10-point italic Times Roman for captions.

When you use two fonts in a single document, make sure that they are contrasting and distinct (for example, sans serif vs. serif) and serve two separate purposes (for example, headlines vs. body text). Fonts that come from the same family but are slightly different tend to be visually distracting.

Don't use more than two fonts per page! With more than two fonts, your document will start to look like a ransom note.

If you are working with technical documents, make sure that your font clearly shows the difference between the zero (0) and the letter O; the uppercase letter Z and the number 2; and the lowercase letter l, the uppercase letter I, and the number 1.

If you use a copier to duplicate your documents, see how the font that you have chosen copies. Since copied text tends to be lighter than the original, is the text still easy to read? If not, select a font with heavier lines.

Consider your audience. For example, if your readers are older people, think about increasing the point size. Certain fonts look smaller than others, even if they are the same point size. Select fonts for your readers' comfort.

If the text in the body of the document is 10-point type, subtitles should be 10 to 12 points, and the main title 14 points. As a general guideline, increase the point size two to four points as the text element changes. Table 7.3 gives general guidelines.

Most important, let your eye and good sense lead the way!

FYI
IDEAS

You can easily create a letterhead for yourself. Type your company name and address information at the top of a document. Select your company name, apply boldface, and select a headline font and point size. You can even go through the steps to kern the text; however, expand the spacing rather than reducing it. Then select the address information, apply boldface. Once you have formatted all the text the way you want it, save it as an AutoText entry. Then every time you start a letter, just add the AutoText entry and then start typing the body of the letter.

Finding Paragraph Formats

Select one or more paragraphs, select Edit Find (Alt), E, F or Ctrl+F). Select the Format button and select Paragraph. Fill in the formats and select OK or press Enter). Select Find Next.

Replacing Paragraph Formats

Select one or more paragraphs, select Edit Replace (Alt), E, E or Ctrl+H). Click in the Find What box, select the Format button, select Paragraph, select formats, and select OK or press Enter). Click in the Replace With box, select the Format button, select Paragraph, select formats, and select OK or press Enter). Click on the Find Next button, the Replace button, or Replace All button.

Finding Character Formats

Select one or more paragraphs, select Edit Find (Alt), E, E or Ctrl+F). Select the Format button and select Font. Fill in the formats and select OK or press Enter). Select Find Next.

Replacing Character Formats

Select one or more paragraphs, select Edit Replace (Alt), E+E or Ctrl+H). Click in the Find What box, select the Format button, select Font, select formats, and select OK or press Enter). Click in the Replace With box, select the Format button, select Font, select formats, and select OK or press Enter). Click on the Find Next button, the Replace button, or Replace All button.

Creating a Bulleted or Numbered List

Select one or more paragraphs and click on the Bulleted List or Numbered List button on the Formatting toolbar.

Advanced Formatting

In the last few chapters, you learned the basics of formatting documents, sections, paragraphs, and characters with Word for Windows. This chapter completes the job with a variety of advanced formatting concepts.

You'll see that you can use the **Edit F**ind and Edit R**e**place commands to find and replace more than text. Word also enables you to search for and replace paragraph and character formatting, nonprinting symbols, special symbols (covered later in this chapter), fonts, and point sizes.

Word enables you to create numbered or bulleted lists automatically. You can use the bullets that Word provides, or you can easily define a custom bullet.

You'll learn the ways to add special symbols (such as copyright and trademark symbols) to a document: via the **I**nsert **S**ymbol command or by inserting a symbol directly.

Finally, you'll see how to create documents with multiple columns and how to manipulate those columns.

Finding and Replacing Formats and Symbols

As you have learned, a document can go through many changes—in content and in appearance. You have seen how to select and manipulate text in order to edit the content of a document. Then, through formatting, you created a specific look for a specific document. In this section, you'll learn how to find a particular format and replace it with a new format.

Suppose a company has hired a graphics designer to modernize its logo, stationery, and forms. Formats of all documents will change from indented paragraphs to block format, and all italicized text will be converted to boldface. If you're responsible for converting each document to the new format, you can start at the top of a document and manually change every occurrence, or you can use Word's **E**dit **F**ind and **E**dit **R**eplace commands to quickly make every change.

Most times, you'll search for formats, fonts, or symbols in order to replace them throughout a document, so we'll emphasize the **E**dit **R**eplace command in the next sections. However, there are times when you'll want to search without replacing. For example, what if you've taken a lunch break and upon reopening a document, you can't remember the last page or section in which you worked? You can look for the first occurrence of the old format, and then start replacing after that point.

Finding and Replacing Formats

In Chapter 3, you searched for and replaced text, and in the last two chapters, you learned how to format paragraphs and characters. You can combine these two pieces of knowledge to search for paragraph and character formats and, if you want, to replace them with other formats. As you did in Chapter 3, you'll fill in either the Find dialog box (which is shown in Figure 8.1) or the Replace dialog box (shown in Figure 8.2) to determine the combination of the text and formats to be found or replaced. In this way, you can quickly change the appearance of a document.

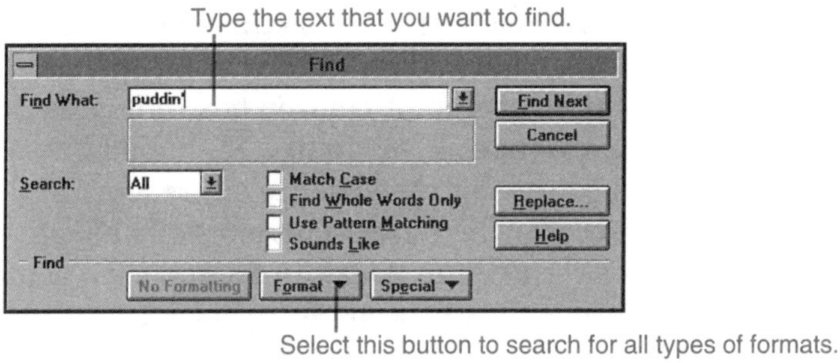

Type the text that you want to find.

Figure 8.1
The Find dialog box, which is used for finding text, formats, fonts, and symbols.

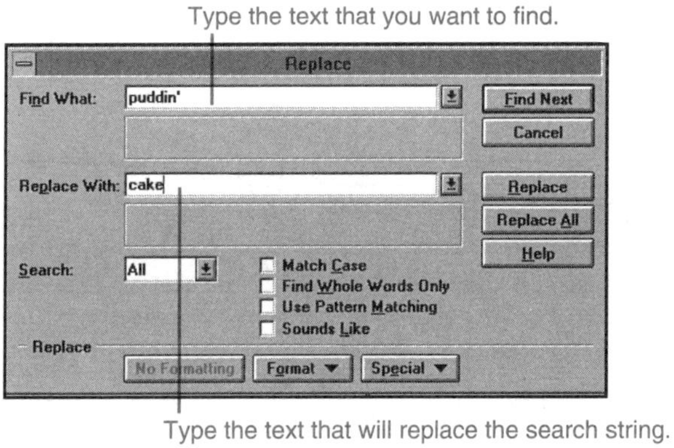

Select this button to search for all types of formats.

Type the text that you want to find.

Figure 8.2
The Replace dialog box, which enables you to find and replace text and formats.

Type the text that will replace the search string.

You can specify a combination of paragraph and character formats to find and/or replace by selecting the **Fo**rmat button at the bottom of the Find dialog box. This reveals a list (shown in Figure 8.3) from which you can open the Find Font dialog box (shown in Figure 8.4), the Find Paragraph dialog box (see Figure 8.5), the Find Language dialog box (Figure 8.6), or the Find Style dialog box (Figure 8.7) to specify search and/or replacement criteria.

When you first see any of these dialog boxes, no values are specified: The boxes next to the options are blank and the check boxes are shaded. Fill in these dialog boxes in the same way you defined the original formats. To put a value in an option box, type the value, display a list, or cycle through the values. When filling in a check box, be aware that it has three states: checked, clear, or shaded. A checked box indicates that Word includes the presence of this value in its search. A cleared box indicates that Word will search for an absence of this value. A shaded box indicates that Word will not search for the absence or presence of this value. For example, to look for the next occurrence of a paragraph preceded by a page break, the **P**age Break Before check box must contain a check; to look for the next occurrence of a paragraph not preceded by a page break, the check box must be clear. If you don't want to include this paragraph format option in your search, make sure that the box is shaded. Once you have selected the formats for which to search, select OK or press Enter. Word redisplays the Find dialog box.

Figure 8.3

The list of format choices in the Find dialog box.

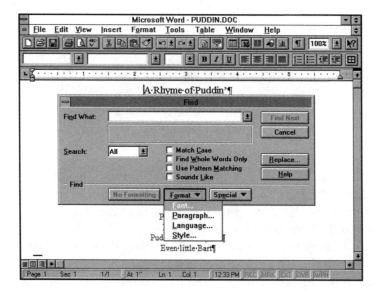

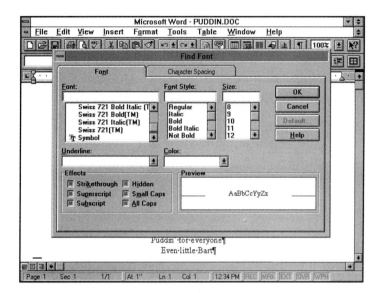

Figure 8.4
The Find Font dialog box.

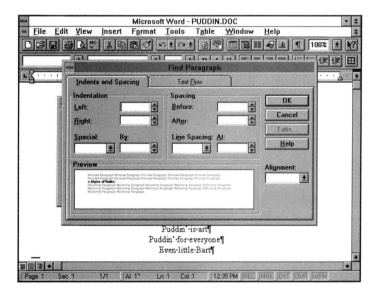

Figure 8.5
The Find Paragraph dialog box.

Figure 8.6
*The Find
Language
dialog box.*

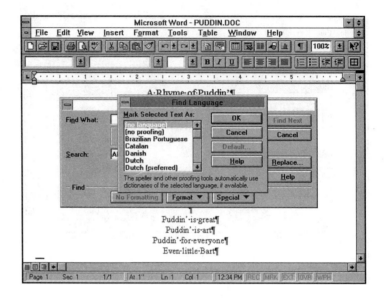

Figure 8.7
*The Find Style
dialog box.*

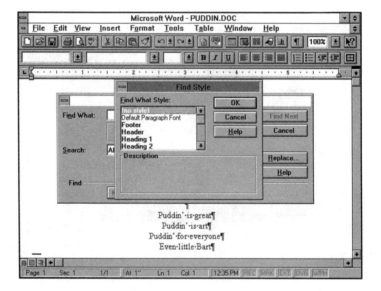

Finding and Replacing Paragraph Formats

In our example, a company is in the process of changing the appearance of all its documents. Because new letterhead has replaced the old, some paragraph formats will also change. You also can use this opportunity to search for and replace text, as you learned in Chapter 3. To search for text only, fill in the **Find** What box. To search for formatting only, make sure that the **Find** What box is empty. Note that if you search for both paragraph formats and text, Word finds only the occurrences of formats and text that match the search criteria.

Use the following Quick Steps to search for paragraph formats and, optionally, text.

Finding Paragraph Formats

1. Select part of the document to be searched; otherwise, Word searches the entire document.

   If you have selected text, Word highlights it.

2. From the **E**dit menu, select Find (Alt , E , F or Ctrl + F).

   Word opens the Find dialog box.

3. To search for text, type it in the Find What box.

   To make room for text, Word scrolls the text out of the box to the left as you type.

4. To match on a whole-word basis or by case, place a check in the Find Whole Words Only or Match Case check box.

   Word surrounds your last choice with a dotted-line choice with a dotted-line border.

5. Select the Format button at the bottom of the dialog box.

   Word displays a list from which you can choose.

6. Select Paragraph from the list.

   Word opens the Find Paragraph dialog box.

continues

---

continued

7. Fill in the combination of formats for which you want to search (Figure 8.8).

Word changes the illustration in the Preview box.

8. Select OK or press ↵Enter.

Word returns to the Find dialog box. Notice that the formats you selected are displayed below the **Find** What box (Figure 8.9).

9. Select Find Next.

In your document, Word finds the first occurrence after the insertion point of the formats and text for which you are looking. Word highlights the text. If the search is unsuccessful, Word displays a message.

10. To continue the search, repeat step 8. Otherwise, select Cancel.

Word returns to the current document.

Figure 8.8
The Find Paragraph dialog box with search format specifications.

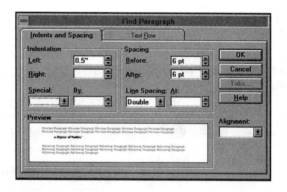

The searched for formats

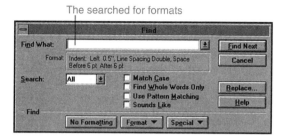

Figure 8.9
The Find dialog box with the paragraph search format specifications.

You'll probably use **E**dit **R**eplace more often than you'll use **E**dit **F**ind. For example, to modernize a document by changing from first-line paragraph indentation to block indentation, you would find all occurrences of first-line indentation and replace each with block indentation.

The main difference between finding formats and both finding and replacing them is that in the latter procedure you'll have to define the formats for which you are looking and the formats that will replace them. For this reason, the location of the insertion point in the Replace dialog box is very important. If the insertion point is in the **Fi**nd What box (whether or not you type text to be found), Word displays the Find Paragraph dialog box when you select Paragraph from the list; if the insertion point is in the **R**eplace With box (whether or not you type text to replace the search string), Word displays the Replace Paragraph dialog box when you select **P**aragraph.

To search for and replace only text, fill in the Find What and Replace With boxes. To search for and replace only formatting, make sure that both the **Fi**nd What and **R**eplace With boxes are empty. To replace paragraph formats, use the following Quick Steps.

NOTE: If you search for and replace both paragraph formats and text, Word finds only the occurrences of formats and text that match the search criteria.

Replacing Paragraph Formats

1. Select part of the document to be searched; otherwise, Word searches the entire document.

   If you have selected text, Word highlights it.

2. From the Edit menu, select the Replace command (Alt, E, E or Ctrl+H).

   Word displays the Replace dialog box.

3. To search for text, type it in the Find What box.

   In order to make room for extra text, Word scrolls the text out of the box to the left as you type.

4. To match on a whole-word basis or by case, place a check in the Find Whole Words Only and Match Case check boxes.

   Word surrounds your last choice with a border.

5. To search for paragraph formats, select the Format button, first making sure to move the cursor to the Find What box.

   Word displays a list from which you can choose.

6. Select Paragraph from the list.

   Word displays the Find Paragraph dialog box (Figure 8.8).

7. Fill in the combination of formats for which you want to search.

   Word changes the illustration in the Preview box.

8. Select OK or press
⏎Enter.

Word returns to the Replace dialog box. The formats that you selected are displayed below the **Find** What box.

9. To replace the text search string with a replace string, type it in the Replace With box.

In order to make room for text, Word scrolls the text out of the box to the left as you type.

10. At the bottom of the dialog box, click on the Format button.

Word opens a list from which you can choose.

11. Select Paragraph.

Word displays the Replace Paragraph dialog box, which looks exactly the same as the Find Paragraph dialog box.

12. Fill in the combination of formats with which you want to replace the search text and formats (Figure 8.10).

Word changes the example in the Preview box as you choose options.

13. Select OK or press
⏎Enter.

Word returns to the Replace dialog box. Notice that the formats you selected are displayed below the **Find** What box and the **Replace** With box (Figure 8.11).

14. Click on the Find Next button.

Word finds the first occurrence for which you are looking and highlights it. If the search is unsuccessful, Word displays a message.

continues

continued

15. To replace this occurrence of found text and/or format, click on **R**eplace.

Word replaces the text and/or format.

16. To replace all occurrences of found text and/or format, click on Replace **A**ll.

Word replaces the text and/or format.

17. To replace either the search format or the replace format, move the cursor to the Fi**n**d What or Replace With box and then click on the No Formatting button.

Word dims and clears the formats for which you were searching and with which you were replacing, and dims the No Formatting button. If you were not searching for text, Word also dims the Fi**n**d Next, **R**eplace, and Replace **A**ll buttons.

18. To stop searching and replacing, select Cancel.

Word returns to the current document.

Figure 8.10

The Replace Paragraph dialog box with the format replace specifications.

The replacement formats are to not keep lines together and not keep with next.

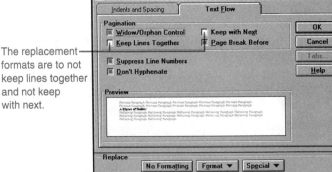

No text is being searched for.

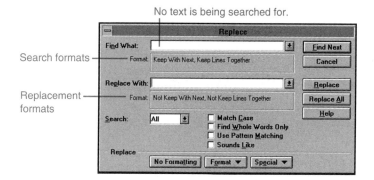

Search formats

Replacement formats

Figure 8.11
*The Replace dialog
box with both the
paragraph format
search and replace
specifications.*

Finding and Replacing Character Formats

Word provides the means to search for and optionally replace
character formats in conjunction with or separately from paragraph formatting. For example, as long as you are searching for
indented paragraphs, you can look for a character format (for
example, changing from italics to bold) to be replaced when you
convert to block paragraphs. In addition, since you are already
using **E**dit **F**ind, you can look for text as well.

The procedures for finding character formats are almost the
same as those used in finding paragraph formats. Rather than
selecting **P**aragraph from the **Fo**rmat list at the bottom of the
Find or Replace dialog boxes, you'll select Character. Just as the
Find and Replace Paragraph dialog boxes are almost identical to
the Paragraph dialog box, the Find and Replace Character dialog
boxes are about the same as the Character dialog box.

Use the following Quick Steps to search for character formats
and optionally text.

Finding Character Formats

1. Select part of the document to be searched; otherwise, Word searches the entire document.

   If you have selected text, Word highlights it.

2. From the **E**dit menu, select **F**ind (Alt, E, F).

   Word opens the Find dialog box.

3. To search for text, type it in the Find What box.

   In order to make room for text, Word scrolls the text out of the box to the left as you type.

4. To match on a whole-word basis or by case, place a check mark in the Find **W**hole Words Only or Match **C**ase check boxes.

   Word surrounds your last choice with a dotted-line border.

5. To search for character formats, click on the Format button.

   Word opens a list from which you can choose.

6. Select **F**ont from the list.

   Word displays the Find Font dialog box.

7. Fill in the combination of formats for which you want to search.

   Word changes the illustration in the Preview box.

8. Select OK or press ↵Enter.

   Word returns to the Find dialog box. Notice that the formats you selected are displayed below the Find What box (Figure 8.12).

9. Select **F**ind Next.

In your document, Word finds the first occurrence after the insertion point of the formats and text for which you are looking. Word highlights the text. If the search is unsuccessful, Word displays a message.

10. To continue the search, repeat step 9. Otherwise, select Cancel.

Word returns to the current document.

As you learned when replacing paragraph formats, you must define the character formats for which you are looking and the character formats that will replace them. To replace character formats, use the following Quick Steps.

TIP: The position of the insertion point controls whether the Find Character or Replace Character dialog box is displayed.

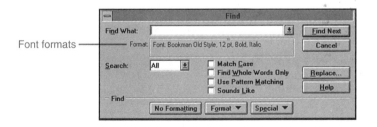

Font formats

Figure 8.12

The Find dialog box with the formats you specified.

Replacing Character Formats

1. Select part of the document to be searched; otherwise, Word searches the entire document.

   If you have selected text, Word highlights it.

2. From the **E**dit menu, select the **R**eplace command (⌐Alt⌐, ⌐E⌐, ⌐E⌐ or ⌐Ctrl⌐+⌐H⌐).

   Word displays the Replace dialog box.

3. To search for text, enter it in the Find What box.

   In order to make room for text, Word scrolls the text out of the box to the left as you type.

4. To match on a whole-word basis or by case, place a check in the Find **W**hole Words Only or Match **C**ase check box.

   Word surrounds your last choice with a border.

5. To search for character formats, select Format.

   Word opens a list from which you can choose.

6. Select Font from the list.

   Word displays the Find Font dialog box.

7. Fill in the combination of formats for which you want to search.

   Word changes the illustration in the Preview box.

8. Select OK or press ⌐↵Enter⌐.

   Word returns to the Replace dialog box. The formats you selected are displayed below the Find What box.

9. To replace the text search string with a replace string, type it in the Replace With box.

   In order to make room for text, Word scrolls the text out of the box to the left as you type.

10. Select the Format button. Select Font.	Word opens a list. Word displays the Replace Font dialog box (Figure 8.13).
11. Fill in the combination of formats for which you want to search.	Word changes the example in the Preview box as you choose options.
12. Select OK or press ↵Enter.	Word returns to the Replace dialog box. Notice that the formats you selected are displayed below the Find What box and the Replace With box (Figure 8.14).
13. Select Find Next.	Word finds the first occurrence for which you are looking and highlights it. If the search is unsuccessful, Word displays a message.
14. To replace this occurrence of found text and/or format, select Replace.	Word replaces the text and/or format.
15. To replace all occurrences of found text and/or format, select Replace All.	Word replaces the text and/or format.
16. To replace either the search format or the replace format, move the cursor to the Find What or Replace With box and then click on the No Formatting button.	Word dims and clears the formats for which you were searching and with which you were replacing, and dims the No Formatting button. If you were not searching for text, Word also dims the Find Next, Replace, and Replace All buttons.
17. To stop searching and replacing, select Cancel.	Word returns to the current document.

Using Shortcut Keys to Find and Replace Formats

When you search for and replace paragraph and character formatting, you can also fill in the Find What and Replace With boxes in the Find and Replace dialog boxes with shortcut keys to represent fonts, point sizes, and other character formats. For example, press Ctrl + B to add Bold or No Bold or delete any bold choice from your search or replace string. For a complete list of formats and shortcut keys, see Table 8.1.

TIP: Word will search for and replace spaces, just as it does characters. For example, it is standard practice to insert one space between sentences. If you inadvertently inserted two spaces, you can have Word search for two spaces and replace them with one. In the Replace dialog box, just fill in the Find What text box by pressing the spacebar twice, and fill in the Replace With text box by pressing the Scroll Lock once. Remember, though, that if you select the Replace All button, Word will search for all instances of two spaces and replace them with one space, wherever the two spaces occur.

Figure 8.13

The Replace Font dialog box filled in with font format choices.

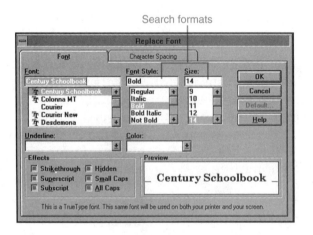

Search formats

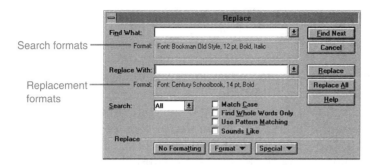

Search formats

Replacement formats

Figure 8.14
The Replace dialog box with all the formats that you selected.

Keys	Format
Ctrl+B	Bold
Ctrl+I	Italic
Ctrl+U	Single Underline
Ctrl+⇧Shift+=	Superscript
Ctrl+=	Subscript

Table 8.1
Shortcut find-and-replace keys.

NOTE: You can edit text while the Find dialog box or Replace dialog box is open. Just click on the text that you want to change and then click in the dialog box to resume your search or replace.

You can search for and replace formats to change the look of a document quickly. For example, if your current headings are too large and the wrong font, rather than edit them line by line, search for the current font and point size and then replace them with a new font and point size.

Finding and Replacing Symbols

Word also allows you to find and optionally replace symbols in the document. Once again, fill in the Find What and Replace With boxes in the Find and Replace dialog boxes, but this time insert a code for a special symbol. For example, to replace a trademark symbol with a copyright symbol, just search for the trademark symbol and replace it with the copyright symbol. For a complete list of key codes, refer to Table 8.2.

TIP: You can search for or replace special characters by clicking on the Special button and selecting from the list.

This Key Code	Represents
^_	An optional hyphen
^?	Text ending in a question mark
^^	A caret (^) mark
^[TILDE]	A nonbreaking hyphen
^0nnn	A character from the ANSI character set, where nnn is the code for the ANSI character
^1	A graphic
^2	Automatic footnote reference mark
^3	Footnote separator
^5	Annotation reference mark
^9	A tab symbol
^10	A linefeed symbol (a character that tells the printer to move to the next line) (_)
^11	A newline symbol, which is also known as a line break mark (°)
^12	A page or section break symbol
^13	A carriage return symbol, also called a paragraph mark (_)

This Key Code	Represents
^14	A column break symbol
^19	A field symbol
^21	An end of field symbol
^c	The contents of the Clipboard
^d	Manual page break or section break
^m	Search text to be used as part of the replace text
^n	Line break (see newline symbol)
^p	Paragraph mark (see carriage return symbol)
^s	Nonbreaking space
^t	Tab mark
^w	White space

Adding Special Characters

Sometimes you'll need to add a special character (like a copyright symbol or trademark) to your document. Special characters, which are not on your keyboard, and standard keyboard characters make up a character set. There are more characters in most character sets than there are keys on the keyboard, so Word provides two methods to add special characters: the **S**ymbol command on the **I**nsert menu and the direct insertion of an ANSI (American National Standards Institute) symbol via the numeric keypad.

When you use Insert Symbol to display the Symbol dialog box, shown in Figure 8.15, notice that one symbol is highlighted. If you select OK or press ↵Enter now, this symbol is inserted into your document. If you press and hold down the left mouse button or press an arrow key, that symbol is "magnified" (see Figure 8.16) so that you can see it in detail.

Figure 8.15

The Symbol dialog box for the Symbol font.

The current font

The current symbol

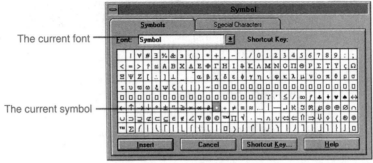

Figure 8.16

The Symbol dialog box with a selected and magnified character.

The selected symbol

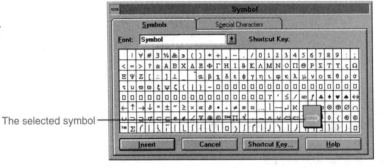

Most standard text fonts have their own unique set of ANSI symbols—some extensive and some not. When you find a font that has the symbol you need, use the following Quick Steps to embed the symbol. If you wish to insert a symbol from a particular font, make sure that the surrounding text is of the same font. If the symbol and the surrounding text don't match in fonts, and if you later change fonts, the symbol might change in appearance.

A few fonts, which may include some text characters, don't use the ANSI character set. A prime example of this type of font is Zapf Dingbats, which is often used to insert special symbols to emphasize parts of documents. Unfortunately, not all of Word's character formatting capabilities are available for enhancing these non-ANSI symbols. However, you can apply some formats, such as bold and italics. The following Quick Steps show you how to use the Symbol command.

Adding Special Characters to a Document

1. Move the insertion point to the place at which you want to embed the symbol. Then select Insert and Symbol (Alt , I , S).

   Word displays the Symbol dialog box.

2. In the Font drop-down list box, type the name of the font from which you want this symbol, or click on the list arrow (the underlined down arrow) to display a list of fonts from which you can select.

   Word changes the symbol display as you select the font.

3. Select the desired character. Either move the mouse pointer to your choice and click the left mouse button or press any combination of arrow keys.

   As you select a choice, Word displays your choice in a magnified view.

4. Select Insert or press ⏎Enter .

   Word returns to your document and inserts the symbol.

5. Select Close.

TIP: You can insert some commonly used special characters by pressing shortcut keys. Press Alt + Ctrl + C to insert a copyright symbol, press Alt + Ctrl + T to insert a trademark symbol, and press Alt + Ctrl + R to insert a registered trademark symbol.

Creating Bulleted and Numbered Lists

One of the most effective ways to emphasize text in a list is to precede each list item with a bullet or a number. Normally, you'd use numbered lists to show the steps in the order in which you perform them to accomplish a task. Bulleted lists emphasize points that are in no particular order.

Creating a Bulleted List

Word provides a shortcut way to create both bulleted and numbered lists using the Format menu and the Bullets and Numbering command. Then, when you produce a bulleted list, you can use either a standard bullet from the Bullets and Numbering dialog box or a special bullet by clicking on the Bullet button in the Modify Bulleted List dialog box. For example, if you publish a newsletter for contract bridge players, you could use hearts, spades, clubs, or diamonds for bullets.

Click on the Bulleted List button to create a bulleted list from one or more selected paragraphs. Each paragraph becomes an item in the list.

The following Quick Steps show you how to create bulleted lists.

Creating Bulleted Lists

1. Select the part of the document that you want to have bullets.

Word highlights the selected text.

2. From the Format menu, select the Bullets and Numbering command (Alt), (O), (N)).

Word opens the Bullets and Numbering dialog box (Figure 8.17).

3. If needed, click on the Bulleted tab.

Word changes to the Bullets and Numbering dialog box for **B**ulleted.

4. To select a standard bullet, choose one of the six samples. Move the mouse pointer to the appropriate bullet or press ← or →.

Word highlights the selected bullet.

5. To choose a special bullet, select the bullet that you wish to replace in the Bulleted group, and select Modify.

Word opens the Modify Bulleted List dialog box, as shown in Figure 8.18. Notice that the bullet that you selected in the previous dialog box is still selected in this dialog box.

6. Select a different bullet or for more choices, click on Bullet.

Word opens the Symbol dialog box.

7. Click on a symbol and select OK or press ←Enter.

Word returns to the Modify Bulleted List dialog box and replaces the selected bullet with your new choice.

continues

continued

8. To change the size of the bullet, either type a value from 1 to 1638 in the Point Size box or use the arrow button to display the list from which you can choose.

As you select a new point size, Word changes the illustration in the Bullet Character box.

9. To format each list item with hanging indents (a good option for bulleted lists), check the Hanging Indent box.

Word shows the format in the Preview box.

10. To align the bullet, select Left, Centered, or Right from the Alignment of List Text drop-down list box.

Word shows the format in the Preview box.

11. To adjust the amount of indentation of the text, select a value from 0 to 22 inches in the Distance from Indent to Text list box.

Word shows the format in the Preview box.

12. To adjust the distance from the bullet to the first line of text, select a value from 0 to 22 inches in the Distance from Bullet to Text list box.

Word shows the format in the Preview box.

13. Select OK or Cancel.

Word returns to the current document. If you have selected OK, Word applies the bullets. If you have selected Cancel, Word does not apply the bullets.

To jazz up a newsletter or any other document, you can substitute any special symbol found in the Symbol dialog box for a common bullet. For example, if you are rating computers, you can use the computer symbol from the top line of the TrueType Wingdings symbols set.

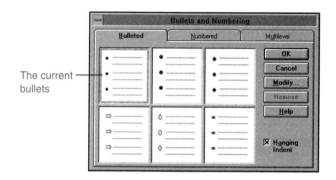

The current bullets

Figure 8.17
The Bullets and Numbering dialog box (Bulleted) from which you can define bulleted and numbered lists as well as special bullet characters.

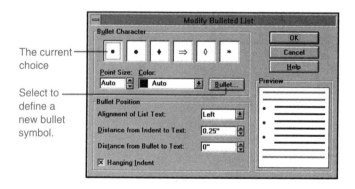

The current choice

Select to define a new bullet symbol.

Figure 8.18
The Modify Bulleted List dialog box from which you can define special bullet characters.

Creating a Numbered List

To create a numbered list, use Format Bullets and Numbering. This time, however, click on the Numbered tab. When Word displays the Bullets and Numbering dialog box (**N**umbered) (shown in Figure 8.19), you can select a numbering format. To start the numbering at a specific number, click on the Modify button and

Word displays the Modify Numbered List dialog box (shown in Figure 8.20). Enter a value in the Start At box (Word's default is 1). To precede each number with text, type characters in the Text Before box; to add a suffix to each number, type characters in the Text After text box. To format each list item with hanging indents (a good option for numbered lists), check the Hanging Indent box. Every time you change a format, Word shows the format in the Preview box. If you select OK, Word returns to the document and applies the numbers. If you select Remove, Word removes the numbers from the selected text.

To replace a bulleted list with a numbered list, or to replace a numbered list with a bulleted list, select the list to be reformatted, open the Bullets and Numbering dialog box, click on the tab of the type of list that you desire, and select OK or press ⏎Enter.

Figure 8.19

The Bullets and Numbering dialog box for a Numbered List.

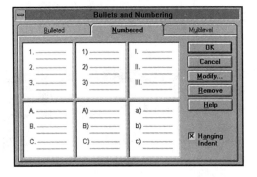

Click on the Numbered List button to create a numbered list from one or more selected paragraphs. Each paragraph becomes an item in the list.

NOTE: To create a multi-level list, which can include a combination of bulleted and numbered items, select Format Bullets and Numbering (Alt, O, N), click on the Multilevel tab, and select the desired list.

Using Multiple Columns in a Document

Not every document consists of text that extends between the margins. Just think of your favorite newspaper or the last brochure you received. To create a newsletter or any document with multiple columns of equal width, you'll have to know how to use columns. The columns that Word creates are called snaking columns, which means the text continues from the bottom of one column up to the top of the next.

If you are combining single-column format, which is the format you've used so far (one line of text stretching from left to right margin), and multiple columns, insert a section break between the two types of column format. Type and correct all your text before formatting columns so that you can see how the column width and spacing looks on the page without worrying about the content of each column. Then, with Format Columns, select the number of columns.

 Click on the Columns button to define the number of columns (from one to six).

While the Columns dialog box (shown in Figure 8.21) is displayed, fill in the Apply To box with information about how you wish to apply the format: to the whole document, to selected sections (if you have selected text), or from the insertion point through the rest of the document (if you have not selected text).

To start a new column at the insertion point, select Selected Text in the Apply To box. Then check the Start New Column box.

Use the following Quick Steps to add columns to a document and to change the column formats.

QUICK STEPS Adding Columns to a Document

1. Select a section of text to become columns or move the insertion point to the section in which you want to create columns.

Word highlights the selected text.

2. Select the Format menu and the Columns command (Alt, O, C).

Word displays the Columns dialog box (Figure 8.21).

3. Type a value in the Number of Columns box or use the arrow keys to cycle through the valid values (from 1 to 45).

Word changes the document in the Preview box and calculates the width of the columns and the space between the columns.

4. In the Width and Spacing group, type a width in the Width list box or use the arrow keys to cycle through the valid values (from 0 to 22 inches).

Word changes the document in the Preview box.

5. In the Width and Spacing group, type a value for the space between columns in the Spacing list box or use the arrow keys to cycle through the valid values (from 0 to 22 inches).

Word changes the document in the Preview box.

6. To insert a vertical line between the columns, check the Line Between box.

Word changes the document in the Preview box.

7. To keep the column widths equal, place a check mark in the Equal Column Width check box.

Word changes the document in the Preview box.

8. Select the part of the document to apply formatting in the Apply To box.

Depending on your selection, Word changes the document in the Preview box.

9. If you have completed filling in the box, select OK or press ⏎Enter.

Word returns to your document and creates the columns as you desire. Word also places section marks at the beginning and end of the selected text.

The default, one column

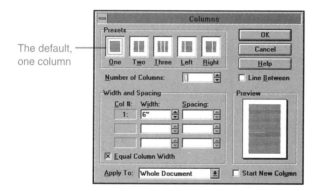

Figure 8.21
The Columns dialog box, which allows you to define the number of columns for this section of your document.

NOTE: In Normal view, you won't be able to see multiple columns; you'll have to use **P**age Layout view or Print Preview to see the result.

Changing Column Widths

While you are looking at your columns and text in **P**age Layout view, you might decide that the lines of text are not long enough (generally, there should be at least 20 characters on a line), and you may want to make the columns wider. The easiest way to change the column widths and the spacing between columns is to use the Ruler. Since Word formats columns in equal widths, changing one of the columns will change all of them. However, you can use the **Ta**ble menu to create columns of uneven widths. You'll learn about setting up tables in Chapter 10.

Changing Column Width

1. Select the **V**iew menu and **P**age Layout or click on the Page Layout button in the horizontal scroll bar to ensure that you are in **P**age Layout mode. If you don't see the Ruler, turn it on by selecting **V**iew and making sure that there is a check mark next to **R**uler ([Alt], [V], [R]).

   Word returns to the current document, displays columns (if you have defined columns) and displays the Ruler with the margins of all columns (Figure 8.22).

2. Select the text that will have new margin settings, move the mouse pointer to one of the column marks (in the gray areas on either end and in the middle of the Ruler) until it turns to a double-ended arrow. Then drag the mark to a new position on the Ruler.

   Word adjusts all column widths to match the new width.

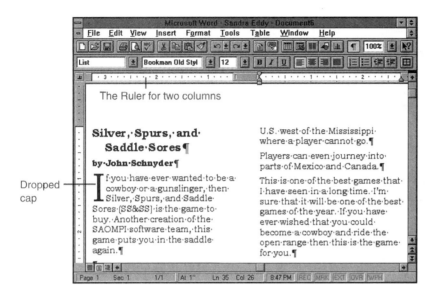

Figure 8.22
The Ruler with two columns defined.

Breaking Columns

If you want to end one column (perhaps because the subject matter changes) and start a new one, you can enter a column break. When the insertion point is at the location at which you want to end a column, select the Insert menu and the Break command (Alt), (I), (B)). In the Break dialog box, click on the Column Break button, and select OK or press (↵Enter).

Defining an Active Printer

Select **F**ile **P**rint (Alt, F, P, Ctrl+P, or Ctrl+⇧Shift+F12). Press **P**rinter, select the name of a printer, click on the Set as **D**efault Printer button. Select Close then OK or press ↵Enter twice.

Viewing a Document As It Will Print

Select **F**ile Print Preview (Alt, F, V).

Print Preview Toolbar Buttons

- Print prints a document using the current printing defaults.
- Magnifier magnifies or reduces the displayed document and turns on or off editing mode.
- One Page fits the page on the screen.
- Multiple Pages displays from one page to 18 pages.
- Zoom Control drop-down list box reveals a list of scaling options.
- View Ruler either displays or hides the Ruler.
- Shrink to Fit attempts to fit the document on just one page.
- Full Screen switches to a screen that includes only the toolbar.
- Close returns you to your document.
- Help displays information about the clicked-on item on the screen.

Printing a Document

Select **F**ile **P**rint (Alt, F, P, Ctrl+P, or Ctrl+⇧Shift+F12). Select options from the Print dialog box. Select OK or press ↵Enter.

Previewing and Printing Documents

In Chapter 2, you learned how to view your document using the **F**ile Print Pre**v**iew command. Once you were satisfied with the document, you could print it with the **F**ile **P**rint command. In this chapter, we will go into further detail about both of these commands as well as related options and features. You will also learn about changing the current active printer. This is done via printer drivers, which are files that contain information about the way a specific printer works with Word.

The Print Preview feature enables you not only to view a document's format but to change positions of margins, headers and footers. When you change the appearance of a document in this way, you can immediately see the results.

Word provides several print options that allow for customization of the print job. For example, you can print just the information associated with a document, a range of pages within a document, or multiple copies of a document (either collated or not), or you can print to a file. In addition, you can customize other printer and printing options via the **T**ools **O**ptions command and the Options dialog box for the Print category.

This chapter concludes with a short troubleshooting guide. If your printer does not print, refer to this checklist for solutions to most common printing problems.

Defining the Active Printer

When you installed Windows, you installed your printers (i.e., installed the necessary printer drivers, and Windows detected the printer ports to which the printers are attached). If you have more than one printer installed, you can check to see which printer is active by selecting the Print command from the File menu and then pressing the Printer button. The name of the Default Printer appears at the top of the Print Setup dialog box, and the other installed printers appear in the **P**rinters list.

You may want to make another printer the default printer. For example, you may change from a dot-matrix printer, on which you print draft copies, to a laser printer, on which you print the final draft of a document. Or, you may want to change from a laser printer to a dot-matrix printer so that you can print forms on the printer having the continuous-feed paper.

To select a printer, you don't have to have an active document. Select File Print (Alt, F, P, Ctrl+P, or Ctrl+⇧Shift+F12). When Word displays the Print dialog box (see Figure 9.1), press the Printer button to open the Print Setup dialog box (see Figure 9.2) in which all the printers—active and inactive—are listed. When you select a printer, Word (through Windows) knows its printer port, the place in the back of your computer where you plug in your printer. Ports are communications gateways through which information from one part of the computer system flows to another part. There are two types of printer ports: parallel (designated as LPT, which stands for line printer) and serial (called COM, which stands for communications). Most laser printers can use either type of port.

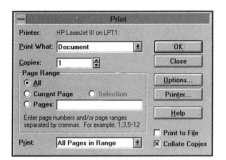

Figure 9.1

The Print dialog box from which you can print and define the default printer and set printing options.

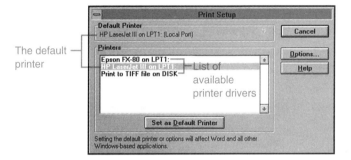

The default printer

Figure 9.2

The Print Setup dialog box with a list of available printers.

NOTE: You can find out the port to which your printer is attached through the Windows Control Panel. In Control Panel, double-click on the Printers icon. In the Printers dialog box, in which you also can specify the default printer, click on the Connect button. The Connect dialog box shows the name of the default printer and a list of ports. The port that is highlighted is the active port for the default printer.

Word also supports the port DISK, which enables document files (along with all formats) to be "printed" to the hard drive so that they can be printed later. Printing to files is covered later in this chapter.

Your computer can have more than one of each type of port. Multiple ports are referred to as LPT1, LPT2, COM1, COM2, and so on. Word allows you to connect multiple printers to multiple ports. You can also assign more than one printer to the same port; but only one of the printer drivers for that port can be active at a time.

To display or change options for the active printer, select the **O**ptions button in the Print Setup dialog box. The Setup dialog box (Figure 9.3) enables you to customize the printer driver to serve your needs better. See your printer manual for information about the options you can select for your printer.

Figure 9.3
The Setup dialog box for an HP LaserJet III.

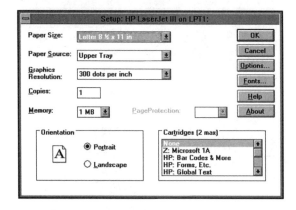

If you have more than one printer driver installed, you can select the printer that you want to use when you print. Use the following Quick Steps to select an active printer driver.

Selecting an Active Printer Driver

1. From the File menu, select Print (Alt, F, P or Ctrl+P).

Word displays the Print dialog box, from which you can print, define the default printer, and specify printing options.

2. Click on the Printer button.	Word displays the Print Setup dialog box, which lists all the available printer drivers. Note that the highlighted driver indicates the active (i.e., the default) printer whose name also appears in the Default Printer box at the top of the dialog box.
3. To replace the current active printer with another, select its name. If the list of printers is too long to be displayed in the box, click on the up and down arrows on the scroll bar to move through the list.	Word highlights your selection. Click on the Set as Default Printer button.
4. To display or change options for the selected printer, select Options.	Word displays an Options dialog box for the printer you have just selected.
5. Select OK or press ⏎Enter.	Word returns to the Print Setup dialog box.
6. Select Close.	Word returns to the document window.

To install configure, or remove a printer, or to specify a new active port, see your Windows documentation. All these actions take place from within the Windows Control Panel Printers application.

Previewing Your Document Before Printing

As you learned in Chapter 2, the **F**ile **P**rint Preview command lets you look at your document's format before you print. Word reduces the page so that it fits on your computer screen. You may not be able to recognize words and characters, but you can see the page's format—how paragraphs, titles, headers, footers, and other parts of the document are positioned on the page. Print Preview lets you adjust margins and the position of headers and footers, and format or edit text. You can also access some commands from within the **F**ile, **E**dit, **V**iew, **F**ormat, **T**ools, and **H**elp menus. For example, select File Page Setup to set specific margin dimensions, and you can select **E**dit **U**ndo (Ctrl+Z) to undo your changes to the margins.

To display the **P**rint Preview window, select File Print Preview (Alt, F, V). Depending on the way the last document was viewed in Print Preview, Word displays one or more pages of your document, as shown in Figure 9.4.

Figure 9.4

The Print Preview screen with toolbar and document displayed.

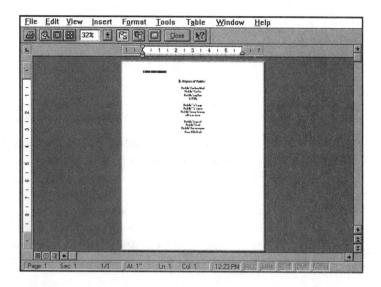

At the top of the Print Preview window is a toolbar you can use to work on the document (see Figure 9.5). Here is an overview of the buttons in the Print Preview toolbar:

Print—Click on this button to print a document from this window using the current printing defaults.

Magnifier—Click on this button to magnify or reduce the displayed document and to turn off the editing mode. Click again to turn off zooming and start editing the document. For example, you can click on this button to magnify the document, then click on it again to enhance selected text.

One Page—Click on this button to fit the page on the screen and to show the page in **P**age Layout view.

Multiple Pages—Click on this button to display from one page to 18 pages. Click on the button and then drag the resulting box to the number of pages you want displayed on the screen at one time. You can use this feature to show and edit facing pages (i.e., one even and one odd is the way they would look if bound in an open book).

Zoom Control drop-down list box—Click on the arrow to the right of the text box to reveal a list of percentages and values by which you can scale the page or pages on display.

View Ruler—Click on this button to either display or hide the Ruler.

Shrink to Fit—Click on this button to have Word attempt to fit your document on just one page.

Full Screen—Click on this button to switch from the standard screen with a title bar, menu bar, toolbar, and status bar to a screen that includes only the toolbar.

Close—The Close button returns you to your document.

Help—Click on this button and then click on a section of the screen to display information about the clicked-on item. For example, you can find out that the paragraph in which you clicked is aligned to the left margin, and that the font of the selected text is Arial, 14 point. Click the mouse button again to close the help box.

On the right side of the Print Preview window is a vertical scroll bar, which you can use to display the previous page or the next page in the document. You can also press PgUp or PgDn to move through the document.

Figure 9.5

The Print Preview toolbar buttons identified.

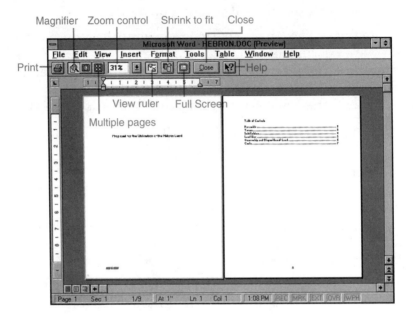

Zooming a Document

Zooming a page in Print Preview is a way to view the text for possible changes as well as to get ready to edit. There are two ways to magnify or reduce the size of the document in Print Preview: the Zoom Control drop-down list box and the Magnifier button.

Open the Zoom Control drop-down list box and select a percentage between 10 and 200 or the width of a page, the entire page, or two side-by-side pages.

Press the Magnifier button and then click the mouse pointer, which looks like a magnifying glass, to magnify or reduce the page. Press the Magnifier button again and switch to editing mode in which you can change text and adjust margins.

Table 9.1 presents Print Preview's zoom options and describes how to get them.

Select	Description
Page Width	Select this option from the Zoom Control drop-down list box to display the widest line within the dimensions of the document window.
Whole Page	Select this option from the Zoom Control drop-down list box to display the entire page within the document window.
200% - 10%	Select these options from the Zoom Control drop-down list box to display the document at twice its normal size to one-tenth its normal size.
Magnifier	Click on this button and click the magnifying glass pointer on the document to switch between viewing it at approximately 31% or 32% and 100%. Click on this button again to change to editing mode.

Table 9.1
Magnification Options

Editing in Print Preview

You can edit a document in Print Preview. If necessary, magnify the document by "pressing in" the Magnifier button. Then click on the Magnifier button again so that the mouse pointer turns into an I-beam when it's located in the text. At this point you can edit as you would in the document window.

Changing Margins in Print Preview

While you're in Print Preview, you can change the positions of margins by either selecting Format Paragraph or by dragging the margin markers on the Ruler. (You learned both techniques in Chapter 6.). Just make sure that the Magnifier button is not "pressed in". Using Print Preview to change formats is a good way to look at the formats of a document as you change them. When you change margins using the Print Preview Ruler, you'll see lines representing margins (see Figure 9.6).

Figure 9.6

The bottom margin being adjusted in Print Preview mode.

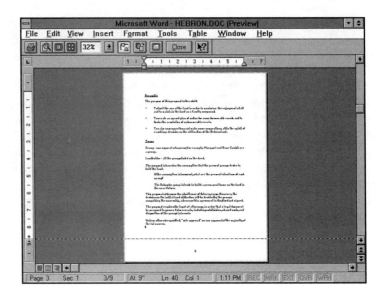

To adjust margins move the mouse pointer to either the horizontal or vertical Ruler and drag the margin to a new location. (You'll know when the mouse pointer is actually adjusting the margin by the dotted lines you see on the screen.)

FYI IDEAS

> One important reason to use Print Preview is to see if text on a page is balanced between the left and right margins as well as between the top and bottom margins. For example, if you are writing a relatively short letter you might find that the bottom margin is far larger than you wish. In Print Preview you can look at the letter and adjust the margins if necessary.

Printing Your Document

After using **F**ile Print Preview to view your document (and possibly to change its margins, header, and footers), you can print it either from within Print Preview (using the printing defaults) or using **F**ile **P**rint.

In Chapter 2, you learned about Word's printing options and how to print a document using the defaults. Now you'll review that procedure and learn several ways to customize printing. First, the File Print command (Alt , F , P , Ctrl + P ,) or Ctrl + ⇧Shift + F12). Word displays the Print dialog box, shown in Figure 9.1, from which you can change the options described in the next sections.

> **TIP:** If the **P**rint and the Print Pre**v**iew commands are dimmed, check to make sure that you have an active printer. You may have to use the Control Panel's Printers application to correct your problem.

At the top of the Print dialog box, Word displays the name of the default printer. You learned at the beginning of this chapter how to specify the default printer.

Printing Selected Parts of Your Document

In Chapter 2, you learned how to print an entire document using the defaults. In this section, you'll see how to print information that is attached to your document, selected pages or ranges of pages, or multiple copies of the document. This is useful when you are testing the format or layout of one or two pages in a long document. Why print the entire document when a range of pages will do?

Printing the Entire Document or Information About a Document

Using the **P**rint What box in the Print dialog box, you can choose to print either the entire document or information that is attached to the document. The default selection is Document, which prints the entire document. Select the down arrow to see the other choices: Summary Info, Annotations (comments about a document), Styles (paragraph formats covered in Chapter 12), AutoText

Entries (described in Chapter 3), and Key Assignments (macro names, the keys they're assigned to, and a description). For a description of annotations see the Microsoft Word for Windows User's Guide. For macros, see Chapter 13. Click on the list arrow to open the Print list box and make a selection. Then select OK or press ↵Enter.

Printing Multiple Copies of a Document

In the Copies group, click on the up or down arrow to cycle through the values (between 1 and 32767), or type a value in the text box. Then select OK or press ↵Enter.

When you print more than one copy of a document, Word's default is to print an entire document from the first page through the last and then start all over again with the next complete document. If you clear the Collate Copies check box, Word prints all the copies of the first page, then all the copies of the second page, and so on until it has printed all the copies of the last page.

Printing a Range of Pages

You can print the entire document, the current page, selected text, selected pages, or a range of pages. To print the entire document you don't have to make any changes, because All is the default.

To print just the page in which the insertion point is located, select Current Page. If you selected text to print, you can print only the selection by clicking the Selection radio button. If you haven't selected anything, the Selection button is dimmed. Select OK or press ↵Enter to print selected text.

By typing page numbers in the Pages text box, you can either print specific pages or ranges of pages. To print a specific page, type the page number. To print several specific pages, type the page numbers separated by commas. To print a range of pages, type the first number in the range, type a dash (–), and then type the last number in the range. You can fill in the text box with any combination of specific pages and ranges of pages.

Printing to a File

Check the **Print to File** box to print this document to file rather than to the printer. This means that you have saved the document with its print format and can print it at a later time. This topic is described in detail later in the chapter.

Additional Printing Options

Remember that Word provides an Options dialog box for the Print category, which is shown in Figure 9.7. From the **File** menu, select **Print** (Alt, F, P, Ctrl+P, or Ctrl+⇧Shift+F12). When Word displays the Print dialog box, select Options. You'll be more likely to set these just once or rarely. For example, in Chapter 5, you saw how Widow/Orphan Control works. You'll probably want this setting for every document, and once you've set it, you won't have to change it again.

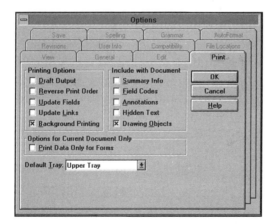

Figure 9.7
The Options dialog box for the Print category.

The options on the Options dialog box for the Print category are:

Draft Output—If you check this box, Word prints a document without graphics or text formatting, such as italics or boldface. Because Word doesn't need to spend processing time on text formatting, printing is usually faster, depending on the printer you are using. Experiment to see if this option is faster for your active printer.

Reverse Print Order—If you check this box, Word prints the document from the last page to the first. When you are using a printer that stacks pages face up after printing, select this option to save yourself the trouble of reordering your document.

Update Fields—If you check this box, Word updates field results in the document before printing occurs. For example, if you embed the system date in a header, a check means that Word always embeds the current system date.

Update **L**inks—If you check this box, Word updates any links to other documents and applications before printing occurs. For example, if you embed a graphic from Paintbrush or another Windows drawing or paint program using Object Linking and Embedding (OLE), a check here will cause Word always to embed the most recent version if you have updated the graphic in the source program. For more information, refer to the *Microsoft Word for Windows User's Guide* and your Windows documentation.

Background Printing—If you check this box, Word prints while other actions take place on your computer. As long as you keep Windows open, printing continues while you do another job.

Print Data Only for Forms—If you check this box, Word prints only the data associated with forms but not the forms. For more information, refer to the *Microsoft Word for Windows User's Guide*.

Summary Info prints a separate page of information about the document. Note that this information is the same as that resulting from the **F**ile Summary **I**nfo command and the Summary Info selection in the **P**rint What drop-down list box of the Print dialog box.

Field Codes prints the document and all its field codes (such as {DATE}) instead of printing field results (February 17, 1992). The **I**nsert **F**ield command in the Word Main Menu lists all Word field codes. For more information, refer to the *Microsoft Word for Windows User's Guide*.

Annotations prints annotations (comments or notes that are added to a document) after printing the document. For more information, refer to the *Microsoft Word for Windows User's Guide*.

Hidden Text includes the hidden text when the document prints.

If you have installed an envelope feeder for the active printer or want to feed paper one sheet at a time, select from the Default Tray drop-down list box. Otherwise, keep Upper Tray as the default. Chapter 14 describes printing envelopes.

Printing to a File

Most times, you'll print a document on a printer. However, there are times when you'll want to print a document, including all its print formats, to a file. For example, you might be working on several files that you want to print at the same time. If you are visiting a site that doesn't have the same make printer you use, or has no printer at all, save the print file and copy it onto a floppy disk. When you get back to your office, print on your own printer. Conversely, if you create a document to be printed at a remote site, save it to a floppy disk to print later.

Use the following Quick Steps to print the current document to file.

QUICK STEPS

Printing to a File

1. From the File menu, select the Print command (Alt, F, P, Ctrl+P, or Ctrl+⇧Shift+F12).

   Word displays the Print dialog box.

2. Select the print options you desire and place a check in the Print to File box.

   Word places a border around the last option that you select.

3. Select OK or press ⏎Enter.

   Word asks you for an output file name in the Print To File dialog box (Figure 9.8).

4. Type a unique file name that is one to eight characters in length.

   Word automatically adds the .PRN extension.

5. Select OK or press ⏎Enter.

   Word displays status information and then returns to the current document.

Now you have a file that you can print any time. To print this file, either exit Windows or double-click on the DOS icon from within Windows. Then type a DOS command to print. Examples of DOS commands that can be used to print this file are:

COPY filename.PRN PRN

TYPE filename.PRN > PRN

TYPE filename.PRN > LPT1:

If you travel extensively, another reason to print to a file is to control the use of disks. If you have enough room on your hard drive, print all your reports and memos to files and print when you return to the home office. In fact, you can send the files to the office via an online service and have them printed and distributed before you get back.

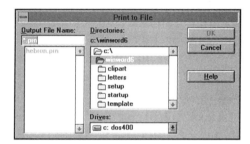

Figure 9.8
The Print to File dialog box.

Troubleshooting Common Printer Problems

Although Word for Windows problems are rare, many that do occur relate to using the printer. If Word displays the message that it is printing but does not print, give it a chance to print. Some printers take longer than others to begin. Some documents or pages take longer to print, particularly if they contain graphics. If your printer does not print after a reasonable time, refer to this checklist:

1. Make sure your printer is plugged in and turned on.

2. Turn your printer off and on. Sometimes this clears a *buffer* (storage area in memory) that might be causing a problem. You can also try rebooting your computer.

If Word has been trying to print for a long time, it may display a message stating that it cannot print. Go through the following items and then answer the prompt.

3. Make sure all cables connecting your computer and printer are plugged in.

4. Make sure the printer's On-line light is on. You might have to press a button if it is not.

5. Make sure there is paper loaded and that it is properly aligned in the paper tray.

6. Make sure that all covers are closed. Some printers cannot print unless every component is in its correct place. If you are using a laser printer, make sure the toner cartridge is correctly installed.

7. Run a self-test on the printer to see if it is working correctly independent of the computer. Maybe the problem is with communication from the PC. To see how to run a self-test, look at your printer's documentation.

8. See if the printer works when you enter a DOS print command (for example, type `DIR > PRN` to print the current directory), which will tell you whether the computer is communicating with the printer).

9. Evaluate your AUTOEXEC.BAT and CONFIG.SYS files. A line may be missing or incorrect in one of these files. For help, refer to your DOS documentation.

10. Make sure the cables are attached firmly to the correct ports. You may have to ask your local guru to help you.

11. Make sure the active printer is attached to a port. At the top of the Print dialog box, you should see the name of the printer and the name of its port. If you are not sure how to proceed, ask your local computer expert.

12. Check to ensure that you are using the correct printer driver for the active printer. You'll have to go into the Windows Control Panel and click on the Printers icon. You may have to ask for help.

CAUTION

If you edit AUTOEXEC.BAT, which is a text format (ASCII) file with Word, be sure to keep the file in the text format. If AUTOEXEC.BAT is not in ASCII format, it will contain extra formatting characters that your computer will misinterpret.

If this list does not prompt you to solve your problem, refer to your printer's manual.

Using WordArt

Select Insert Object (Alt, I, O). Select Microsoft WordArt 2.0 and select OK or press Enter. Type text in the box, then choose from the WordArt toolbar to modify the text. To exit from WordArt, click anywhere in the document window.

Using Microsoft Drawing

Click on the Drawing button on the Standard toolbar. Click on any drawing button (line, rectangle, free-form, etc.) to start work on the graphic. Click on other buttons to edit the graphic.

Importing a Picture

Select Insert Picture (Alt, I, P). Select a picture and select OK or press Enter.

Selecting an Object

Click within the object or move the insertion point to either side of the object and press Shift+→ or Shift+←.

Cropping an Object

Select the object.

- Using the mouse, move the pointer to a sizing handle, press Shift, drag the border toward the center of the object.
- Select Format Picture (Alt, O, R) and select positive values in the Crop From group.

Adding White Space Around an Object

Select the object.

- Move the mouse pointer to a sizing handle between the corners. When the pointer is a double-sided arrow, press Shift and drag the handle away from the object center.
- Select Format Picture (Alt, O, R) and select negative values in the Crop From group.

Illustrating Your Document

In previous chapters, you learned how to create, edit, and format documents within Word for Windows. In this chapter, you'll get an overview of ways to further enhance your documents using the WordArt text formatting feature, Microsoft Drawing, and Word's collection of clip art.

Word allows you to produce and edit graphics, such as pictures, charts, and text that has been turned into graphics while remaining within the Word program. You can also import and optionally edit many pictures and graphics from other Windows applications.

WordArt and Microsoft Drawing create and use items called objects, which are individual components that make up a graphic (or a document). Examples of objects are rectangles, lines, and ellipses in Microsoft Drawing (and other paint and drawing applications) and a piece of text that is converted to a single graphic in WordArt. Other objects include fields in database programs, dialog boxes, icons, and buttons; almost every item on your computer screen is an object.

Although WordArt, Microsoft Drawing, and Word clip art are all used to enhance a document, there is little similarity among them. You even access them in different ways:

You start WordArt by selecting the Insert Object command,

You click on a toolbar button to display the Microsoft Drawing toolbar, and

You select the Insert Picture command to insert clip art into a document or a table cell.

NOTE: Although we don't cover it in this book, Word also includes Microsoft Chart, which inserts charts into documents. To learn about Microsoft Chart as well as Microsoft Drawing's intermediate and advanced techniques, see your Microsoft *Word for Windows User's Guide.*

Converting Text to Graphics with WordArt

Word's WordArt feature enables you to manipulate text and insert it in a document as a graphic. You can use WordArt to enhance a heading, or to design a certificate, a handout, or even a simple logo. To start WordArt, select the Object command ([Alt], [I], [O]) From the Insert menu. When Word displays the Object dialog box (Figure 10.1), select Microsoft WordArt and select OK or press [↵Enter]. Word adds a WordArt toolbar to the document window (Figure 10.2) and puts a box in the middle of the document window.

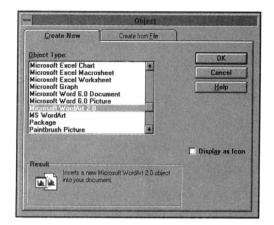

Figure 10.1
The Object, Create New dialog box from which you can start Microsoft Drawing, Microsoft Graph, or WordArt.

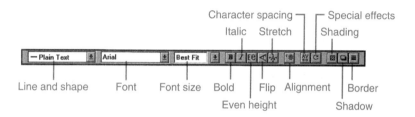

Figure 10.2
The WordArt toolbar.

Type the text you wish to convert into the box, and Word then changes the text into a graphic. You can now edit the whole, but not the parts, by selecting combinations from the following list of formatting options:

Line and Shape—Open this drop-down list box (Figure 10.3) and select from the patterns that you want the text to follow. For example, you can print on a stop sign, a triangle, or bend your text in various ways.

Font—Select a font from this familiar drop-down list box.

Font Size—Select the size of the text or let Word decide by selecting Best Fit.

Bold—Click on this button to switch between normal and boldface.

Italic—Click on this button to switch between normal and italics.

Even Height—Click on this button to apply uppercase and lowercase to alternate letters.

Flip—Click on this button to turn the text on its side.

Stretch—Click on this button to stretch the text vertically.

Alignment—Click on this button to open a menu from which you can choose from six types of alignment.

Character Spacing—Click on this button to open the Spacing Between Characters dialog box (Figure 10.4), which allows you to set the spacing between characters.

Special Effects—Click on this button to open the Special Effects dialog box (Figure 10.5), which enables you to rotate and change the angle of the text.

Shading—Click on this button to open the Shading dialog box (Figure 10.6) from which you can select patterns and colors.

Shadow—Click on this button to display types of shadows. If you select More, WordArt opens the Shadow dialog box (Figure 10.7).

Border—Click on this button to display the Border dialog box (Figure 10.8) from which you can select border styles and colors.

Whenever you select an option, WordArt changes the sample in the document window. To exit from WordArt, click anywhere on the document window.

To edit a WordArt graphic, simply double-click on it. Word opens the Object dialog box and you can start editing.

Figure 10.3
The Plain Text drop-down list box.

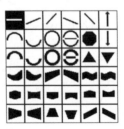

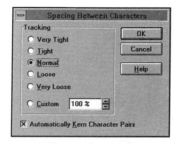

Figure 10.4
The Spacing Between Characters dialog box used to expand or condense the spacing between characters.

Figure 10.5
The Special Effects dialog box used to rotate and angle text.

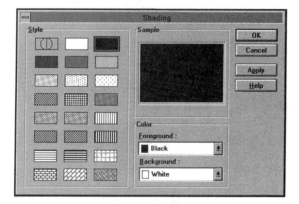

Figure 10.6
The Shading dialog box used to select patterns and colors.

Figure 10.7
The Shadow dialog box, which offers several types of shadows.

Figure 10.8

The Border dialog box used to select border styles and colors.

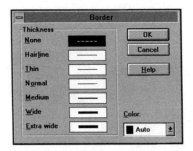

For a logo that is based on your company name or your initials, use WordArt. Type the text in the Object dialog box, and experiment with the many options until you are satisfied with the design. One of the most important factors in designing a logo is how it will move from your business card to your letterhead and even to the sign in front of your business.

Creating and Editing Pictures with Microsoft Drawing

The Microsoft Drawing application creates and edits pictures within Word documents. For example, you can create flow charts, diagrams, organization charts, and illustrations for reports and proposals using Microsoft Drawing.

 Click on the Drawing button to display or close the Drawing toolbar.

Starting Microsoft Drawing

Microsoft Drawing is based on the toolbar; there is just one menu command (**Fo**rmat Drawing **O**bject). To display the Microsoft Drawing toolbar (see Figure 10.9), click on the Drawing button on the Standard toolbar. The Drawing toolbar includes the buttons described in Table 10.1.

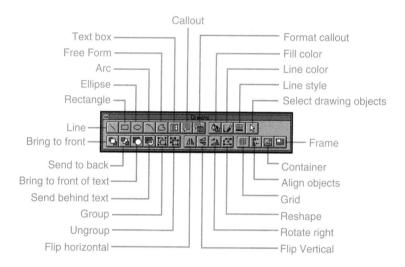

Figure 10.9
The Microsoft Drawing toolbar.

Button	How to Use This Tool
Line	Draws a line in the document window.
Rectangle	Draw a rectangle or square in the document window.
Ellipse	Draw an ellipse or circle in the document window.
Arc	Draw an arc in the document window.
Free Form	Draw a free-form object in the document window.
Text Box	Insert a box in which you can type text in the document window.
Callout	Insert a callout in the document window.
Format Callout	Format a callout in the document window.
Fill Color	Change the color that fills a Drawing object in the document window.

Table 10.1
Microsoft Drawing Toolbar Buttons

continues

Table 10.1
Continued

Button	How to Use This Tool
Line Color	Change the border color of a Drawing object in the document window.
Line Style	Change the line style for a Drawing object in the document window.
Select Drawing Objects	Encompass several graphics in the document window.
Bring to Front	Bring the selected object to the front of the other objects.
Send to Back	Send the selected object to the back of the other objects.
Bring to Front of Text	Bring the selected object one text layer forward.
Send Behind Text	Send the selected object one text layer back.
Group	Group two or more selected objects into one object.
Ungroup	Ungroup an object into its individual objects.
Flip Horizontal	Flip an object 180 degrees horizontally.
Flip Vertical	Flip an object 180 degrees vertically.
Rotate Right	Rotate the selected object 90 degrees.
Reshape	Select several lines that make up a free-form object.
Snap to Grid	Attach a grid to the drawing area.
Align Objects	Align selected objects to each other or to the page.
Create Picture	Place an empty picture in the document window.
Frame	Insert an empty frame or to surround selected text with a frame.

TIP: To hold down a button on the Drawing toolbar until you decide to "unselect" it, double-click on the button when you select it.

Creating a Graphic

To create a graphic, click on one of the buttons on the Drawing toolbar, move the mouse pointer to the drawing area, and start working.

When you draw a line, start at one end of the line, press and hold down the mouse button and then drag to the other end of the line. To force a line to be drawn at an angle based on a multiple of 45 degrees (where a complete revolution is 360 degrees), press ⇧Shift, click the left mouse button, and drag from the starting point of the line to the desired length and angle.

To draw an ellipse or rectangle, click on the Ellipse or Rectangle button, move the mouse pointer to a starting point and then press the mouse button and drag in the desired direction. To draw a circle or a square, press ⇧Shift and drag the object until it is the size that you want. To draw an ellipse or rectangle that extends in opposite directions from the starting point, press Ctrl and then drag to draw the object. To draw a circle or square extending in either direction from the starting point, press both Ctrl and ⇧Shift, click the left mouse button, and drag until the object is the size that you want.

To draw a rounded rectangle, draw a rectangle using the preceding directions and then select Format Drawing Object (Alt, O, O). Word opens the Drawing Defaults dialog box. Click on the Line tab and place a check mark in the Round Corners check box (shown in Figure 10.10).

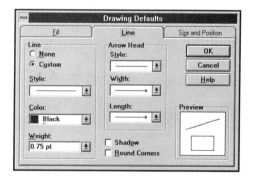

Figure 10.10

The Drawing Defaults Line dialog box

Use the *arc tool* to draw filled (a quarter of a circle or ellipse with lines running from the center of the circle) or unfilled arcs (without lines from the center), if the fill setting matches the background. Click the left mouse button and drag from the beginning point of the arc to the other end to draw an arc based on an ellipse. To draw an arc based on a circle, press ⇧Shift, click the left mouse button, and drag until the arc is the desired size.

The *free-form tool* draws all sorts of free forms, which consist of any combination of straight or curved lines. Click the left mouse button and drag to draw free-form in any direction. Release the left mouse button and drag to draw straight lines, or release the left mouse button, press ⇧Shift, and drag to draw a line based on a multiple of 45 degrees. To draw straight lines from one point to another, click the left mouse button at the position at which you want the angle of the line to change. Double-click to end free-form drawing.

Use the *text box tool* to type characters inside a box that you draw on the computer screen. Using this tool is the same as drawing a rectangle. However, when you have completed the text box, you'll notice a blinking insertion point at the top left corner of the text box. Just start typing up to 255 characters. You don't have to worry about pressing ↵Enter at the end of each line; Word provides the wordwrap for you.

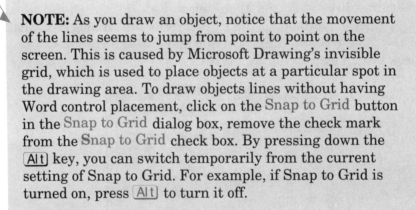

NOTE: As you draw an object, notice that the movement of the lines seems to jump from point to point on the screen. This is caused by Microsoft Drawing's invisible grid, which is used to place objects at a particular spot in the drawing area. To draw objects lines without having Word control placement, click on the Snap to Grid button in the Snap to Grid dialog box, remove the check mark from the Snap to Grid check box. By pressing down the Alt key, you can switch temporarily from the current setting of Snap to Grid. For example, if Snap to Grid is turned on, press Alt to turn it off.

Editing a Picture

Once you have inserted objects in the drawing area, you'll want to move them around or change their appearance. As you learned in earlier chapters, before you can manipulate text, you must select it. The same is true for Microsoft Drawing pictures.

To select an object within a picture, move the mouse pointer to the object and click the left mouse button. Microsoft Drawing places resize handles (Figure 10.11), at either end of a line or around a two-dimensional object. To change the shape of an object, move the mouse pointer to a resize handle, click the left mouse button and drag in any direction. The object is stretched in the direction you drag the mouse pointer. To move the object, place the mouse pointer within the object, click the left mouse button. When the mouse pointer changes to look as it does in Figure 10.12, drag the object to its new location.

The Drawing toolbar also provides editing functions. For example, you can select the Bring to Front button to move the selected object to the front of all other objects in the picture, and selecting the Send to Back button moves the selected object to the back of all other objects in the picture.

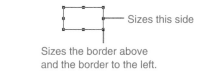

Figure 10.11

A Microsoft Drawing picture with a selected object.

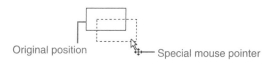

Figure 10.12

A Microsoft Drawing picture as it is moved.

Selecting the Group button allows you to select a group of objects and make them a single object. This command is very useful when you are making a part of a picture out of several objects. Rather than moving individual objects to make room for the new objects, group them and move them as a whole. When you are finished moving them, select the Ungroup button.

For more information about Microsoft Drawing, remember to refer to the Microsoft *Word for Windows User's Guide*.

Inserting Pictures Directly into a Document

You can import pictures from other drawing applications and clip art from Word's clipart subdirectory into a document or a table cell. To insert a picture, select Insert Picture. When Word displays the Insert Picture dialog box (Figure 10.13), either type a file name in the File Name box or select a file name from the list of files below the box. Notice that Word only displays files with certain extensions (e.g., .BMP, .WMF, .WPG). These are not the only files that you can import into your document. Open the List Files of Type drop-down list box to see the types of graphics files you can insert into a Word document. Once you have selected a picture to insert, select OK or press ↵Enter.

One especially useful feature in the Import Picture dialog box is the **P**review Picture check box. If you check this check box, you can select a picture and view it before inserting it. This can save a lot of time if you don't remember a picture name or are choosing from a new group of pictures.

Figure 10.13

The Insert Picture dialog box with a preview of the selected picture.

Selected file ——

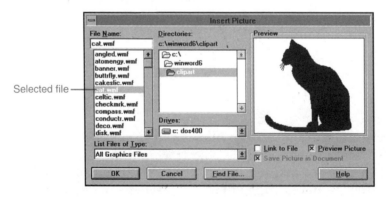

Working with Graphics and Pictures in Word for Windows

Once you have created, edited, or inserted an object into Word, you can make more changes. You can change an object's size, crop (cut) pieces off, and add space between the object and text. You can add a frame and then wrap text around the object at a distance you define.

Selecting an Object

Before making most of the changes described in this section, you'll have to select the object first. There are two ways to select an object: either click the left mouse button anywhere within the object, or move the insertion point to the left or right of the object and then press the ⌈⇧Shift⌋+⌈→⌋ or ⌈←⌋. Word surrounds the object with a border containing eight sizing handles, small rectangles located at each corner and between all corners (see Figure 10.11).

Cropping an Object

When you crop an object, you remove parts that you don't want to display. Cropping is just like cutting pieces off the object. You can crop using the mouse or the Format Picture command (⌈Alt⌋, ⌈O⌋, ⌈R⌋).

To crop an object using the mouse, first select the object. Then move the mouse pointer to a sizing handle between the corners on the side of the object to be cropped. When the mouse pointer changes to a double-sided arrow, press and hold the ⌈⇧Shift⌋ key and drag the sizing handle toward the center of the object. Word removes the section between the original and new location of the sizing handle. To restore the cropped parts of the object, press and hold Shift and drag the sizing handle toward its original position.

To crop an object using a Word command, select the object. From the Format menu, select Picture (⌈Alt⌋, ⌈O⌋, ⌈R⌋). When Word displays the Picture dialog box (Figure 10.14), in the Crop From group, either type or cycle through the values in the **L**eft, **R**ight, **T**op, and/or **B**ottom boxes. Valid values are from –22" to 22". To crop, make sure that the value you specify is a positive number. To restore the cropped parts of the object, select the Re**s**et button in the Picture dialog box.

Figure 10.14

The Picture dialog box.

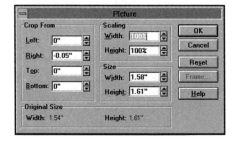

Adding White Space Around an Object

Adding white space is another way to enhance an object. When you move a picture away from any text, there is a greater emphasis on the picture itself. You can use the mouse or the Format Picture command (⌈Alt⌋, ⌈O⌋, ⌈R⌋).

To add white space using the mouse, select the object. Then move the mouse pointer to a sizing handle between the corners on the side of the object to have more white space. When the mouse pointer changes to a double-sided arrow, press the ⌈⇧Shift⌋ key and drag the sizing handle away from the center of the object. Word adds white space between the original and new locations of the sizing handle. If you have previously cropped the object, Word restores the part of the picture that you cropped, and then starts adding white space.

To add white space to an object using a Word command, select the object. From the Format menu, select Picture ([Alt], [O], [R]). When Word displays the Picture dialog box, in the Crop From group, either type a value or cycle through the values in the **L**eft, **R**ight, **T**op, and/or **B**ottom boxes. To add white space, make sure that the value you specify is a negative number.

Resizing an Object

You can increase or decrease the size of objects with the mouse or by using the Format Picture command ([Alt], [O], [R]). This is also known as *scaling* an object.

Select the object and then drag a sizing handle. If you select a sizing handle at the corner of the frame, you'll adjust the object proportionally. If you select a sizing handle between the corners of a frame, you'll adjust that one edge of the object; the adjustment will not keep the original proportions. When you scale an object, Word reports in the status bar the percentages that the height and width change from the original dimensions.

NOTE: You can resize WordArt text using these same techniques.

To increase or decrease the size of an object using a Word command, select the object. From the Format menu, select Picture ([Alt], [O], [R]). When Word displays the Picture dialog box, in the Scaling group, either type or cycle through the values in the Width and Height boxes. Valid values are from 5 to 6545. These values represent the proportion of the object's original dimensions. You can also type or cycle through the values in the Size group. In this case, Width and Height are the true dimensions of the object on the page. Valid values are from 0.12" to 22". Notice that the Original Size area shows the original width and height of the selected object.

At any time, you can return an object to its original size. Select the object and then select Format Picture ([Alt], [O], [R]). When Word displays the Picture dialog box, select Reset. After you select OK or press [↵Enter], Word returns to your document and the object assumes its original size.

Adding a Frame to an Object

In Chapters 6 and 10, you learned how to use the Format Borders and Shading command ([Alt], [O], [B]). You also can use this command to place either a border or lines around an object. However, using this command results in a border or lines that don't allow text to flow around it. Therefore, it's best to use the Insert Frame command ([Alt], [I], [F]) to add both a frame and a border. Adding a frame allows for manipulation of both the object and the text that surrounds it.

> Click on the Frame button on the Drawing toolbar to insert either an empty frame or a frame that surrounds selected text.

Click on the Frame button to insert either an empty frame or a frame that surrounds a selected object (e.g., text, graphics, or table, and so on) in the current document at the specified location. You must be in Page Layout view to insert a frame.

To insert a frame around an object using the menu bar, either select the object or place the insertion point within the object. Select Frame from the Insert menu ([Alt], [I], [F]). If you are not working in Page Layout view, Word displays a dialog box that asks you if you want to change to that view. Answer Yes. Word inserts a frame around the object (Figure 10.15). Notice that with or without a frame, a selected object has sizing handles around its edges. One way of telling whether there is a frame around an object is to look at the margin settings on the Ruler after you have selected the object. The margin settings show the left and right edge of the frame. Otherwise, the margin settings show the left and right margins for the document.

Figure 10.15
An imported picture from the \clipart subdirectory. Notice that a frame doesn't look like a border or a selection with handles.

At any time, you can remove a frame surrounding an object, text, or a table by first selecting it and then using the Format Frame command (Alt , O , M) to display the Frame dialog box (Figure 10.16). Click on the Remove Frame button and Word removes the frame. If there is also a border, it remains.

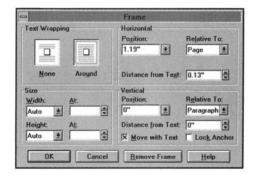

Figure 10.16
The Frame dialog box.

Inserting a Blank Frame

You can insert an empty frame so that you can later add an object or type text. An empty frame reserves space on the page.

Select Insert Frame (Alt , I , F). Word returns to your document and changes the mouse pointer to a cross. This shape helps you to select the exact location of the first corner of the frame. Move the mouse pointer to the first corner of the empty frame. Press and hold the left mouse button, and then drag it to a diagonal corner. As you drag, a dotted rectangle shows you the size of the frame. When you release the left mouse button, Word places a frame surrounded by a border.

To change the size of the frame, click within the frame border. Then move the mouse pointer to one of the handles, and drag the side of the frame (or its border) to its new dimensions. To move a frame, move the mouse pointer until it points up and to the left, and trails a four-headed arrow. Drag the frame to its new location.

Adding a Caption to an Object

To add a caption to the bottom of an object surrounded by a frame, move the insertion point between the lower right corner of the object and the paragraph mark in that area. Press ↵Enter, and Word inserts a paragraph mark and adds room to the bottom of the frame. Move the insertion point between the two paragraph marks, and then type the caption. To center the caption under the object, select the caption and then center it using either the button on the Formatting toolbar or the Format Paragraph command (Alt, O, P).

Positioning Objects on a Page

You can move an object to any location on a page. For example, if you are using facing pages for formatting, you might want to insert an object at the left margin of the left page and another object at the right margin of the right page.

Any object to be moved should first be inserted into a frame. You can move a frame and its contents anywhere on a page by dragging it or by using the Format Frame command (Alt, O, M).

To use the mouse, move the mouse pointer to the border of the frame. When the mouse pointer changes to a four-pointer arrow, click the left mouse button and drag the frame anywhere on the page. When you have moved the frame to the desired location, release the left mouse button.

You can also select the **F**ormat **F**ra**m**e command (Alt, O, M) to move a frame on the page. When Word displays the Frame dialog box, you can select horizontal and vertical alignment of the frame on the page, margin, or column.

In the Horizontal group, use the Position box to align the frame to the left side, right side or centered between the left and right sides of the page, margin, or column. You can also align the frame along the inside or outside edge or type an actual value in the Position text box. In the Relative To box, specify Margin, Page, or Column. Use the Distance from Text box to determine the amount of white space between the frame and the text wrapping around the frame.

In the Vertical group, you'll also find Posi**t**ion, **R**elative To, Distance **f**rom Text boxes. You can define a position aligned with the top, bottom, or center of the margin, page, or paragraph. In the **R**elative To box, you can select Margin, Page, or Paragraph. If you check the **M**ove with Text check box, and if you move the text with which this frame is associated, the frame moves as well. If the **M**ove with Text checkbox is clear, the frame remains in its present position. If you select Remove Frame, Word deletes the selected frame.

Wrapping Text Around an Object

When you insert an object without a frame into a document, Word makes room for the object by clearing the area of the object, from the left margin to the right margin. If you insert a frame around an object, Word's default is to wrap text around the object (Figure 10.17). To adjust the distance of text from the frame, select Format Frame (Alt, O, M). When Word displays the Frame dialog box, you can turn off text wrapping by selecting None. You also can define a distance between a frame and text by typing or cycling through the values in the Distance from Text boxes. Valid

values are between 0 and 22". Then select OK or press ⏎Enter.
Once you have returned to the document, move the object around
the page if you want to adjust the length of the lines of text.

Figure 10.17

*An example of text
wrapping around
an object.*

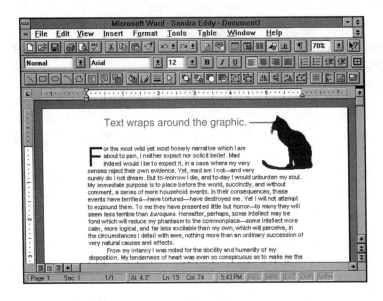

Creating a Table

Move the mouse pointer to the table location and:

- Select Table Insert Table (Alt, A, I), define the number of columns and the number of rows, and select OK or press ↵Enter.
- Click on the Table button in the Standard toolbar, drag the number of columns and the number of rows. Release the mouse button.
- Select File New (Alt, F, N). Select Table Wizard and answer the prompts. Select Finish.

Converting Text to a Table

Select text to be converted, and then select Table Convert Text to Table (Alt, A, V). Optionally, select the mark that represents the separation between cells, and select OK or press ↵Enter.

Adding Rows to a Table

Move the mouse pointer to the location of the new rows, and:

- select Table Insert Cells (Alt, A, I), select Shift Cells Down or Insert Entire Row, and select OK or press ↵Enter.
- select the number of rows to be added and then click on the Table button on the Standard toolbar.
- press Tab⇥ if the mouse pointer is in the last cell of the table.

Chapter 11

Creating Tables

Up to this point, you have learned how to create and format documents that consist of a single column of text, extending from margin to margin. In Chapter 8, you were introduced to the first multiple-column format, snaking columns. Remember that there is no way to make these columns unequal widths; every time you adjust the width of one column, all other columns assume the new width.

In this chapter, you will learn how to create, format, and edit another multiple-column format: tables. Unlike snaking columns, Word's table columns can be of unequal widths and can extend up to the full width of a page. You can select, edit, manipulate, and format tables and their contents in the same ways you work with other text in your documents.

Creating Tables

A table is a good way to present information in an easy-to-read format. Unlike some word processors that have you create a table from scratch by using tabs, Word lets you create a table as if it were a spreadsheet. Like spreadsheets, Word's tables are made up of cells, arranged in rows and columns. With Word, it is easy to edit tables that you've created.

Inserting a Table in a Document

Creating tables is similar to creating multiple columns. When you create a table using the Table menu and the Insert Table command, Word divides the space between the margins into equal columns. If you are working in a multiple-column format (such as snaking columns), the total width of the table is the width of the single column where the insertion point was located when you created the table. The height of a cell expands to hold all the text you have entered for that cell. The height of a row is the height of the largest cell in the row.

To create a table, select Table Insert Table ([Alt], [A], [I]). When Word displays the Insert Table dialog box (shown in Figure 11.1), define the size of the table. In the Number of Columns box, type a value or cycle through the range of values (from 1 to 31). In the Number of Rows box, type a value or cycle through the range of values (from 1 to 32767). To define the width of a column, type a value or cycle through the range of values (from 0 to 22 inches) in the Column Width box. You can also accept Word's column width, Auto, which is based on the width between the margins and the number of columns. Keep in mind that the ranges of values for the Insert Table dialog box are also affected by computer memory, paper width and height, and other factors. Therefore, you may not be able to use the full range of values that Word provides.

Figure 11.1

The Insert Table dialog box, which enables you to define the columns and rows for a table to be inserted in the current document.

Define the number of columns across the table.

Define the number of rows down a table.

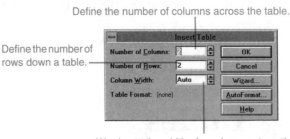

Word sets the width of a column automatically.

You can make a Things to Do page by using a table and a series of Word commands. First, create a table consisting of a single row. Select the table. Choose Format Borders and Shading, select a single line, and then select OK or press ⏎Enter. Word surrounds the table with a single line. Making sure that the table is still selected, choose Edit Copy (Ctrl+C or Ctrl+Num Lock) and Edit Paste Row (Ctrl+V or ⇧Shift+Num Lock). Then select Edit Repeat (F4) to insert as many rows as you want (we used 48). You can create a header to hold the text Things to Do. Define a font, point size, and alignment. Then print the sheet.

Follow these Quick Steps to define a table and insert it into the current document.

Defining a Table and Inserting It into a Document

1. Move the insertion point to the place in your document where you want the table.

The insertion point flashes on and off.

2. From the Table menu, select the Insert Table command (Alt, A, I).

Word displays the Insert Table dialog box (Figure 11.1).

3. Type a number in the Number of Columns, Number of Rows, and Column Width boxes, or use the up and down arrow buttons to cycle through the values. The defaults are 2 columns, 1 row, and Auto.

As you insert values in the Number of Columns and the Number of Rows boxes, remember that you may not be able to use the full range of values because of computer limitations and other factors.

4. Select OK or press ⏎Enter.

Word returns to your document and inserts a blank table template with the characteristics that you specified (Figure 11.2).

Figure 11.2

A table template created by using the Table menu and the Insert Table command.

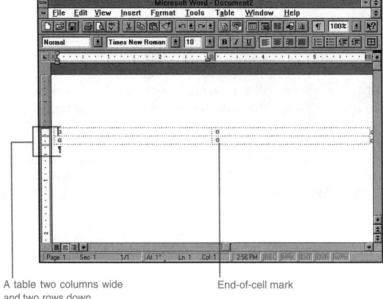

A table two columns wide and two rows down

End-of-cell mark

Click on the Table button to insert the table template into the document at the insertion point. When Word displays the table template, drag the mouse to define the number of rows and columns in the table. Drag to the left or right to determine the number of columns, drag up or down to set the number of rows, or drag diagonally to change both rows and columns.

When a table is inserted in your document, notice that dots surround each cell. The dots show the boundaries of the cell and do not print. To turn off the dots, select the Table menu and remove the check from the Gridlines command (Alt , A , L).

TIP: You can create a table using the Table Wizard, which is available when you select File New (Alt , F , N). When you use a wizard to design a document, Word leads you through the creative process, making suggestions every step of the way. For more information about wizards, see Chapter 12.

Navigating a Table

You can use the keyboard or the mouse to move around a table. Note that you cannot move down to the next cell in a table by pressing Enter; when you press Enter, the cell containing the insertion point just gets larger.

The easiest way to get around a table is to use the mouse pointer. Move the mouse pointer to the place in which you want to add text and click the left mouse button to place the insertion point.

You may find it awkward to switch between the keyboard and the mouse. If you are adding text to a table, you may want to use only the keyboard. Table 11.1 provides a list of table-navigation keys.

Key	Description
↓	The insertion point moves down one line within the table or out of the table.
↑	The insertion point moves up one line within the table or out of the table.
→	The insertion point moves to the next cell.
←	The insertion point moves to the previous cell.
Tab↹	The insertion point moves to the next cell.
⇧Shift+Tab↹	The insertion point moves to the previous cell.
Alt+Home	The insertion point moves to the first cell in the current row.
Alt+End	The insertion point moves to the last cell in the current row.
Alt+PgUp	The insertion point moves to the top cell in the column.
Alt+PgDn	The insertion point moves to the bottom cell in the column.

Table 11.1
Word's Table-Navigation Keys

NOTE: Use Ctrl+Tab↹ to insert a tab in a table.

Converting Text to a Table

If the current document contains text that would look better as a table, there is an easy way to convert that text into table format. When you select text to convert it to a table, make sure that the segments of text that will make up table cells are separated by paragraph marks, tabs, or commas. If there is a combination of tabs and paragraph marks, or commas and paragraph marks, Word treats each paragraph mark as the end of a row. If all three of these marks are used to divide the text, Word asks you to choose the mark that represents the division between cells.

To convert text to a table, select the text to be converted and then choose the Table menu and the Convert Text to Table command ([Alt], [A], [V]). If Word detects a combination of characters used to separate the text, it displays the Convert Text To Table dialog box; otherwise, it returns to your document and converts the text to a table. You can also select a table and convert it to text. When you select a table, Word changes the Convert Text to Table command to Convert Table to Text.

TIP: To select an entire table, click anywhere within the table and press [Alt]+[5] (numeric keypad).

Follow these Quick Steps to convert text in a document to a table.

Converting Text to a Table

1. Select the text to be converted to a table.

    Word highlights the text (Figure 11.3).

2. Select the Table menu and the Convert Text to Table command ([Alt], [A], [V]).

    If you have more than one type of separator (for example, commas and tabs) between units of text, Word displays the Convert Text to Table dialog box (Figure 11.4).

3. If the Convert Text To Table dialog box is displayed, select the mark that represents the division between cells. Then select OK or press ⏎Enter).

Word returns to the current document and makes a table (Figure 11.5).

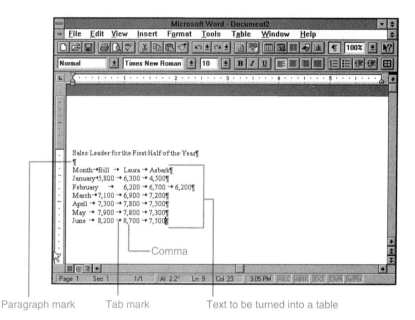

Figure 11.3

Text before it is converted to a table.

Paragraph mark   Tab mark   Text to be turned into a table

Word calculates the number of columns and the number of rows.

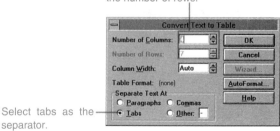

Figure 11.4

The Convert Text to Table dialog box from which you select the symbol that separates text.

Select tabs as the separator.

Figure 11.5

Text converted to a table with adjusted columns.

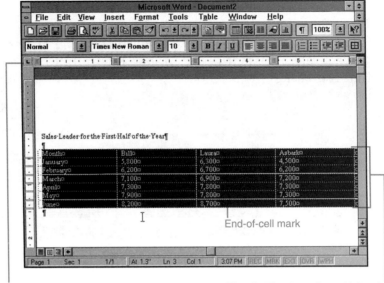

Ruler with four columns

End-of-cell mark

Text that has been turned into a table.

To adjust the width of a column, move the mouse pointer to the Ruler. Find the area between segments of the Ruler, press and hold the left mouse button and drag the area to the left or the right (Figure 11.6). When the column width is satisfactory, release the left mouse button. Or you can place the mouse pointer on the vertical line you want to move and drag the pointer until it looks like a double-headed arrow. Then drag the line to its new position (Figure 11.7). Word adjusts the column width as you wish.

TIP: To convert selected text to a table, click on the Table button on the Standard toolbar.

Left margin   Right margin

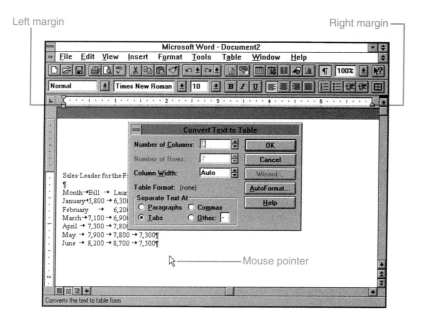

Figure 11.6
Adjusting columns from within the Ruler.

Left margin   Right margin

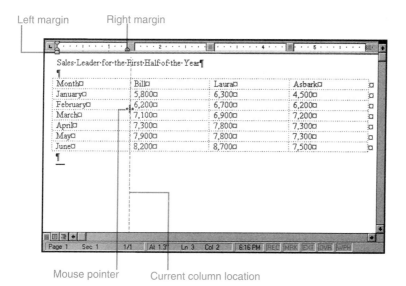

Mouse pointer   Current column location

Figure 11.7
Adjusting columns by dragging on the grid.

Editing Tables

In this section, you'll learn how to select and manipulate text and the components of a table. You'll find editing tables almost the same as editing text in other parts of a document.

Selecting Text in a Table

As you learned in Chapter 3, to copy or cut text when using Word, you must select the text first. Selecting text in a table is like selecting text anywhere else in your document. When you select text using any of the keys in Table 11.2, the selection starts at the location of the insertion point and extends from there. You can also turn Extend Selection mode on when selecting text in a table. In Chapter 3, you learned that you turn Extend Selection mode by pressing the F8 key or by double clicking on the Ext indicator in the status bar. Remember that when Extend Selection mode is turned on, you can turn it off by pressing Esc or by double-clicking again on the Ext indicator in the status bar. Table 11.2 provides a list of table selection keys.

Table 11.2
Word's Table
Selection Keys

Key	Description
Without Extended Selection mode	
Alt+5 (on the numeric keypad with Num Lock toggled off)	Selects the entire table
⇧Shift+↑	Selects the current cell and the cell above and with every press, selects the prior cell. Removes the selection from the cells selected by pressing Shift+↓.
⇧Shift+↓	Selects the current cell and the cell below and with every press, selects the next cell. Removes the selection from the cells selected by pressing Shift+↑.
⇧Shift+←	Selects the current cell one character at a time and with every press each adjacent cell to the left. Removes the selection from the cells selected by pressing Shift+→.

Key	Description
⇧Shift+→	Selects the current cell one character at a time and then with every press each adjacent cell to the right. Removes the selection from the cells selected by pressing Shift+←.
⇧Shift+Alt+Home	Selects all the cells from the insertion point to the first cell in a row.
⇧Shift+Alt+End	Selects all the cells from the insertion point to the last cell in a row.
⇧Shift+Alt+PgDn	Selects all the cells from the insertion point to the last cell in a column.
⇧Shift+Alt+PgUp	Selects all the cells from the insertion point to the first cell in a column.
Tab⇄	Selects the contents of the next cell.
⇧Shift+Tab⇄	Selects the contents of the previous cell.
In Extended Selection Mode	
↑	Selects the current cell and the cell above and then with every press each adjacent cell above.
↓	Selects the current cell and the cell below and then with every press each adjacent cell below.
←	Selects the current cell one character at a time and then with every press each adjacent cell to the left.
→	Selects the current cell one character at a time and then with every press each adjacent cell to the right.

To select text with the mouse, click the left mouse button on specific cells, or click the left mouse button and drag the pointer across several cells of a table.

To select a row of cells, move the mouse pointer to the selection bar in the left margin. When the mouse pointer changes to an arrow pointing up and to the right, click the left mouse button. Word highlights the entire row.

To select a column of cells, move the mouse pointer to the top border of the top cell. When the mouse pointer changes to a down arrow, click the left mouse button.

Editing Cells

There are two aspects to manipulating cells; you can edit the text within a cell, or you can edit the cells themselves.

Cutting, copying, and pasting text from one cell to another is just like cutting, copying, and pasting in other parts of the document. Select all the text in a cell including the end-of-cell mark. Then use either the Edit Copy or Edit Cut command. At this point the **Edit Paste** command becomes **Edit Paste** Cell. When you paste, the cell that you are pasting overwrites the cell to which you are pasting. When you copy or cut multiple cells, the area into which you paste must have the same row-by-column dimensions as the cut or copied cells. If the dimensions are different, Word may add new cells to the table in order to contain the contents of the cut or copied cells.

TIP: To see the end-of-cell marks in a table, select the Show/Hide button on the Standard toolbar. This displays all nonprinting symbols including the end-of-cell mark. See Figure 11.2 for an example of an end-of-cell mark.

You can also insert cells and shift selected cells at the same time. Select the location of the cells to be inserted. From the Table menu, select Insert Cells ([Alt], [A], [I]). When Word displays the Insert Cells dialog box (shown in Figure 11.8), select Shift Cells Right to insert cells and shift the selected cells one cell to the right; select Shift Cells Down to insert cells and shift the selected cells one row down. You'll learn about the Insert Entire Row and Insert Entire Column options in the next section.

TIP: A shortcut method for adding new rows or columns to a table is to move the mouse pointer to the table, select some columns and rows equaling the number that you want to add, and then click on the Table button on the Standard toolbar. For example, to add one row, select a row and then click on the Table button. To add a cell to a table, select an existing cell, click on the Table button, and select a button in the Insert Cells dialog box. To add a row to the end of a table, move the mouse pointer to the last cell on the right side and press Tab⁺.

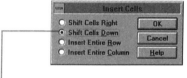

Select this radio button to insert cells and
shift the selected cells one row down.

Figure 11.8

The Insert Cells dialog box with Shift Cells Down selected.

To delete cells and shift the remaining cells at the same time, select the cells to be deleted. From the Table menu, select Delete Cells (Alt, A, D). When Word displays the Delete Cells dialog box (shown in Figure 11.9), select Shift Cells Left to delete cells and shift the remaining cells one cell to the left; select Shift Cells Up to delete cells and shift the remaining cells one row up. To delete a row of cells, select Delete Entire Row, and to delete a column of cells, select Delete Entire Column.

TIP: To delete the contents of a table but not the table itself, select the table and press Del. One simple way to delete a table and its contents is to select the table and one piece of text (even a single character or paragraph mark) and then press Del.

Figure 11.9
*The Delete Cells
dialog box with
Shift Cells Left
selected.*

Editing Rows and Columns

It is easy to add more rows and columns, or both, to a table. First, select the cell in the place in which the new row or column is to be placed. Select the Table Insert Cells command (Alt, A, I). When Word displays the Insert Cells dialog box, select the Insert Entire Row option to insert a row, or the Insert Entire Column option to insert a column.

Depending on the type of selection you have made (rows, columns, or cells), the command on the Table menu changes. For example, if you select rows, you'll see the **Insert Rows** or **D**elete Rows command. If you select columns, the commands are **Insert Columns** or **D**elete Columns. If you select a cell, you'll see **Insert Cells** or **D**elete Cells.

Formatting Tables

Certain problems are typical of tables. For example, information in some tables is hard to read because cells and text are squeezed together. Or one cell may contain too much text, resulting in a row that is half a page high and a table that looks lopsided. If the table is long, important information may be lost in it if pertinent facts aren't highlighted. The upcoming sections show how to use formatting to call attention to your table and its components, solve typical problems, and make the table easier to read.

There are two methods for formatting a table: You can use the Menu bar (specifically, the **F**ormat and **T**able menus) or a combination of the Ruler and Formatting toolbar. In the upcoming sections on table formatting, you'll learn about both methods.

Formatting a Table Automatically

Before you learn the specifics of formatting by cells, columns, and rows, you should know that there is an automatic way to format a table as a single entity. Word provides the **Ta**ble Table Auto**F**ormat command to format tables using ready-made templates. Simply select all or part of a table and then select the Table AutoFormat command from the Table menu (Alt, A, F). When the Table AutoFormat dialog box appears (see Figure 11.10), select a format from the list in the Formats list box, apply other formats to the entire selection or parts of the table. You can try varying combinations of borders, shading, text enhancement, color, and the way the table fits on the page. The best way to learn about the **Ta**ble Table Auto**F**ormat command is to experiment with it. Figures 11.11 and 11.12 show you two more samples of AutoFormat.

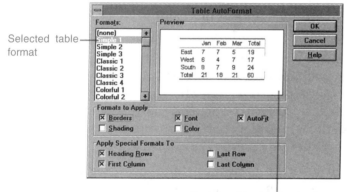

Selected table format

Sample table showing the format

Figure 11.10

The Table AutoFormat dialog box with the first table format in the Preview box.

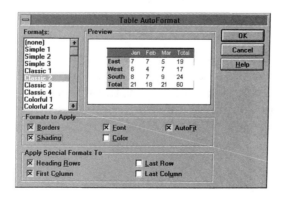

Figure 11.11

Another sample in the Table AutoFormat dialog box.

Figure 11.12

The third sample table in the Table AutoFormat dialog box. The choices are almost unlimited.

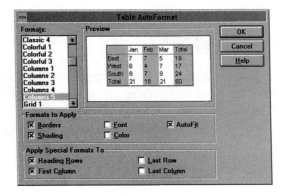

Changing the Width of a Column or Cells

If you need to change the width of a column, you can use several methods. The first method relies on the mouse, the second uses the mouse with the Ruler, and the third is a command in the **T**able menu. When you change the size of a column, you can also decide whether to let that change affect the overall width of the table.

To change the size of a column using the mouse in the table, move the mouse pointer to the border of the cell that you would like to resize. When the mouse pointer changes to two parallel lines with arrows pointing left and right, click the left mouse button and drag the border to its new location. This technique works only on vertical (width) lines and not on horizontal ones.

If you hold down the ⇧Shift key while you resize a table using the mouse, the table keeps its original width. If you hold down the Ctrl key while resizing a column with the mouse, not only will the table remain its original width, but the space to the right of the resized column will be equally divided among the remaining columns in the table.

To use the mouse with the Ruler (see Figure 11.13), first make sure that the insertion point is within a table or that cells are selected. To increase or decrease the size of a column, locate on the Ruler the Column Width marker that is directly above the corresponding vertical column line in the table. Then drag the marker to a new location on the Ruler.

Sales·Leader·for·the·First·Half·of·the·Year¶			
Month□	Bill□	Laura□	Asbark□
January□	5,800□	6,300□	4,500□
February□	6,200□	6,700□	6,200□
March□	7,100□	6,900□	7,200□
April□	7,300□	7,800□	7,300□
May□	7,900□	7,800□	7,300□
June□	8,200□	8,700□	7,500□

Active column

Figure 11.13
The Ruler with column marks for each column.

To change the cell widths of certain rows in a table, select those rows. Then drag the Column Width markers on the Ruler, to a new location to increase or decrease the size of a column.

You can use the **T**able Cell Height and **W**idth command to change the width and height of rows and columns in a table. With this method, the changes made to a column (or row) affect the entire width (or height) of the table. You can also change the width of certain cells in a table by selecting only the cells that you want to change.

Use the following Quick Steps to change the width of columns or cells with the **T**able Cell Height and **W**idth command.

Changing the Widths of Columns or Cells

QUICK STEPS

1. Select the column or cell whose width you want to change.

   Word highlights the selection.

2. Select the Table menu and the Cell Height and Width command (Alt, A, W).

   Word displays the Cell Height and Width dialog box (shown in Figure 11.14).

3. If needed, click on the Column tab at the top of the dialog box.

   Word displays the Cell Height and Width dialog box for Column.

continues

continued

4. Type a new width for the selected column or press the up or down arrow to cycle through the valid values (0" to 22").

Depending on the limitations of your computer system, paper dimensions, and other factors, Word may not allow the width that you entered.

5. To change the width of any other columns, select the Previous Column or Next Column button.

Word changes the column width you just set, highlights the new column in the document, and displays the column number of the column that you are changing in the dialog box.

6. Repeat steps 3 and 4 until you have changed all the columns widths that you want. Select OK or Close, or press ⏎Enter.

Word closes the dialog box and returns to the document.

Figure 11.14
The Cell Height and Width dialog box.

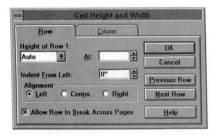

Adjusting the Space Between Columns

To increase or decrease the space between columns, select any column in the table and select Table Cell Height and Width (Alt),

A, W). In the Space Between Columns text/list box, type the value of the space between columns (ranging from 0" to 22"), and select OK or press ↵Enter. When you return to the document, all the columns in the table have the new spacing. You can also change the spacing of one row by selecting the row (or any cell in that row). When you change the spacing, only that row changes.

When you change the spacing between rows, you affect the width of the text area in a column. Thus, a column with a width of two inches and space between columns of 0.25 inch has a text area of 1.75 inches.

Changing the Height of a Row

The height of a row is normally determined by the height of the tallest cell in a row. With **T**able Cell Height and **W**idth (Alt, A, W), you can adjust the height of a row automatically (Word's default—Auto), or you can adjust a minimum height or a fixed height. If you use a fixed height, some items in large cells may be clipped on-screen and when the table is printed. A row height can be between 0 and 1584 points.

To change the height of a selected row, select the Cell Height and **W**idth command from the Table menu (Alt, A, W). In the Row Cell Height and Width dialog box (shown in Figure 11.15), select Auto, At Least, or Exactly from the Height of Row list box. Auto is the default selection for all the rows in your table; this selection sets the height of each row using the highest cell of that row. When you want a row height to start at a minimum size but be larger, if needed, select At Least. To set a fixed row height, choose Exactly. If you select either At Least or Exactly, you will have to select a size in the At text/list box.

Notice that the **R**ow Cell Height and Width dialog box has two buttons: **P**revious Row and **N**ext Row. Choosing one of these buttons moves you either one row up or one row down from your current selection. You'll learn about the rest of the options in the Cell Height and Width dialog box later in this chapter.

Figure 11.15

The Row Cell Height and Width dialog box, from which you change the height of a row or alignment of the contents of cells.

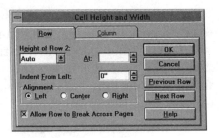

Indenting and Aligning Rows in a Table

You can change the indentation of rows or an entire table to enhance the appearance of one or more tables or to align text in a table with other text in the document.

To change the alignment of rows, first select one or more rows to be changed. Then, select Table Cell Height and Width (Alt), (A), (W)). In the Row Cell Height and Width dialog box, select one of the alignment radio buttons to align the cells' contents against the left or right margin or to center them between the margins. Use the Indent From Left box to define the distance (ranging from 0" to 22") from the left margin to the left edge of the selected row. Remember that the value that you select, even if it is within the range of valid measurements, is also affected by factors such as your computer system's limitations and paper dimensions.

Adding Borders to a Table

To give a table or selected cells extra emphasis, add borders or lines. Use the same procedures described in Chapter 6 for surrounding paragraphs with borders and lines.

To place a border around a table, select the entire table. Next, select Format Borders and Shading (Alt), (O), (B)). In the Table Borders and Shading dialog box (shown in Figure 11.16) for Borders, select the type of box and the type of line that form the border. Then select OK or press (↵Enter).

To place a border around selected cells, first select one or more cells. Next, select Format Borders and Shading (Alt , O , B). In the Cells Borders and Shading dialog box for Borders, select the type of box and the type of line that form the border. Then select OK or press ↵Enter .

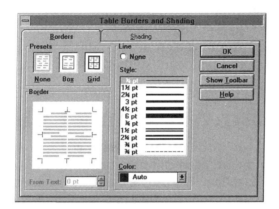

Figure 11.16
The Table Borders and Shading dialog box for Borders with its default settings.

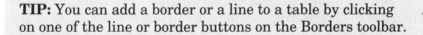

TIP: You can add a border or a line to a table by clicking on one of the line or border buttons on the Borders toolbar.

Once you have perfected a table and its formats and know that you will use the same type of table in the future, save it as an AutoText entry. Then to create a table, all you have to do is to either click on the AutoText button in the Standard toolbar or select Edit AutoText, and select the Name from the AutoText dialog box.

Merging and Splitting Cells in a Table

If you want a cell to extend the width of a table or to be a combination of two cells, you can merge cells. For example, to include a long title at the top of a table, combine cells until the merged cell is the width that you want. Start by selecting the cells to be merged. Then select Table Merge Cells (Alt, A, M). Word returns to the table and merges the selected cells.

If you change your mind about cells that you have merged, Word provides the means to split the merged cells. Start by selecting the cell to be split. Then select Table Split Cells (Alt, A, P). In the Split Cells dialog box, type the number of columns into which you wish to split the cells, and select OK or press ⏎Enter. Word returns to the table and splits the selected cells.

Formatting Text in a Cell

One thing to keep in mind is that each cell in a table is like a miniature document; each cell has its own margins and format. Text within cells follows the cell format, not the document format. Just as you would format the text in a document, you can format cells or the contents of cells in a table.

Select the entire cell or the text within a cell to be formatted. Then use the formatting commands you learned in Chapters 6, 7, and 8. For example, to apply boldface to selected text or cells, use the Format Font command or select the Bold button from the Formatting toolbar. To change the alignment of the text in a cell, use the Format Paragraph command or select the appropriate button from the Formatting toolbar. You can use the Ruler to change the margin settings for selected text. Just drag the margin pointers to format text the way you want.

Sorting Items in a Table

When creating tables, you might like to order the information within the table—alphabetically, numerically, or by date. Select the Table menu and the Sort command (Alt, A, T) to sort selected information. Word displays the Sort dialog box, which is shown in Figure 11.17. Word ignores blank spaces, tabs, and indents; it sorts by the first alphanumeric character that it finds.

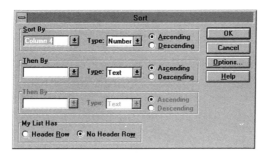

Figure 11.17
The Sort dialog box with its default settings.

There are two different sort orders—**A**scending and **De**scending—available in the Sort dialog box. **A**scending sorts from the lowest to the highest alphanumeric character; **D**escending sorts from the highest to the lowest alphanumeric character.

Normally, Word treats lowercase and uppercase letters as the same. However, you can specify that Word be sensitive to case. Just select the Options button to open the Sort Options dialog box (see Figure 11.18) in which you can check the Case Sensitive check box; Word puts uppercase letters before lowercase (for example, S before s, but not before B or b).

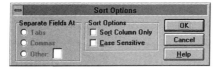

The Number option in the **T**ype drop-down list box sorts by number, regardless of the location of the numbers in the paragraph; all characters that are not numbers are ignored. For Word to sort by dates, it must be able to recognize dates in the table. The date formats in Table 11.3 are the only formats that Word recognizes as dates; all other text is ignored.

Table 11.3
*Word's Date
Formats*

Format	Example
MM/DD/YY	04/17/67
MM-DD-YY	04-17-67
Month Day, Year	April 17, 1967
	Apr 17, 1967
DD-Mon-YY	17 April 67
	17 Apr 67
Month-YY	April-67
	Apr-67
MM-DD-YY hh:mm PM|AM	04-17-67 08:55 PM
Day, Month, Year	Saturday, April 17, 1993

Select Sort Column Only to sort only the columns that you have selected.

Using a Word table, you can produce your own business cards on perforated 8 1/2"-by-11" business card stock with 10 cards on a sheet. Create a table that is three cells wide and five cells long with top, left, and right margins of 0.5", and a bottom margin of 0. From left to right, cell widths are 3.5", 0.5", and 3.5", and the cell height is 144 points (about 2"). The space between columns is .15". Printing requires hand-feeding sheets through a laser printer. Because laser printers require margins of at least 0.5", Word will issue a message. When you acknowledge it, Word will print the sheet of cards.

Creating a Data Source File

With the Mail Merge Helper dialog box displayed:

1. Select Get Data.
2. Select Create Data Source.
3. Define merge fields and select OK or press ↵Enter.
4. Type a file name and select OK or press ↵Enter.

Word enables you to produce documents that are custom-made for each member of your audience. By using a main document and a data source file, you can mention each recipient by name, refer to his or her address, and incorporate special messages in selected letters.

Adding Merge Fields to a Main Document

Type the body text, select the Mail Merge Helper button, and select Edit. Move the mouse pointer to the desired location of the merge field in the document. Select a merge field.

Merging a Main Document and a Data Source File

Select one:

- Click on the Mail Merge Helper button and fill in the Merge dialog box.
- Click on the Merge to New Document button to create a new document using the defaults.
- Click on the Merge to Printer button to create and print a merge document.
- Click on the Mail Merge button to display the Merge dialog box from which you can merge.

In this chapter, you'll learn the basics of creating and printing form letters, mailing labels, and envelopes. Refer to the Microsoft Word for Windows User's Guide for advanced features.

Creating Form Letters, Labels, and Envelopes

Creating and Printing Form Letters

A form letter has two basic components: a main document and a data source file. Once you have opened these documents, you merge them. The merging process is what actually creates a form letter.

The main document is like any other letter, with one exception. It includes all the text that you plan to send to your audience as a whole but omits the information unique to each individual. For example, a main document might include an invitation to a grand opening, a plea for a donation, or a cover letter for an enclosed brochure, but would not include the name and address of any recipients. You can create a form letter using a brand-new or existing main document.

The data source file contains the unique information about each recipient of your letter. A data source file, which is actually a simple database, is a table that includes names, addresses, and information that might not even make its way into your letter. Information like the amount of the last donation, the money the recipient owes your company, or whether an individual pays with a check or a credit card might not appear in a letter but might trigger special messages in a letter (for example, "We appreciate receiving your check" or "You may have overlooked our last bill. Thank you for paying promptly."). The data source file is made up of records (such as name, address, and telephone number) for each individual to whom you will send a letter. Records, in turn, are made up of fields, each of which contains one piece of information about the individual.

The first record in a data source file is the header record, containing all the merge fields, which identify or label the fields and tell Word what field goes where in a main document. Merge fields are between one and 31 characters long and can contain only letters, numbers, and underscores; no spaces are allowed. Examples of merge fields are FirstName, LastName, Address1, and City. Word lists some of the most common fields from which you can choose but also allows you to identify your own merge fields.

The remaining records in the data source file contain the actual information about each individual. Examples are Mary, Smith, 123 Main Street, and Anytown. You can use either a brand-new or existing main document to create a form letter.

Creating and Merging a Main Document and a Data Source File

The first step in creating a form letter is to open a main document. You can create a form letter using a brand-new or existing main document. If you're starting with a new document, you don't need to enter text now. At this stage, you're just identifying the main document and the data source file and creating a link between the two. If your main document does not exist, select the File New command (Alt), F , N) and select OK or press ↵Enter . If your main document already exists, select File Open (Alt , F , O) and select the appropriate file name from the File Name box. Then select OK or press ↵Enter .

> **TIP:** You can use a Wizard (e.g., the Letter Wizard) to create a main document and then edit it to accept merge fields. Just select the File New command (Alt , F , N), and in the New dialog box, select Letter Wizard. Then select OK or press ↵Enter .

At this point, you can start the actual Mail Merge process of attaching a data source file to the main document. Word provides the Mail Merge Helper, which guides you through the process step by step. When you select Tools Mail Merge (Alt , T , R), Word displays the Mail Merge Helper dialog box, which is shown in Figure 12.1. The Mail Merge Helper dialog box points out by the dimmed or undimmed state of the buttons exactly what your next step is before you can merge the two documents.

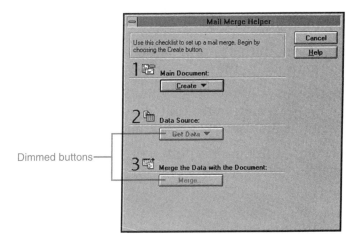

Dimmed buttons

Figure 12.1

The Mail Merge Helper dialog box, which illustrates a print merge operation.

Word provides a unique toolbar (see Figure 12.2) for the Mail Merge Helper. Note that for some buttons to be active, there must be an active data source file. The toolbar buttons are:

Insert Merge Field—Click on this button and Word opens a list of merge fields (i.e., field names) from which you can select for inclusion in your letter.

Insert Word Field—Click on this button and Word opens a list of Word fields and functions from which you can select for inclusion in your letter.

View Merged Data—Click on this button to switch between viewing merge fields and and viewing actual data in the main document. If the button does not look pressed in, you can see the merge fields. Otherwise, you see the contents of the field (e.g., the actual name, address, and so on).

First Record—Click on this button to display the first record in the data source file.

Previous Record—Click on this button to display the previous record in the data source file.

Record Number Window—Click on this button to display current record number in the data source file.

Next Record—Click on this button to display the next record in the data source file.

Last Record—Click on this button to display the last record in the data source file.

Mail Merge Helper—Click on this button to display the Mail Merge Helper dialog box so that you can edit or merge either the main document or the data source file.

Check for Errors—Click on this button to check for errors in a mail merge.

Merge to New Document—Click on this button to create a new document in which the results of the mail merge are placed.This document, which uses the mail merge defaults, shows the fields rather than the data and no longer displays the Mail Merge toolbar.

Merge to Printer—Click on this button to create a merge document, which uses the mail merge defaults, and to open the Print dialog box from which you can print the mail merge document.

Mail Merge—Click on this button to combine the main document and the data source file to produce form letters, mailing labels, envelopes, or catalogs. When you click on this button, Word displays the Merge dialog box in which you can change the defaults. The document consists of a group of sections—one for each selected record.

Search Button—Click on this button to open the Find in Field dialog box in order to search for a search string in a particular field in the data source file.

Open Button—Click on this button to open the Data Form dialog box so that you can edit, delete, or add a record to the data source file.

Use the following Quick Steps to create and link a new main document with a new data source file.

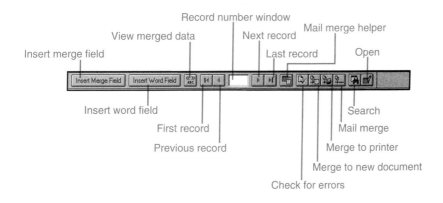

Figure 12.2
The Mail Merge Helper toolbar contains buttons that are unique to editing main documents and data sources files as well as performing steps in the mail merge process.

Creating and Merging a Main Document and a Data Source File

1. To create a new main document select the **F**ile menu and the **N**ew command (Alt , F , N).	Word displays the New dialog box (Figure 12.3).
2. Select a template or a Wizard and then select OK or press ↵Enter .	Word displays a blank document window or the first step in a wizard.
3. Select Tools Mail Merge (Alt , T , R).	Word displays the Mail Merge Helper dialog box.
4. Select the Create button.	Word opens a list (Figure 12.4) from which to choose.
5. Select Form Letters.	Word displays an information box (Figure 12.5).
6. Select Active Window. (To start with a new document, select New Main Document.)	Word displays the Mail Merge Helper dialog box with the Data Source section "undimmed."
7. Select Get Data.	Word displays a list (Figure 12.6)from which to choose.
8. Select Create Data Source to create a new data source file. (To use an existing data source file, select Open Data Source instead.)	Word displays the Create Data Source dialog box (Figure 12.7), which lists some of the most common field names you can use to define headers for the columns in the data source file.
9. Remove all the field names that you can't use from the	Word removes each of your choices from the list box.

Field Names in Header Row list box, pressing the Remove Field Name button after each selection.

10. To add a new field name, type it in the Field Name text box and select Add Field Name.	The name is added to the list.
11. To relocate a field name on the list (to move its column to a new location in the data source file), select it in the Field Names in Header Row list box and press one of the Move arrows.	The field changes position with its neighboring field.
12. When you have completed selecting field names, select OK or press ⏎Enter.	Word displays the Save Data Source dialog box (Figure 12.8).
13. Type a name in the File Name text box and select OK or press ⏎Enter.	Word returns to the Mail Merge dialog box, and then displays an information box (Figure 12.9) from which you can edit the data source file or the main document.
14. Select the Edit Data Source button.	Word displays the Data Form dialog box (Figure 12.10).
15. For each record, type information in the field text boxes. After completing a record, select Add New.	Word displays another blank record.
16. After completing entry of your last record, select OK or press ⏎Enter.	Word closes the Data Form dialog box and returns to the document window. The Mail Merge toolbar (Figure 12.2) *is now displayed to* facilitate the mail merge.

TIP: When you name a data source file, don't worry about typing an extension; Word uses the .DOC extension for data source files.

Figure 12.3

The New dialog box.

Figure 12.4

The list from which you can select the type of main document.

Figure 12.5

The information box that prompts you to select either the current document or a new document.

Figure 12.6

The list from which you can choose to create or open a data source file.

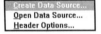

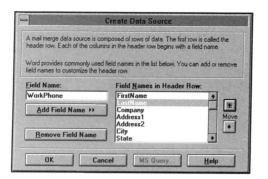

Figure 12.7
The Create Data Source dialog box.

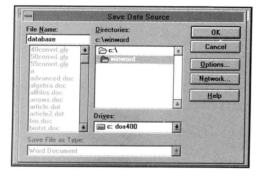

Figure 12.8
The Save Data Source dialog box.

Figure 12.9
The information box from which you can choose to edit either the data source file or the main document.

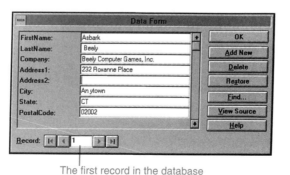

Figure 12.10
The Data Form dialog box.

The first record in the database

There is a special benefit to defining a data source file: many of the buttons become available for use. For example, after you have added a data source file to the mail merge, Word displays a button that allows you to toggle between the main document and the data source file rather than using the **T**ools Mail Me**r**ge command.

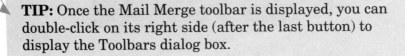

TIP: Once the Mail Merge toolbar is displayed, you can double-click on its right side (after the last button) to display the Toolbars dialog box.

If you already have a database file in another application (either Windows- or non-Windows-based), you can import it into Word and then convert it to Word for Windows format (provided that you have installed the conversion utilities). For more information, refer to the Microsoft Word for Windows User's Guide.

Sorting Records in a Data Source File

Before you print form letters, you may want to sort the records. Let's say that you want to send letters only to those people living in a certain city. Sort the records in the data source file on the City field, identify the range of record numbers for the city, and then print the form letters. Word enables you to define up to three sort criteria, so you can refine a search for specific records. For example, you can sort to find the records for a certain ZIP code within a city, or even to find a specific street within a ZIP code within a city.

To start a sort, first select the Mail Merge Helper button on the Mail Merge toolbar. When Word displays Mail Merge Helper dialog box, select the Query Options button to display the Query Options dialog box (shown in Figure 12.11), and click on the Sort Records tab (if needed). Open the Sort By drop-down list box and select one of the fields. To sort within the first sort specification, select a field from the Then By drop-down list box. To sort within the first two sort specifications, select a field from the Then By drop-down list box. Then choose either Ascending or Descending order. For example, to sort a city and then a PostalCode within that city, define City in the first drop-down list box, PostalCode in the second drop-down list box, and select (none) in the third box. Then select OK. Word returns to the data source file and sorts it as you specified. For more information about sorting within a document, see the Microsoft Word for Windows User's Guide.

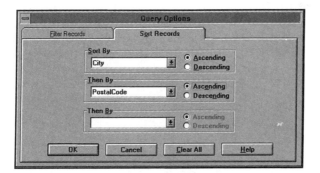

Figure 12.11

The Sort Records Query Options dialog box.

Adding Merge Fields to a Main Document

After creating and/or editing a data source file, you are ready to work on the main document. First, you'll need to type the body of the letter if you haven't already done so. Then, to be able to get information from the data source file, you'll have to insert merge fields.

Unless a dialog box or the data source file is open, the main document should already be displayed on your computer screen. If it isn't, select the Mail Merge Helper button on the Mail Merge toolbar. In the Mail Merge Helper dialog box, select Edit in the Main Document area, and choose the document to be edited from the list.

Start editing the main document. To insert a merge field at the insertion point, select the Insert Merge Field button on the Mail Merge toolbar. Then select a print merge field from the resulting list (see Figure 12.12). Word adds it to the main document. Add more fields until the main document is complete (Figure 12.13).

NOTE: You can add spaces or punctuation between fields where needed.

TIP: To insert a date that is always current in any document, select Insert Date and Time (Alt , I , T). In the Date and Time dialog box, select an appropriate format, check the Insert as Field check box.

Figure 12.12

The merge fields from which you can choose.

Figure 12.13

A completed document with all its merge fields specified.

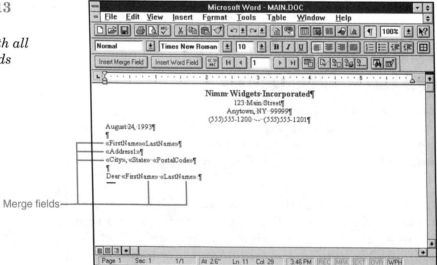

To check for any errors in the main document, select the Check for Errors button on the Mail Merge toolbar. If Word finds any discrepancies between the main document and the data source file, it displays a dialog box explaining the error.

The following Quick Steps explain the procedure used to add merge fields to your main document.

Adding Merge Fields to the Main Document

1. In your document, move the insertion point to the spot where you want to merge a field from the data source file.

   The insertion point flashes on and off.

2. Select the Insert Merge Field button from the Mail Merge toolbar.

   Word displays a list of field names.

3. Select a merge field from the list.

   Word inserts the field name into the main document at the insertion point.

4. Repeat steps 1, 2, and 3 until you have completed the document.

   Word places the insertion point after your last insertion in the main document.

5. To check the document for errors, select the Check for Errors button on the Mail Merge toolbar.

   Word reviews your entries and displays a message.

6. After correcting any errors, save the main document by choosing File Save (Alt , F , S , Ctrl + S , or ⇧Shift + F12).

   Word displays the Save As dialog box.

7. Type a file name in the File Name box.

   If this is the first time you have saved this file, Word may prompt you for summary information. Word returns to the main document.

Merging and Printing Form Letters

After creating and editing the main document and the data source file, you are now ready to merge the two files into your form letter. There are four ways to do this:

- Click on the Mail Merge Helper button to open the Mail Merge Helper dialog box in which you can select the Merge button and open the Merge dialog box (Figure 12.14).

- Click on the Merge to New Document button to create a new document using the mail merge defaults.

- Click on the Merge to Printer button to create a merge document, which uses the mail merge defaults, and to open the Print dialog box.

- Click on the Mail Merge button to display the Merge dialog box in which you can change the defaults before merging.

Figure 12.14

The Merge dialog box with which you can merge to a new document or directly to a printer, select records to be merged, and indicate whether to print blank lines when data fields are empty.

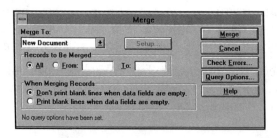

In the Merge dialog box you can choose to merge the main document and the data source file into a form letter that is either printed or saved to a file for later printing. You can also check for potential errors in the merge without printing or saving. In the Records to be Merged group, choose all the form letters, or choose a range of records.

To print a range of form letters, enter a starting number in the From box; if you leave the **F**rom box empty, Word prints from the first record. If you fill in the To box, Word prints to that record; if you leave the **T**o box empty, Word prints through the last record.

You can also decide whether to print blank lines in your data source file. For example, your data source file might include two fields for street address, allowing for post office boxes and apartment or suite numbers. However, many of your records do not use both fields. Word's default (**D**on't print blank lines when data fields are empty) fills in blank spaces with the next field. If you select the **P**rint blank lines when data fields are empty button, the empty second address field is printed as a blank space in the form letter.

The following Quick Steps demonstrate one way to merge the main document and the data source file and print the resulting form letter.

Merging and Printing the Main Document and the Data Source File

1. With the main document in the document window, select the Mail Merge button.

   Word displays the Merge dialog box (Figure 12.14).

2. Open the Merge To drop-down list box and select Printer.

   Word highlights your selection.

3. Limit the merge by typing a range of records in the From and To text boxes.

   Word changes the filled-in radio button from **A**ll to **F**rom.

continues

continued

4. In the When Merging Records group, indicate whether or not to print blank lines when data fields are empty.	Word fills in the selected radio button.
5. Select Merge or press ⏎Enter.	Word displays the Print dialog box.
6. Select the number of copies or the range of pages. Then select OK or press ⏎Enter.	Word starts the merge process and then prints the desired number of copies.

Creating and Printing Mailing Labels

Mailing labels, which Word regards as a type of form letter, also result from the link between a main document and a data source file. However, there are some differences in the way you work with the Mail Merge Helper for mailing labels. Word also provides a method to print single labels and sheets of labels, which are covered later in this section.

To create mailing labels select Tools Mail Merge once again. This time, however, when creating the main document, instead of selecting Form Letters from the list, select Mailing Labels. Word displays an information box in which you are prompted to select the active document in the document window or to start an entirely new document. Remember that even if your document window is empty, if you selected File New, there is a document there, although there may be no contents.

After starting a main document, you return to the Mail Merge Helper dialog box, in which you can select a data source—either a new or existing file. Then Word displays an information box (Figure 12.16) that prompts you to finish setting up the main document by selecting a label and specifying whether your printer is a dot matrix or laser. At this point, you create a label by inserting merge fields and formatting them. To finish, you merge the main document and the data source file.

To create and print mailing labels, use the following Quick Steps.

Creating and Printing Mailing Labels

1. From the File menu, select the New command (Alt , F , N).

   Word displays the New dialog box.

2. In the Template box, select the Normal template. Select OK or press ↵Enter .

   Word opens an empty document window.

3. From the Tools menu select Mail Merge (Alt , T , R).

   Word displays the Mail Merge Helper dialog box.

4. Select Create.

   Word opens a list of documents.

5. Select Mailing Labels.

   Word displays an information box, which asks you whether you wish to use the current document or a new document.

6. Select Active Window.

   Word "undims" the Get Data button.

continues

continued

7. Select Get Data and Open Data Source. (If you select Create Data Source, follow the steps for Creating and Merging a Main Document and a Data Source File, covered earlier in this chapter.)

Word displays the Open Data Source dialog box, as shown in Figure 12.15.

8. Choose a file and select OK or press ⏎Enter.

Word displays an information box (Figure 12.16).

9. Select Set Up Main Document.

Word displays the Label Options dialog box (see Figure 12.17).

10. Select the type of printer that you use and the correct label. (For more information about a label type, highlight it and click on the Details button.) Then select OK or press ⏎Enter.

Word displays the Create Labels dialog box (Figure 12.18).

11. Click on the Insert Merge Field button and select a merge field from the list.

Word adds the field name to the sample label.

12. Repeat step 11 until you have filled the sample label with all desired fields.

Word adds each new field name to the end of the previous field name.

13. To format the label, move the insertion point before a field that you want to place on the next line, then press ⏎Enter. (Do insert spaces between fields on the same line.)

Word formats the fields as you have indicated.

14. Either click on OK or tab to the OK button and press ⏎Enter.

15. Merge the main document and the data source file by selecting the Merge button on the Mail Merge Helper dialog box.

Word displays the Merge dialog box.

16. Fill in the Merge dialog box and select Merge or press ⏎Enter and Close the Mail Merge Helper dialog box.

Word merges the documents and displays the finished label in the document window (Figure 12.19). If you see any problems with the labels, you can edit them.

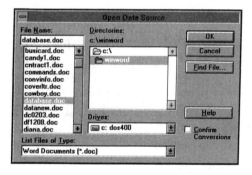

Figure 12.15
The Open Data Source dialog box.

Figure 12.16
An information box which prompts you to finish setting up your main document.

Figure 12.17
The Label Options dialog box.

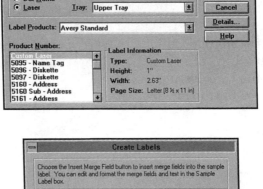

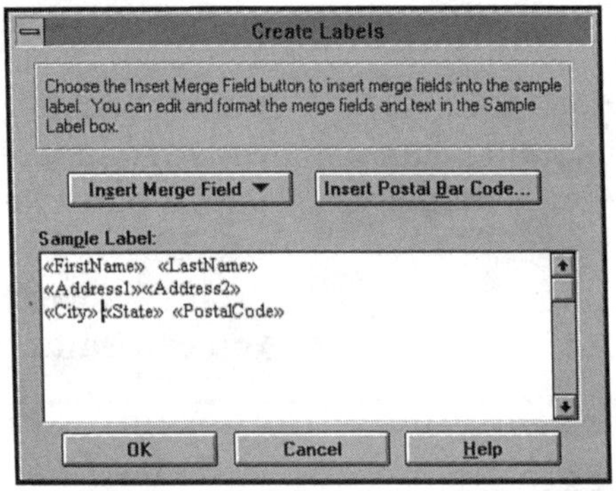

Figure 12.18
A filled-in Create Labels dialog box.

Figure 12.19
Four labels in the document window.

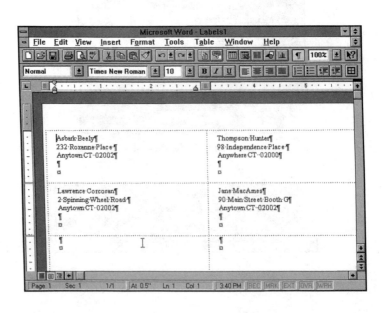

Creating and Printing Single Mailing Labels

Word also enables you to create individual mailing labels or sheets of labels with the same information. This Word feature is useful if you wish to print return labels, or business cards or rotary cards to hand out to prospective clients.

To produce mailing labels this way, select Envelopes and Labels command from the Tools menu. Click on the Labels tab at the top of the Envelopes and Labels dialog box, as shown in Figure 12.20. Then select the label, specify whether to add your return address to the label, and set printing options. Finally, select the Print button.

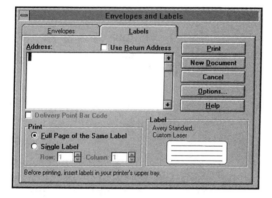

Figure 12.20

The Envelopes and Labels dialog box for Labels.

An inexpensive way to advertise your business is to print sheets of labels that contain your company logo and motto in addition to your return address.

Creating and Printing Envelopes

Mailing labels are often used for addressing form letters but printed envelopes provide a more personal touch. However, if you decide to print envelopes, be aware that you'll be sitting in front of your printer, feeding envelopes one at a time, unless you have an envelope feeder or use continuous form envelopes. Still, you may find it's worth the extra effort unless you're mailing hundreds of letters.

Before getting started, if your printer has an envelope feeder, make sure that it is the current paper source. You can specify the type of feed in the **E**nvelope Options dialog box for Printing Options.

Creating and printing envelopes is very much like creating and printing mailing labels. In fact, you can use the same steps. One difference is that you use the **E**nvelope Options dialog box to select envelope size, fonts for both return and delivery addresses, and the placement of each address on the envelope (Figure 12.21). You also can specify printing options, such as the position of an envelope being fed into the printer, whether you feed face down or face up, and the method by which you feed (Figure 12.22). You insert merge fields exactly as you insert them for mailing labels. When Word displays the Create Envelope dialog box, type the Addressed To and Return Address envelope information. Then select Print Envelope.

Figure 12.21

The Envelopes Options dialog box for Envelope Options.

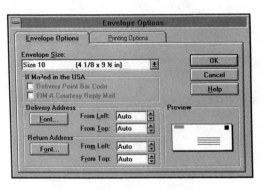

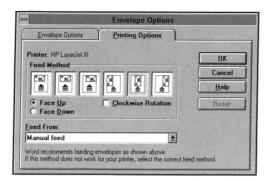

Figure 12.22
*The Printing
Options dialog box
for Envelope
Options.*

NOTE: If you have filled in the Mailing Address box in the Options dialog box for the User Info category, that information will automatically be your return address for envelopes.

Creating and Printing Single Envelopes

Most times, you'll print single envelopes rather than groups of envelopes. Printing one envelope at a time is similar to printing one label or a sheet of the same labels. To get started, select Envelopes and Labels from the Tools menu, and if needed, click on the Envelopes tab. In the Envelopes and Labels dialog box for Envelopes, type the name and address in the Delivery Address box and make sure that the correct return address appears in the Return Address box. If you need to select an envelope size, add a bar code, or change the font for the delivery or return address, select Options and click on the Envelope Options tab. If you want to change the Feed Method, or direction that you feed the envelope, or how you feed, click on the Printing Options tab. After you have specified all the options, you may have to get your printer ready for printing an envelope. For example you may have to open the back door or narrow the wings on the top of the paper tray. (Check your printer's documentation before printing the first envelope.) Feed an envelope into your printer, using the small illustration in the Feed box as a guide, and click on Print or tab to Print and then press ⏎Enter. Then wait for the envelope to feed into your printer.

Installing Word for Windows

Before Installing Word for Windows

Windows should be installed on your computer system already, and you should have followed the Windows guidelines for hardware and software requirements. Here are some recommendations:

- Your computer system should be an IBM-compatible computer based on an Intel 80386 processor or greater.

- Windows version 3.0 or above should be installed.

- Your computer should have at least 2 megabytes of RAM. The more RAM, the better Windows runs.

Random-access memory (RAM) is your computer's main memory; your computer uses RAM to run DOS, Windows and applications software, and to store information temporarily. When you turn off your computer, RAM's contents are deleted.

- Additional memory, in any combination of extended and expanded memory, also helps Windows run better.

There are three types of RAM: conventional, extended, and expanded. Conventional memory (you can have as much as one megabyte) is the regular RAM that your computer uses. Extended memory is an extension to conventional memory. Expanded memory requires special software and often requires a special board; it is an addition to conventional and extended memory.

- Your color monitor and video card should support VGA.

  VGA stands for Video Graphics Array, which produces high resolution images and enables you to use 16 colors at a time on your system.

- A Microsoft-compatible mouse is required for using the toolbars, and invaluable for greater flexibility, speed and ease of operation.

- To get the most from Word for Windows, a printer (either laser or dot-matrix) should be part of your computer system.

TIP: Before you install Word for Windows, make copies of the product disks and store them in a safe place away from your computer.

Installing Word for Windows

Use these Quick Steps to install Word for Windows.

Installing Word for Windows from Within Windows

1. Start Windows.

Windows goes through its regular startup routine.

2. Choose **R**un from the **F**ile menu (Alt, F, R).

Windows opens the Run dialog box.

3. In the Command Line box, type either **a:setup** or **b:setup**, depending on the disk drive selected in step 2. Press ⏎Enter.

The Setup program displays an installation screen asking for your name and organization.

4. Enter your name, tab to Organization, and enter the name of your company. Select Continue (to continue the installation) or Exit (to leave the installation).

Setup asks you to verify the information that you just entered.

5. Select either Continue or Exit. Remember, you can press F3 at any time to exit the installation.

Setup displays directory information and gives you a choice of the directory on which Word will be in stalled.

6. Accept the **WINWORD** directory, and select Continue.

Setup displays a menu giving you the following options: Typical, which will be installed with the most common options; Complete/ Custom, which will be installed with only the options you select; Laptop

continues

continued

(Minimum) which will be installed with minimum necessary options.

7. To overwrite the old program files, select Continue.

8. Select Typical Installation to install the common Word's options. Press ⏎Enter.

Setup gives you the option of accepting the default Program Manager Group of Microsoft Applications or selecting another from the Existing Group.

9. Select Yes or No.

Setup informs you that it is setting up the program. As it installs Word, Setup displays the percentage of installation completed, the file currently being in stalled, its destination, and its features. When Setup is finished installing from one floppy disk, it beeps.

10. Insert the next floppy disk that setup asks for and press ⏎Enter.

If you put the wrong floppy disk in the drive, Setup prompts you to insert the proper floppy disk.

11. Repeat step 11 until you have inserted the last floppy disk.

At the end of the installation, Setup updates files that help Word to run more efficiently, returns to Windows, displays the Group window (Microsoft Applications if you used the default), and informs you that Setup is complete.

Index

I

Standard Toolbar Tools

Create a new document

Open an existing document

Save the active document

Print the active document

Display full pages print as they will print

Check spelling

Cut selected text to clipboard

Copy selected text to clipboard

Insert text from clipboard

Copy formatting of selected text

Reverse the last action

Reverse the last action that was undone

Automatically format a document

Create or insert an AutoText entry

Insert a table

Insert a Microsoft Excel spreadsheet

Change column format

Show or hide the Drawing toolbar

Insert a Microsoft Graph chart

Show or hide Non-printing characters

Scales the editing view

Get Help or Text property information